BUILDING BLOCKS
OF THE **SOUL**

BUILDING BLOCKS
OF THE SOUL

STUDIES ON THE
LETTERS AND WORDS
OF THE HEBREW LANGUAGE

MATITYAHU GLAZERSON

JASON ARONSON INC.
Northvale, New Jersey
Jerusalem

This book was set in 11 pt. Janson Text by A-R Editions, Madison, WI.

10 9 8 7 6 5 4 3 2 1

Library of Congress Cataloging-in-Publication Data

Glazerson, Matityahu.
  [Selections. English. 1997]
  Building blocks of the soul : studies on the letters and words of the Hebrew language / by Mattityahu Glazerson.
    p. cm.
  Component parts of the book previously published separately by the author.
  Includes index.
  Contents: pt. 1. Hebrew : the source of all languages — pt. 2. Revelations about marriage — pt. 3. Riches and righteousness — pt. 4. Repentance in words and letters.
  ISBN 1-56821-932-6 (alk. paper)
  1. Hebrew language—Alphabet—Religious aspects—Judaism. 2. Gematria. 3. Marriage—Religious aspects—Judaism. 4. Repentance—Judaism. I. Title.
  PJ4589.G5662   1997
  492.4—dc21   96-51938

Manufactured in the United States of America. Jason Aronson Inc. offers books and cassettes. For information and catalog write to Jason Aronson Inc., 230 Livingston Street, Northvale, New Jersey 07647.

Contents

Part III

Riches and Righteousness

Part IV
Repentance in Words and Letters

PART I

HEBREW
THE SOURCE OF ALL
LANGUAGES

VARIOUS BOOKS HAVE been written, by both Jewish and gentile teachers of linguistics, that have recorded many examples of the similarity between Hebrew words and words in other languages. Our purpose is to demonstrate that this is because Hebrew, the holy language, is the source of all languages. This phenomenon was not adequately explained by these same linguists; some failed to explain this phenomenon at all, and others explained it superficially or even childishly. Professor Ashbel (Hebrew University), an expert in the field, has published a paper on this subject. He was clearly aware that these similar-sounding words are derived from Hebrew, but simply stated this fact without any explanation. Professor Ashbel is to be commended for not emulating some of his colleagues, who have given far-fetched and inadequate theories for this phenomenon simply to avoid seeming ignorant in this important field.

When someone who knows nothing about Kabbalah and סוד—the esoteric—expresses an opinion on this subject, he is like a person who, not knowing that the atom is the basic building block of matter, attempts to explain a scientific phenomenon. A person who has no knowledge of פרדס (pardes, literally "orchard," which is made up of פשט, peshat, the literal meaning; רמז, remez, the implied meaning; דרש, derash, the interpretation; and סוד, sod, the esoteric meaning) but nevertheless claims to understand these matters is likened to a פרד (pered, a mule, who does not understand פרדס, pardes, with the ס, the סוד, sod, missing). I do not claim to be an expert on סוד and Kabbalah, but I

3

believe that my limited knowledge is sufficient to demonstrate the truth, and the reader can judge this for himself because truth is self-evident once it is pointed out.

Linguistics is taught, in the "enlightened" western countries, according to the systems developed by anti-Semitic professors, who attempted to construct innovative theories to conceal the fact that Hebrew is the source of all languages. People who study linguistics on the basis of these theories may feel threatened by this information, for it negates all that they were taught. If those same people, however, think it through carefully, they will almost certainly find many more examples of similarities between the holy language and other languages. They will come to realize the inadequacy and superficiality of the material they had been fed by their distinguished professors. Many newly observant Jews who had studied linguistics at university (and who had been taught in accordance with the latest theories), after studying in *yeshivot*, came to appreciate the exact meaning and depth of the Hebrew words.

In earlier times, the world's wise men admitted that the Hebrew language contained the wisdom of the world. Kol Yehuda, on the *Kuzari* (2:62), quotes various sources to this effect. Josephus Flavius wrote, in *Against Aphion II*, that the nations received their wisdom from Israel.

1

The Meaning of the Name "God"

IN MANY NON-HEBRAIC languages, the word used to refer to the Almighty is "God" or a similar-sounding word. Where does this name come from, and what does it mean? The source of this word—like the sources of many other non-Hebraic words—is found in the Torah. Incidentally, the English word "source" is clearly derived from Hebrew; its Hebrew equivalent is שרש (*shoresh*), which, when the שs in the word are substituted for שs (the same letter with a different pronunciation), becomes שרש (*sores*), which sounds similar to the word "source."

We find the first reference to the word גד (*God*) in connection with the birth of Jacob's son of that name (Genesis 30:11): "Good fortune (גד, *gad*) has come, exclaimed Leah. She named the child Gad." The word בגד (*bagad*) is traditionally to be read בא גד (*ba gad*), "a troop has come." According to Ibn Ezra, the word *gad* refers to the battalions (גדוד, *gedud*) of the heavens, which are the planets, stars, and constellations (מזלות, *mazalot*). Thus, גד means מזל (*mazal*), in Arabic, as can be seen in Isaiah (65:11): "Those that prepare a table for fortune (גד)." According to one opinion (*ibid.*), this refers to the planet צדק (*Zedek*), Jupiter.

In Aramaic, גדה (*gedah*) means "a god," as is found in the Gemara (*Chullin* 40a): "the god (גדה) of the mountain." The Rashbam does not agree with Ibn Ezra that the word גד (*gad*) is derived from גדוד (*gedud*, battalion), but does agree that גד (*gad*) means מזל (*mazal*). The Midrash Rabba (71:9) also interprets the words ב גד (*ba gad*) as "the מזל (*mazal*) of the house came."

Two further opinions as to the meaning of גד (*gad*) are recorded in the Gemara (*Shabbat* 67a). According to the Tana Kama, the word refers to the reliance of the Amorites (heathens) on the מזלות (*mazalot*), which are predictions according to the constellations. Rabbi Yehuda is of the opinion that גד refers to the name of a specific form of idolatry, as explained by Rashi on that Gemara. However, according to Rashi on the abovementioned verse in Isaiah (65:11), there is no real difference of opinion, as all agree that it refers to the idolatrous worship called by the name of this constellation. The Radak, in his commentary on Isaiah, says in the name of Rabbi Moshe Cohen that גד refers to the planet Jupiter, צדק (*Zedek*), and that this is the Arabic word for it.

Rabbi Yosef Karo, in his book *Maggid Mesharim*—interpretations of the weekly portions that were revealed to him by an angel—says that גד (*gad*) means מזל (*mazal*); according to him, the source of the word is נזל (*nazal*, flow)—that the מזל (*mazal*) is the medium through which abundance is directed to the world. The numerical values of the word מזלא (*mazala*; 40 + 7 + 30 + 1 = 78) and the word לחם (*lechem*, bread; 30 + 8 + 40 = 78) are identical, in order to teach us, as is stated in the Gemara (*Moed Katan* 28b), that the supply of bread, the most basic food staple, is dependent on מזל (*mazal*, luck). There seems to be a contradiction, as the Gemara states (*Shabbat* 156a): "The constellations (מזל, *mazal*) do not have an effect on the Jewish nation." The Tosfot (*ibid.*) resolves this, however, by explaining that the מזל (*mazal*) of an individual can change according to his merit.

In the non-Hebraic languages, the consonants g and d, with different vowels, make up various words meaning GooDness. The small numerical value of the word טוב (*tov*, good; 9 + 6 + 2 = 17; 1 + 7 = 8) is the same as that of God's name, יהוה (10 + 5 + 6 + 5 = 26; 2 + 6 = 8), further showing that God is the source of lovingkindness and goodness. (*Kehillat Yaacov*, L'Baal Male HaRoyim, Ch. 15).

Also, according to their meaning in Hebrew, the letters of the word גד express goodness and lovingkindness. It is stated in the Gemara (*Shabbat* 104a) that the letters ג and ד refer to גומל דלים (*gomel dalim*, giving to the indigent). The shape of the letter ג resembles a man striding toward a poor person to offer him help; the shape of the ד resembles a poor man leaning toward the rich man.

God used his attribute of lovingkindness to create the world, as it is said: עולם חסד יבנה, "The world was built on lovingkindness" (Psalms

89:3). In non-Hebraic languages, the name used for God limits his attribute to that of גמילות דלים (*gemilut dalim*, g and d), whereas in Hebrew, the holy language, God has many different names that describe his many different attributes.

The English word "God," when reversed, spells "dog," spelled דג (fish) in Hebrew. This strange phenomenon makes sense when we examine the order of the Hebrew letters: The ד, the in**d**igent (the poor person), approaches the ג, the **g**iver. A fish (דג, *dag*) always feels that there is insufficient water for him, no matter how big the sea. When it rains, the fish pokes its head out of the water to catch the raindrops. Lack of satisfaction is a trait typical of the dog, as well. According to the *Zohar*, this is even expressed by its bark, "*Hav, hav*" (הב הב), which in Hebrew means, "Give, give." הכלבים עזי נפש, לא ידעו שבעה, "Dogs are fierce creatures who are never satisfied" (Isaiah 51:6). For this reason, the dog is portrayed in the Midrash and the *Zohar* as a symbol of the evil power, Amalek, whose sole wish and purpose is to take and draw away from others. Amalek, the "dog," signifies the antithesis of the kingdom of God; the opposite of the Almighty's trait of "**g**iving to the in**d**igent."

As has already been seen, גד (*gad*) means מזל (*mazal*) in both Hebrew and Arabic. The connection between the two can also be understood from the letters of the word גד (*gad*), which imply "giving generously," and the fact that מזל (*mazal*) is the force that directs abundance to the world. This connection can also be seen in their numerical values: גד = 7 (3 + 4) and מזל = 77 (40 + 7 + 30). The seventh attribute is that of majesty, which is the basis of the Creation of the world. As our holy books state, everything multiplied by ten is on a higher plane than the corresponding smaller number; thus, seventy implies majesty in a more exalted world.

גד (*gad*) is also the Arabic name of the planet Jupiter, צדק (*Zedek*, justice) in Hebrew. Therefore, according to what we have already discussed, *gad* represents the power of **g**oo**d** and lovingkindness inherent in the letters גמל–דלת (*gimel* and *dalet*).

According to the *Sefer Yetzira* (4:46), God created the planet Jupiter with גמל (*gimel*), the letter suggesting the attribute of lovingkindness, which is the יסוד (*yesod*, foundation). The Gemara (*Shabbat* 156a) says that this planet was the constellation of Abraham, who himself was the pillar of lovingkindness.

The English word "God" has an interesting characteristic. If we assign each letter of the Latin alphabet a numerical value corresponding to its position in the alphabet, the value of the word God (g = 7; o = 15; d = 4; 7 + 15 + 4 = 26) is the same as the numerical value of God's name in Hebrew, יהוה (10 + 5 + 6 + 5 = 26). However, only in Hebrew, the holy language, are all the ideas embodied in the name of God revealed.

2

Other Meanings Behind the Letters *Gimel* and *Dalet*

THE LETTER גמל (*gimel*) suggests the power of giving, as can also be seen by the first letter of the English word "give" (גיו), which is a ג, a g. Its form is a combination of a ו (suggesting a hand) giving the י (a "coin"), which is at its base, to a poor man.

As we have just seen, the גמל (ג, *gimel*) is made up of וי, which spells וי (*vay*)—a word that expresses anguish in several languages. The *Ben Ish Chai* says (Drashot, Parshat Yitro), that this teaches us that charity saves a person from suffering and death, and that the גמל (*gimel*, lovingkindness) negates the וי (*vay*).

The letter גמל (*gimel*) also suggests גדלות (*gadlut*, greatness), as we can see from the form of the letter (*Resh Milin*, Gimel). The word גמל (*gamal*), which has the same letters as the letter גמל (*gimel*), means "camel" in English. The letters גמל and c are related: They are both gutturals, and are the third letter of their respective alphabets. The word גמל (*gamal*) is associated with the word גדל (*gadal*, grew or became great), according to the rule of איק בכר as מ = 40 and ד = 4.

According to *Sefer Yetzira*, Jupiter, the largest of the planets, was created with the letter ג. This can be clearly understood, for this letter symbolizes giving and greatness, greatness and lovingkindness being interdependent. This is also apparent from the order of the מדות (*midot*, attributes), in which the first attribute, חסד (*chesed*, kindness), is identical to greatness: לך הי הגדולה והגבורה וכוי—"Yours, o God, is the greatness and the power" (1 Chronicles 29:11). Similarly, we find that our forefather Abraham, the epitome of kindness, is referred to in our holy writings as הגדול האדם (*haadam hagadol*, the great man).

Rabbi Samson Raphael Hirsch gives a different meaning to the word גד (*gad*) in his commentary on Genesis (30:11). He says that גד (*gad*) comes from the word meaning "sever," as it is used in Daniel (4:11): אילנא גדו: "Hew (*gedu*, גדו) down the tree." The letters גד (*gad*) are the first two of the root of the word גדע (*gada*, cut down or demote), which may be associated with the word קטע (*kata*, cut short; ק and ג are interchangeable, as are ד and ט, as they belong to the same phonetic groups).

According to this interpretation, גד (*gad*) means מזל (*mazal*): מזל (*mazal*) is a force that has a sudden effect on the world, as if an extraterrestrial force were severed from another world and imposed on ours. The Seforno gives a similar explanation in reference to the word בגד (*bagad*) (Genesis 30:11): The word גד (*gad*) refers to a chance happening. There is a connection between גד, meaning "sever," and גד, meaning "chance," because a מקרה (*mikre*, chance happening) occurs suddenly, as if it were נקרא (*nikra*) severed from somewhere else. According to this explanation, the word גד (*gad*), used in a negative sense, means a "disconnected body"—like an idol, which has no connection with the truth. In the positive sense *gad* means a higher power, one separated from the physical world. This is the meaning of God's name עתיק ימין (*atik yomin*), as he is מנותק (*menutak*, cut off or separated) from the physical world.

The letters גד also suggest a chance occurrence, as can be seen by exchanging them with the letters קר (according to a key called ת–ב–ש–א, whereby the first letter of the alphabet is exchanged with the last, the second with the penultimate, and so on). קר is the root of the word מקרה (*mikre*, a chance happening).

גד (*gad*), meaning "cutting and severing," is related to the English word "cut" (כת, in Hebrew), for the letters belong to the same phonetic groups (כ and ג are gutturals, and ד and ת are palatals). The Hebrew word כת (*cut*) comes from the word meaning "section" or "sect." The word כרת (*karet*), a strong form of cutting off, is given its strength by the ר in the middle of the word.

The Bet Yosef says (*Magid Mesharim*, Exodus) that גד (*gad*) refers to the attribute of יסוד (*yesod*, foundation), the sixth מידה (*midah*). This attribute is said to bring goodness and abundance to the world, as is expressed by the letters ג and ד. The power of bestowal inherent in the ב can be seen by its shape—that of a ו, a "hand giving a coin," the י below. The numerical value of ו is 6 (parallel to the sixth attribute of יסוד); the י, whose numerical value is 10 (עשר, *eser*), represents abundance (its letters are the same as עשר, *osher*, wealth).

3

Words and Letters of Light

THE WORD ראי־ה (*reiya*, seeing), in the Bible, includes the concept of understanding and wisdom, as stated with reference to King Solomon (Ecclesiastes 1:16): "My heart has seen much wisdom and knowledge." The attribute of כתר (*keter*, crown), which is the source of חכמה (*chochma*, wisdom), בינה (*binah*, understanding), and דעת (*daat*, knowledge), is also called קרן (*keren*, a ray of light). Thus, this attribute projects its light to the source of all wisdom, understanding, and knowledge. The English word "ray" sounds similar to the Hebrew word ראה (*raah*, saw), which has the same letters as the word ארה (*ora*, light), which is connected to the word קרן (*keren*) through the rule of איק־בכר (when the letters of the same basic numerical value—i.e., 1, 10, and 100; 2, 20, and 200; and so on—are related; ארה = 1 + 200 + 5; קרן = 100 + 200 + 50). The letters of the word ארה (*ora*) are similar to that of קרן (*keren*); therefore the English word "ray" is clearly connected to the Hebrew word קרן.

The א and the ה of the word ארה (*ora*) are unit values equal to 1 and 5, respectively. Unit values represent the lower world. In the word קרן (*keren*), the ק, whose value is one hundred, and נ, whose value is five tens, suggests the upper world. The middle letter of the two words ארה (*ora*) and קרן (*keren*) is ר, its shape suggesting a horn, a קרן in Hebrew. The letter after ר is שׁ (*shin*; 300 + 50 = 350), which has the same numerical value as the word קרן (*keren*; 100 + 200 + 50 = 350).

According to *Sefer Yetzira* (3:48), שׁ is the letter with which the element אש (*esh*, fire) was created, and light (אר, *ohr*) is contingent upon fire. The shape of the letter שׁ, which is the basis of fire (אשׁ, *esh*) and, therefore, of light (אור, *ohr*), resembles a flame. The שׁ, as written in the Torah, is made up of the letters זיי, which spell the word זיו (*ziv*, sheen). The English word "sheen" is certainly derived from Hebrew, and expresses the essential meaning of the שׁין (*shin*).

The source of light (*ohr*, אור) from fire (*esh*, אשׁ) can be seen in the fact that they are both written with an א, and the ר and שׁ are consecutive letters in the Hebrew alphabet. It is interesting to note that the letters following those of שׁין (ס, כ, ת) spell the word סכת (*seket*), which means ראי–ה (*reiya*, seeing) (Rabbenu Bechaya in *Kad HaKemach* with reference to Sukkot).

In English, too, there is a relationship between the שׁין (*shin*) or שׁין (*sin*) and seeing, as in the word "seen." Moreover, the main letter of the word "see" is the s, which is the equivalent of the שׁ, both having the same position in their respective alphabets. (The phenomenon of a relationship existing between letters in the same position in the Hebrew and Latin alphabets applies to most of the other letters, as well.)

Another Hebrew word meaning "sight" is שׁקף (*shikef*, observed). If one exchanges the שׁ (sh) for a שׂ (s), and the פ (f) for a פּ(p), the word resembles the word "scope," which means "seeing." The word שׂקף, made up of שׂ and קף, suggests the word הקף (*hekef*, observation in all directions). The English meaning of the word "scope," range, is derived from this.

"Shine" is another English word related to שׁ, and this, too, is related to the concept of seeing.

Using the key of איק–בכר (whereby the letters of numerical value 1, 10, and 100; 2, 20, and 200; etc. are related), the letters of the word שׁין are related to the letters of the word לאה (Leah), which, re-arranged, spell the word אהל (*ohel*). According to Jewish mysticism, אהל (*ohel*) is the manifestation of the celestial light (*Kehillat Yaakov*, Ch. אהל). The name לאה, Leah (having the same letters as אהל), suggests our Matriarch Leah, who, in Jewish mysticism, is regarded as having been particularly connected to the esoteric world, while our Matriarch Rachel was specifically connected to the physical world.

This concept has reached English in the form of the word "halo" (האלו), which in Hebrew has the same letters as the word אוהל (*ohel*, celestial light). The English word "halo" refers to the celestial light that surrounds a person, and is similar to another English word, "aura," which is also related to the Hebrew word ארה (*ora*, light). אהל is related to הלה (*hila*, shining light and brightness), which is mentioned in several places in Job: "If I beheld the sun when it shone (יהל)" (31:26); "When His lamp shone (בהילו) above my head" (29:3); and "Flash forth light (טהל אור)" (41:10).

The numerical value of אהל (1 + 5 + 30 = 36) suggests "light," as there were thirty-six hours in which the original light (the light of Creation, not that of the sun) shone for Adam, the first man. Words meaning light (מאורות, *meorot*; אור, *ohr*; נר, *ner*) are mentioned thirty-six times in the Torah (*The Book of Rokeach*, Kabbalah received from the prophet Elijah). Thirty-six righteous men form the basis of the world, and it is through them that the light of Creation continues to shine, enabling the world to continue to exist. This light might cease because of the thirty-six types of sin for which the Torah demands כרת (*karet*, cutting off), thus endangering the continued existence of man and of the world. This phenomenon was manifested during the destruction of the Temple, as it is said: על אלה חשכו עינינו, "For these things (אלה, whose numerical value is 36) our eyes became dim" (Lamentations 5:17). The thirty-six sins that are punishable by כרת (*karet*, corresponding to the numerical value of the word אלה) led to the destruction of the Temple. The numerical value of the word איכה (*aichah*, the first word as well as the title of the Book of Lamentations) is also 36 (Midrash Rabba, Lamentations), and refers to these thirty-six sins.

The Hebrew word אלה (*aileh*, these), with different vowels, may be read אלה (*alah*, curse), and is perhaps the derivation of the English word "alas." אלה, having the same letters as אהל, is an expression of destruction of the basis of the celestial light, אהל. Similarly, the word כרת (*karet*, cutting off) has the same letters as כתר (*keter*, majesty). כרת is the severe punishment meted out for those sins negating God's majesty, the root of אור (*ohr*, light). The strong severance as a result of כרת is expressed by the letter of movement, the ר, which comes between the letters כת, which stem from the verb כתת (*katat*, cut flat or pound). This is also clearly associated with the English word "cut." It is interesting to note the connection between the words containing the same letters: אהל (*ohel*) and אלה (*aileh*); כתר (*keter*) and כרת (*karet*).

The Gemara explains (*Sota* 12a) that there is a connection between the number 36 and the concept of כתר (*keter*, majesty) as it says: "Thirty-six crowns were hung on the coffin of the Patriarch Jacob" (*Shem Olam*, 7). The number 36 is related to the number 63 (when a numeral is multiplied by ten, it has the same meaning as the original numeral, only on a different plane; thus, 30 is the same as 3, and 6 is the same as 60). The number 63 is the full numerical value of the name of God (יהוה; יוד = 10 + 6 + 4 = 20; הי = 5 + 10 = 15; וו = 6 + 6 = 12; הי = 5 + 10 = 15; plus 1 for the number—*kollel*—20 + 15 + 12 + 15 + 1 = 63) that refers to the world of בריאה (*bria*, Creation). The word בריאה contains the letters האיר, which is the root of the word האויר (*haavir*, the air). As we shall discuss, אויר (*avir*, air) is related in Hebrew to אור (*ohr*, light). In English, one can see a clear connection between the words "air" and "aura" (light). This connection exists in other languages, too.

The root of the word הלה (*hila*, celestial light) and אהל (*ohel*, celestial light or tent) are related to the root of the word הלל (*hallel*, expression of praise and thanksgiving), similar to the word "halloo" in English. "Halo" has letters similar to "halloo," which means "calling aloud"; the doubling of the letters "o" and "l" serve to emphasize the intensity of the action.

The words הלה (*hila*, celestial light) and אור (*ohr*, light) are related to the word הלל (*hallel*) in Hebrew because the purpose of הלל (thanksgiving) is to emphasize and to light up the greatness of the One who is being thanked or praised. Thus, we see that the word הללויה (*halleluja*, praising God) means הללו, "throwing light on," or recognizing, the יה, the attributes of God represented by these letters. The English word "hail" is a greeting, and to greet someone is to give him honor. The aura (הלה, *hila*) of a man is what gives him his honor, as implied by the words of Rabbi Chaya, who referred to his clothing as "that which honors him": עוטה אור כשלמה, "Who cover Yourself with light as with a garment" (Psalms 104:2). A person's clothes represent the celestial light that surrounds and honors him (*Zohar* on Toldot 142b).

An anagram of נגה (*naga*, shine) forms the root of the word להגן (*lehagen*, to shield), suggesting that the celestial light that surrounds a person forms a sheen and a halo around him, thereby protecting (*magen*, מגן) him. The Ramban explains this with reference to the verse: "Their defense (צילם) is departed from them and the Eternal is with us" (Numbers 4:9). צל (*tzel*, shade) is a form of protection. This concept may be contained in the English words "shell" and "shield."

The Hebrew word צד (*tzad*) has the same meaning as, and sounds similar to, the English word "side," which sounds similar to "shade" (צל, *tzel*). If the ל and ד are exchanged (both palatals), then צל becomes צד. צל is also interchangeable with שד (*shade*) because צ and ש are dental letters, and ד and ל are palatals. The Hebrew word שד (or שר), according to Kabbalah, means "demon," and is related to the divine

Name שדי (without the י). The missing י, which represents holiness, suggests that demons are derived from negative forces. The English word "shed" suggests "shelter," and it appears to be associated with the Hebrew צל. "Shed" can also mean "to throw off," and in this sense is similar in meaning to the Hebrew אשד (*eshed*, cascade).

4

Wisdom and Strength Related to *Shin*, the Letter of Light

THE LETTER ש resembles not only flames of light, but the root of a plant, suggesting that the world is rooted in light. According to Kabbalah, the beaming light of the crown (כתר, *keter*), whose numerical value is 620, represents the number of *mitzvot* (613 Torah laws and seven Rabbinic injunctions), suggesting the 620 lights attached to the crown (*Kehillat Yaakov*, Keter).

The letter ש, the source of fire, also represents strength, which is symbolized by fire. This is the derivation of the word שן (*shen*, tooth), the strongest part of the body. שן (*shen*) is used to mean strength in the Bible, for example: "You broke the teeth of the wicked" (Psalms 3:9). The concept that the ש represents strength can be seen in its having the same letters as שני (*shani*, scarlet), which, according to Kabbalah, is the color that represents strength. A further anagram of שין is the word שני (*sheni*, second), and the second of the attributes is גבורה (*gevura*, strength), the one after lovingkindness. So, in Hebrew, there is a connection between שן (*shen*, tooth), שניים (*shinayim*, teeth), and שניים (*shnayim*, two). In English, too, there is a clear connection between "tooth" and "two." Linguists are also aware that there is a connection between "tooth" and "two," but most of them believe that it is based on the fact that a person has two rows of teeth. This explanation is superficial and narrow, denoting ignorance of the hidden depth of meaning of the Hebrew language.

Within the seven attributes of emotion, the attribute of strength occupies second (שני, *sheni*) place. However, when we include the three attributes of rationality—כתר (*keter*, majesty); חכמה (*chochma*, wisdom); and בינה (*binah*, understanding), making ten attributes, then wisdom occupies second (שני) place. According to this order, the שנים (*shinayim*, teeth) are associated with wisdom. There is a connection between the facts that an adult has thirty-two teeth and that there are thirty-two paths to wisdom (*Kehillat Yaakov*, שן), the basis of the power of understanding with which a person can acquire esoteric wisdom. Just as teeth are needed to chew and grind food, so, too, a person who wants to gain knowledge has to revise—"chew and grind"—the material.

The word שן (*shen*, tooth) is related to משנן (*meshanen*, revise). Revision is closely associated with understanding; according to Kabbalah, the attribute of understanding is the basis of the attribute of strength (*Kehillat Yaakov*, גבורה). The words שן and בינה (understanding) are connected: They have a נ in common, and the ש of שן is interchangeable with the ב of בינה, for both are the second letter of the alphabet in their respective directions (the ש being the second-to-last letter and the ב, the second letter). Their common letter, נ, represents understanding.

The word יין (*yayin*, wine), also containing a נ, suggests בינה (*binah*, understanding), and its red color suggests strength. This is the basis of the similarity between the English words "wine" and "vine," the French word *vin* (wine), and the Hebrew word יין (*yayin*). Interestingly, the letter וו (*vav*) is spelled out as a double ו, and the Hebrew word וו means "hook," the purpose of which is to connect two objects. The letter ו similarly means "and," which is a conjunction. The English letter v sounds like a וו, and is also two-pronged, like the word וו spelled out.

יין (*yayin*), whose numerical value is 70 (10 + 10 + 50), suggests understanding, for it corresponds to the seventy ways in which the Torah can be interpreted and understood. It also has the same numerical value as the word סוד (*sod*, secret, esoteric, or hidden), suggesting that there is a deeper meaning in the expression נכנס יין יצא סוד, "When wine goes in, that which is hidden is exposed."

According to Chazal, the fact that the word נשים (*nashim*, women, here, the partners of men) has the same letters as the word שנים (*shnayim*, two) shows that their basis is strength and understanding. The rabbis say that in the word אשה (*ishah*, woman), the letters אש (*esh*, fire) appear side-by-side, while in the word איש (*ish*, man), the א and ש are separated by a י. אש (*esh*, fire), the basis of strength, is stronger in a woman than in a man. The German word for "woman" is *frau*, which is based on the letters פ and ר (פר, *par*, bull), also indicating strength. (The letters פ and ר are closely related to the English letters p and r.) The English word "feminine" begins with the letter f (פ), suggesting strength.

The connection between אשה (*ishah*, woman) and אש (*esh*, fire); נשים (*nashim*, women) and שנים (*shnayim*, two) explains the woman's role as protector and supporter of her husband. King Solomon said: "A virtuous woman is her husband's crown" (Proverbs 12:4). The word עטרה (*atara*, crown) suggests an encompassing protection. The Midrash (Bereishith Rabba 17:6) attributes the letter ס (סמך, *samech*) to women because they help men to withstand שטן, Satan (סטן, the round letter ס that is the first letter in the word, resembles a surrounding, protecting wall). The circular shape of the ס, a stronger letter than the ש, represents the encompassing light latent in the ש and ש. This encompassing light is unique to women (*Kehillat Yaakov*, אשה). The term אהל (*ohel*, celestial light, lit. tent) is used in many places in the Bible to mean woman, e.g., וידעת כי שלום אהלך, "And you shall know that there is peace with your wife" (Job 5:24). Therefore, אהל is related to ש, the letter of fire and light.

5

The Absence of Light

IN THE TORAH WE FIND the word סות (*sut*): "And in the blood of grapes (סותו) his rainment" (Genesis 49:11). The word סות (*sut*) is connected to the word מסוה (*masve*, veil), which refers to a person's essential clothing (*Ohr Hachayim, ibid.*). This gave rise to the English word "suit," which as a noun means "garment," and as a verb means "is fitting," "is suitable."

According to the mystical writings, the word סות (*sut*) refers to the power that counteracts immorality (*Kehillat Yaakov*, סות). The force of temptation (סתה, *sate*), tempts (מסית, *mesit*) a person to sin. The letters preceding the root of this word—i.e., סית—is שטן (ש–ת; ט–י; נ–ס). The English words "entice" and "incite" have similar connotations, and are connected phonetically to סית, *sit*. The basic root of סתר (*seter*, hidden) is סת, which is connected to words like "esoteric," "mystery," and "secret." The words סוד (*sod*), סתר (*seter*), and סות (*sut*)—all expressing the idea of "secret," hidden, or covered up—are connected, as is apparent in the numerical value of the words סוד (ד = 4) and סות (ת = 400), which, according to the key of איק–בכר, are interchangeable.

Light (*ohr*, אר) was the basis of Creation, as we can see by analyzing the root of the word בריאה (*bria*, Creation). The root ברא, when divided, forms the word ב–רא, which means the ב (*bet*, which is *bayit*, house) of אר (*ohr*, light)—i.e., the world. Therefore, light is the essence of Creation, and the absence of light and truth—the basis of the existence of the world—brings destruction. This explains why the Hebrew word סתר (*seter*, hidden, or absence of light) also means

20

destruction. This idea is also reflected in the English word "destroy." The kabbalistic expression סתרא אחרא (*sitra achra*, the other side; סתר, in Aramaic, means "side"), refers to Satan, which is a destructive external force that conceals God's light from the world.

Included in these negative forces are the stars. The first two letters of the word "star"—spelled, in Hebrew, סטר—are the same as the first two letters of the word סטן (Satan), which turns people away from the correct path (סטה, *satah*).

Kabbalah makes a connection between אור (*ohr*, light) and the continued existence of the world. The word הלה (*hila*) means "light" and is connected to the word הלל (*hallel*), which means to praise or enlighten the qualities of God. The words הלל (*hallel* (5 + 30 + 30 = 65) and אדני (a name of God that describes him as the Master) (1 + 4 + 50 + 10 = 65), have the same numerical value. Accepting God as Master is the basis of the world's existence, and הללויה (*halleluja*), which highlights the attribute of יה, is the basis of the continued existence of the world. The holiness inherent in the word הלל (*hallel*) is the source of the English words "hallow" and "holy." Both are related to "halo" and אור (*ohr*, light).

In Hebrew, the word חלל (*chalal*, profane) is the opposite of the word הלל (*hallel*). The ח of הלל is associated with the word חטא (*chet*, sin) and gives the word הלל its negative connotation. There is no English letter that corresponds to the Hebrew letter ח; the letter h is used instead. The words "hollow" and "hole" signify emptiness (חלל, *chalal*).

6

The Number Eight
and the Oil:
A Link to Holiness

THE *Zohar* (LECH LECHA, 96) says that because King David was anointed with a קרן (*keren*, horn), his kingdom endured. קרן (*keren*) is the source of the Latin word "cornu," which means "horn" (note the similarity of sound between this word and the word "coronation" (of kings).

If we substitute the מ, which immediately precedes it in the alphabet, for the letter נ in the word קרן (*keren*), the word מקר (*makor,* source or beak) is formed. This suggests that the horn receives its sustenance from the מקר (*mekor,* source) of blessings, which is from Above. The letters of מקר precede the letters ן, ש, and ר, the main letters of the word ראשון (*rishon,* first). The word ראשון includes an א, which is connected to the wonder of high, the crown.

The English word for מקר (*mekor*) is "source" (שרש, *shoresh*). The letter ש is interchangeable with the letter s (ש); therefore, the word "source" is similar to the word שורש (*shoresh,* root). Even the shape of the letter ש suggests a root.

כתר (*keter*) means "crown" or something round, which suggests that the attribute of כתר (*keter,* majesty) is the source of the enveloping light (*Kehillat Yaakov, ibid.*). This is also apparent from the fact that the letters אורה (*ora*) are numerically similar to the letters of קרן (*keren*).

אָרה = 1 + 200 + 5 = 1 + 2 + 5
קרן = 100 + 200 + 50 = 1 + 2 + 5

The idea of anointing kings with oil (שמן, *shemen*) is also seen in the small numerical value of the word כתר (*keter*; 20 + 400 + 200 = 620; 6 + 2 + 0 = 8), which is 8, שמנה (*shemona*)—which has the same letters as השמן (*hashemen*, the oil). The association of oil with holiness can be seen in the English language, too: The words "oil" and "holy" are both related to "halo," which refers to celestial light.

The word משחה (*mishcha*, oily substance) is used as a synonym for oil, and as a verb means to anoint kings and to make vessels holy. The connection between שמן (*shemen*) and משחה (*mishcha*) can be seen in the letters of which they are composed. משחה (*mishcha*) has the same letters as חמשה (*chamisha*, five), and השמן (*hashemen*, the oil) has the same letters as שמנה (*shemona*, eight). The attribute of glory, הוד (*hod*, glory), is the eighth of the ten attributes, and the fifth of the seven attributes of emotion. Oil (connected to the number eight), the source of anointing and holiness, is the "glory" and "splendor" of kingship and priesthood.

The importance of השמן (*hashemen*) can be understood by the fact that its letters are the same as those of נשמה (*neshama*, soul) and also שמנה (*shemona*, eight), the number representing that which is above nature. The numeral 6, corresponding to the six days of the week—the lower, physical world—contains a circle in its lower half; the numeral 9, the highest of the numerals, representing the world-to-come—the higher world—has a circle in its upper half. The numeral 8, with a circle in both its lower and upper halves, represents a link (it even looks like a link) that joins the two worlds.

The numeral 8, which is made up of two circles, denotes the two worlds. In German, eight is *aCHT*, which is similar to the Hebrew letter ח (*CHeT*), whose numerical value is 8. "Eight" and *acht* are similar words because gh is sometimes read as a ח. In a positive sense, ח refers to חיות (*chayut*, life), which refers to the נשמה (*neshama*, the soul) which is the source of life. נשמה and שמנה (*shemona*, eight) have the same letters.

There are a few ideas about how the number six represents the physical world. "Six" sounds similar to its Hebrew equivalent שש (*shesh*) if the ש is read as ש, and is true which in many other languages. The word שש (*shesh*) consists of a double set of three branches, which clearly represents the number six. Moreover, its numerical value of 600 (300 + 300) suggests that which it represents; the physical world.

According to Kabbalah, the number six corresponds to the attribute of foundation, upon which the continued existence of the world depends. שת (*shat*, basis, foundation) is related to the word שש (*shesh*) in that the first letters of the words are identical, and the second letters are adjacent in the Hebrew alphabet. In English, the word "sex," which has connotations related to "founding," is related to the word "six."

That the number nine stands for the higher, eternal world is apparent from the fact that the small numerical value of all multiples of nine is 9—e.g., 18 is 1 + 8 = 9; 27 is 2 + 7 = 9, etc. The small numerical value of אמת (*emet*, truth) is also 9 (1 + 40 + 400 = 1 + 4 + 4 = 9).

The numerals 6 and 9 are parallel, as can be seen by their shape. The sixth of the seven attributes is actually the ninth when the three attributes of rationality (חכמה, בינה, כתר) are included.

This world—represented by the number six—is a basis of or corridor to the next world, the world of truth, which is represented by the number nine. When the material aspect of this world is elevated and sanctified, the "6" is elevated to "9."

A person's נשמה (*neshama*, soul), which is located in the brain, is a link between the parts of his soul outside his body (יחידה, *yechida*, and חיה, *chaya*), and those inside his body (רוח, *ruach*, and נפש, *nefesh*), which are located in the heart and liver. The נשמה's (*neshama*) function is, therefore, similar to that of the oil in a lamp, which links the fire to the wick (נשמה, *neshama*, soul, and השמן, *hashemen*, the oil, have the same letters). Just as the purity of the oil adds to the quality and strength of the flame, so does the purity of the soul affect a person's saintliness. Note the similarity between the English words "oil" and "holy."

7

The "Saturated" Number Seven and the "Rich" Number Ten

BETWEEN THIS WORLD and the world-to-come will be the time of the Messiah and of תחית המתים (*techiat hametim*, Resurrection of the Dead). These days are associated with the number eight, as Chazal have deduced from the verse: למנצח על השמינית, "For the leader, on the *shminit* (a musical instrument with eight שמנה, strings)" (Psalms 12:1) (*Erechin* 13b). They say that in the time of the Messiah, the harp will have eight strings, as opposed to the present-day harp, which has only seven strings. Chazal say that in the verse שבע, שמחית את פניך הי, "Fullness (שבע, *sova*) of joy is in Your presence" (Psalms 16:11), the word שבע (*sova*, fullness or satisfaction) should be read as שבע (*sheva*, seven). This shows the connection between the number seven and the feeling of satisfaction and satiety. The number seven, the attribute of majesty, which includes all the attributes, is a basis of this world. This concept can be further understood by the facts that the full range of colors in the rainbow is seven, and that there are seven basic notes in the full musical scale, which provides a person with a feeling of complete harmony or satisfaction. One can also see the similarity between the word "seven" and its Hebrew equivalent, שבע (*sheva*).

The word שבע can be divided into "the ש (which means the שרש, *shoresh*, the source) of the עב" (*av*, cloud), which also refers to Creation. The word עב refers to the cloud that covers God's light in the world (עולם, *olam*). The word עולם, whose root is עלם (hidden), also refers to a "covering." The numerical value of the word עב (70 + 2) is 72, which refers to the seventy-two letters of God's name as well as the seventy-two names of God, each of which contain three letters. These names are found in three verses in the incident of the splitting of the Red Sea, each verse consisting of seventy-two letters. These forces of God, represented by each name, are involved in Creation. As we have seen, the שׁ is the letter of light; therefore, שׁבע is "the light behind the cloud," which refers to Creation.

The letters following the word שׁבע (פ, ג, ת) form the word גפת (*gufot*, bodies), also demonstrating that the basis of Creation is the number seven. גפות refers to the birth of a human being, which is creation. עב, the letters preceding גף (*gaf*, wing or side), are also related to the word כנף (*kanaf*, wing), a covering that hides the body. The English word "fog" (פג), meaning a thick cloud, has the same letters as גף.

Reading a Hebrew word from left to right will sometimes produce an English word. An example of this is the word "FaLSe," a reversal of the letters of סלף (*self*, distortion, falsification), which is also a reversal of פלס (*peles*, straight), implying ישׁרות (*yashrut*, straightness), which is the opposite of falsehood.

Chazal (*ibid.*) relate the number ten to the time of the Resurrection, as is said: עלי עשׂור, עלי נבל, "With an instrument of ten strings and with the psaltery [a large harp-like instrument]" (Psalms 92:4), and also זמרו לו בנבל עשׂור—"Sing praises to Him with the psaltery of ten strings" (*ibid.* 33:2). The Gemara says that the harp will have ten strings at the time of the Resurrection, as at that time all ten spheres will be revealed clearly (today, they are still covered). The number ten expresses the unity of all the numerals and attributes. The English word "rich" (רישׁ), reversed, resembles the Hebrew word עשׁיר (*ashir*), which has the same meaning. The number ten (עשׂר, *eser*), which is the total number of attributes, has the same letters as עשׁר (*osher*, riches); שׁבע (*sheva*) is the number of the attributes of emotion.

The numerals 1, 4, and 7 are made up of straight lines, and all the other numerals are rounded. These numbers, as can been seen by their shape, do not have a meaning unto themselves like the 6, 9, or 8, which represent the connecting link between the two worlds. The numeral 7 resembles the Hebrew letter ד, and is probably derived from the attribute of kingship (מלכות, *malchut*), which they both symbolize. The letter ד, which means דל (*dal*, poor), is related to the attribute of מלכות (*malchut*), as this is the only attribute that is dependent on the others. (*Kehillat Yaakov*, Dalet). The word מלכות means תם כול (*kol tam*, all perfect), which means "everything." The English word "dull" also denotes something that has no particular intrinsic value.

The very shape of the numeral 4 somewhat resembles the letter ד (*dalet*), whose numerical value is 4. The four elements are the basis of Creation, the seven being the expansion; therefore, the concept of kingship is also implied in the number four. Even the corresponding letters of these numbers are similar in shape, i.e., the ד (four) is similar to the ז (seven). The initials of the words that describe the four elements—fire (אש, *esh*); wind (רוח, *ruach*); water (מים, *mayim*); earth (עפר, *afar*)—make up the word ארבע (*arba*, four) if ב is substituted for the מ (both ב and מ are palatals).

The shape of the numeral 1 alludes to the unity of all ten attributes, as is suggested by the letters of the word אחד (*echad*, one). The א (*alef*) refers to the highest sphere, that of the crown, for it refers to God, the אלוף (*aluf*, chief) of the world. The ח (whose numerical value is 8) refers to the eight spheres under it. The ד represents the four corners of the world over which God rules—i.e., his kingdom.

In many languages, the word for the number one sounds similar to the Hebrew word הן (*hain*); for instance, in Japanese *hain* is the word for the number one. Chazal tell us (*Masechet Shabbat* 31b) that the verse הן יראת הי היא חכמה, "The fear of God is wisdom," meaning that the הן (*hain*, one) being referred to is יראת ה' (*yirat Hashem*, fear of God), which is considered as wisdom. *Sefer HaAruch* (Ch. הן) says that the word הן (*hain*, one) stems from the holy language; these letters are different than the other letters in the Hebrew alphabet, as each does not have a pair. The unit letters are paired off so that their total is ten (א-ט; ב-ח; etc.), except for the ה. The same idea is seen in the "tens": The י is paired off with the צ; כ-פ; etc., totaling a hundred, except for the נ. Thus, ה and נ remain "alone."

It is possible that the English word "one" (והן) is related to the word אין (*ayn*, nothing), which is the root of יש (*yaish*, that which exists), as the world was created יש מאין (*yaish mayayin*, something from nothing). The numerical value of הן, 55, also hints at the Creation of the world; The Gemara Minchat says that the world was created with the letter ה, בהבראם (*behibaram*: ב-ה-בראם, *behai baram*). Each letter of the word אין (*ayn*) is the source of a different attribute: the א of כתר (*keter*, crown); the י of חכמה (*chochma*, wisdom); and the נ of בינה (*binah*, understanding), the three attributes that are the foundation of everything.

The shape of the numeral 1 resembles the Hebrew letter ו (*vav*), which signifies unity by both its form and its numerical value

(6). Six is a perfect number, as it is the sum of its factors, 1, 2, and 3 (Ibn Ezra, Exodus 3:15).

Multiplying the numerical value of ו (*vav*), 6, by ten yields sixty (denoted by the circular letter ס, *samech*), which represents unity in a higher world. The five final letters מנצפך, may be given equivalent values in the hundreds: ש = 300; ת = 400; ך = 500; ם = 600; etc. The final ם (*mem*) resembles the circular shape of ס (*samech*), whose value is 60, and can therefore be assigned the value 600. This represents unity in the highest world.

The round, closed shape of the ס (*samech*) suggests unity and perfection. For example, the total number of books of the Mishnah is six, and there are sixty tractates in the Gemara. We find a similar comment in the *Zohar Chadash* (108a) on the verse (Genesis 46:26): "All the souls that came with Jacob to Egypt . . . were sixty-six." Sixty is clearly a significant number, generally accepted as representing unity. Regarding the calculation of time, there are sixty seconds, sixty minutes, and sixty days (when two months are coupled). This is discussed by the holy Ari, who said that the twelve months of the year are made up of six male months and six female months—the six summer and six winter months. The twenty-four hours of the day are divided into four time periods of six hours each: before noon, after noon, before midnight, after midnight.

The letters סו (expressing the number sixty-six) are central to the word יסוד (*yesod*, foundation), the attribute they represent. The shape of these letters, סו, resembles the number ten, which signifies completion and perfection.

The letter o is a circle, as is the letter ס; both are in the fifteenth position in their respective alphabets. On a deeper level, we see that the ס (*samech*), in its negative sense, represents the power of Satan, whose entire strength lies in the external, the superficial—that which has no content. The shape of the ס also represents an empty outer shell. The English o is pronounced with the tongue withdrawn, which leaves the mouth empty. The sound "o" in Hebrew is written with a ו (*vav*), a חולם, ו, whose numerical value is 6, the numeral with a rounded base.

8

The Letter *Hei*, Life;
The Letter *Mem*, Death

THE LETTER ה, whose numerical value is 8, in a positive sense represents חיות (*chayut*, life). Eight, שמנה, has the same letters as נשמה (*neshama*, soul), the source of life. A perfect life is one that unites the material with the spiritual, as is suggested by the joining of two circles in the numeral 8.

It is significant that a *brit mila* is held on the eighth day, for this *mitzvah* sanctifies the physical, infusing it with the holiness of the spiritual world. The נשמה (*neshama*, soul), based in the brain, is higher than the emotion of the heart. The basis of true life, connected with the brain, is revealed by inverting the letters of the word מח (*moach*, brain) and inserting two י s (i.e., God's name, which is made up of two י s), forming the word חיים (*chayim*, life). The word חכם (*chacham*, wise person; 8 + 20 + 40 = 68) is similar to חיים (8 + 10 + 10 + 40 = 68) and has the same numerical value, teaching us that life ought to be based on wisdom.

It is interesting that "live," the English word for חיים (*chayim*), is similar to the word "love," an emotion of the heart, which is לב (*lev*) in Hebrew. In German, "love" is *liebe* and "living" is *Leben*, both of which are based on the word *lev*. (In Hebrew, b (ב) and v (ב) are the same letter.)

The letter ה also suggests strength, for it is derived from the word חתת (*chatat*, trepidation), which is fear engendered by the strength of the enemy. The חתים (Hittites) were so called, according to the Chozeh of Lublin in his book *Torat Emet*, because the peoples of

29

the world were afraid of their strength. The same idea can be seen by the fact that the letter ח, as written in the Torah, is made up of two זז. זין (*zayin*) means weapon, and, thus, the ח signifies two opposing forces, which are the cause of fear.

As we have seen, the letter ח (whose numerical value is 8, שמנה) is connected to נשמה. According to Kabbalah, the נשמה (*neshama*, soul) is connected to the attribute of בינה (*binah*, understanding), as can be seen from the book of Job: נשמת שד–י תבינם, "The soul of God will understand them." The attributes of בינה and גבורה (*gevura*, strength) are also related, both being on the left (*Kehillat Yaakov*, Neshama).

The English word "heat" sounds similar to ח′ת (*chet*). Warmth and fire are connected to strength, as we have seen. The connection is also made by the fact that the planet Mars, which is reddish, is associated with the attribute of fire and strength (*Sefer Yetzira*).

In the negative sense, ח (*chet*) is the initial letter of, and represents, חטא (*chet*, sin) (*Letters of Rabbi Akiva*, Chet), which is the outcome of the "heat" of passion and destruction. This is expressed in the English words "hit" and "heat."

The letter ט (*tet*), whose numerical value is 9, which signifies טוב (*tov*, goodness) (*Kehillat Yaakov*, ט), did not appear in the first set of tablets; neither did the word טוב (*tov*) (*Bava Kama* 55a), for these tablets were destined to break. The ninth attribute of יסוד (*yesod*, foundation) is the root of טוב (*Kehillat Yaakov*, *ibid.*), and is identical to the sixth attribute. Perhaps this is why the shape of the numeral 6 and that of the letter ט (when written in script) are similar: Both are based on the same attribute. The *Kehillat Yaakov* says (*ibid.*) that if the attributes are reversed, the ninth is חכמה (*chochma*, wisdom). חכמה (*chochma*) is made up of the words כח–מה (*koach mah*, Strength, what is it?), implying that wisdom has no physical dimension, as is said: "But wisdom, where (מאין, *m'ayn*, from nothing) shall it be found" (Job 28:12). He also explains that the letter ט (*tet*, spelled טית) is the same as it if would be spelled out טיט (*teet*), which also means "clay." Similarly, *Letters of Rabbi Akiva* says: "Do not read טית, but טיט." The concept of wisdom is associated with clay, which suggests היולי (*hiyuli*, a primeval force), the unprocessed material from which everything was created, as the Ramban says, at the beginning of Genesis. This may be why the English word "nine" sounds so similar to the Hebrew אין (*ayn*, nothing) and to the German "nein" (meaning both "nine" and "no").

The letter ט (*tet*) suggests death. The Ramban says (*Emunah U'Bitachon*, Ch. 19) that in early times, kings would write the letter ט

against the name of a person whom they sentenced to death: וטטתה
במטטה השמד, "And I will sweep it with the broom of destruction" (Isaiah 14:23). This may be the origin of the German word *tot* (dead), the English words "dead" and "death," and similar-sounding, like-meaning words in other languages (the "d," "t," and "th" sounds are related, all being dental sounds).

In a positive sense, the letter ט (*tet*) denotes the annihilation of the physical, which is the basis of wisdom and of life. "This is the Law (Torah) when a man dies (ימות, *yamut*) in a tent" (Numbers 19:14) shows that the words of the Torah are fulfilled only when a person dedicates himself (ממת, *maimit*, lit., "makes himself die") to it absolutely (*Berachot* 43b). This implies that a person must annihilate the physical in himself in order to achieve the spiritual values of Torah.

In English, too, the words "mortar" (clay) and "mortal" are related. It is interesting to note that the Hebrew word מות (*mavet*, death) is contained in both of these words.

9
—

The Strength and
"Power" of פאר

THE LETTERS OF פלא (*pele*, wonder), when rearranged, spell אלף, and relate to the attribute of כתר (*keter*, crown). This hints at the wonderful, נפלא (*nifla*, majestic) attribute within man. For this reason, this attribute is kabbalistically called עתיק (*atik*), for it is distant and removed from man's perception and understanding. The English word "antique" (ענתיק) is derived from עתיק (*atik*). The attribute of עתיק (כתר, *keter*, crown) influences the attribute of תפארת (*tiferet*, beauty), whose root is פאר, whose letters follow those of עתק in the alphabet (א follows ת). The English word "fair" (פאיר) sounds like and has a similar meaning to פאר (*p'er*), a balanced and beautiful state. By the order of its letters, the word פאר reveals this balanced state—the א separating the פר, the letters of strength. The letter פ is a strong letter, as expressed by its strong labial pronunciation. Also, its numerical value is 80, ten times that of the letter ח, which also expresses strength. The letter ר (*raish*) is pronounced by the movement of the tongue, and is a letter of movement. Examples of English and Hebrew words expressing speed and movement are: "rash," "rush," "race," רץ, ממהר.

The letters פר are also the source of the English word "**fire**" (פיר)—fire being the source of strength. The letter פ (*peh*, פה) means "mouth," and is an explosive sound made with the lips. The shape of the ר (*raish*) resembles rays of light spreading out; the shape of the R is like a head at the top, with two feet at the bottom, as if it were running. Similarly, the Hebrew word ריש (*raish*, or ראש, *rosh*) means "head." The brain, which controls movement, is located in the head.

The word "ash" (אש) stems from the word אש (*esh*, fire). Just as the א separates the letters פר in the word פאר, so does the "a" separate the word "fire," making it "fair" ("a" and א are parallel in their respective alphabets).

The letter א, the central letter, the foundation of the word פאר (*p'er*), has its source in the upper פלא (*pele*, wonder, whose letters are the same as אלף, as we have seen), the wonders of God—i.e., the highest sphere. The numerical value of the name of God, יהוה (26), is the same as the letters that make up the letter א (א is made up of יוי = 10 + 610 = 26). When the two יs of God's name are included in the word מח (*moach*, brain), the word חיים (*chayim*, life) is formed. Theses two letters hint at the upper חכמה (*chochma*, wisdom), which is the foundation of life.

The physician (רופא, *rofe*) has the power to heal (רפא, *rafe*), which stems from the attribute of פאר (*p'er*, harmony), which is dependent on the foundation of life. The unbalanced פאר is the negative state of פרא (*pere*, wild), whereby the פר, the source of strength, rules over the foundation of the א (*alef*), whose source is in the מח, the brain. From this are derived the English words "ferity" (פאריתי), which means the state of being wild (פראות, *peraot*) or savage, and "feral," like a wild, untamed beast.

In Latin, *par* (פאר) means equal or regular, which is the state of the attribute of פאר, which is placed between that of חסד (*chesed*) on the right and גבורה (*gevura*) on the left. The English word "power" (פור) is derived from the Hebrew פר, the source of strength and power. The numerical value of פר (*par*; 80 + 200 = 280) is ten times that of כח (*koach*, strength; 20 + 8 = 28) to teach us that פר is the source of כח—a compulsive force, כפי–ה (*kefiya*), hinted at by the letter כף (*kof*), and the active strength of the ח. The letter ח is made up of זז, like two swords facing each other (זין, as we saw, means "weapon"), which symbolizes the war between strength (גבורה, *gevura*) and life (חיים, *chayim*). In Hebrew, the word לחם (*lechem*, bread) is similar to מלחמה (*milchama*, war, whose root is לחם), and מזון (*mazon*, food) is similar to instruments of זין (*zayin*, war). This similarity is also found between the word "feed" (פיד) and the word "fight" (פית), which is related to war.

In Kabbalah, the expression of פר symbolizes the five final letters of מנצפ"ך (*Bnei Yissacher*, Adar, third article). The letter פה (*peh*) symbolizes life, which is revealed by the power of speech, the פה (*peh*, mouth). The Targum, in reference to the verse (Genesis 2:6): לנפש חיה

ויהי האדם, "And man became a living being," says: והוית באדם לרוח ממללא, "A speaking spirit entered man."

פר, together with the negative aspect of the צ (*tzadi*), forms the word פרץ (*peretz*), פריצות (*pritzut*, breaking the code of morality, and defilement), which is a result of enticement (פתוי, *pituy*) and ensnarement (צדיה, *tzediya*). (The positive aspect of the צ being צדקות (*tzidkut*, righteousness.) This word also suggests the negative connotation of פר, the bad within a person that rules over the צ, the צדיק (*tzadik*), the person's goodness.

A synonym for harlotry (פריצות, *pritzut*) is "prostitution," a word that is clearly related. The word פרץ (*peretz*) is similar to חרץ (*charatz*, cut into, engrave) (פ = 80 and ח = 8 are interchangeable, according to the key of איק בכר), and, rearranged, it spells רצח (*retzach*, murder). The sins of harlotry, immorality, and nakedness (ערוה, *erva*), are the core of evil (רע, *ra*) in the world, and lead to the undermining (ערער, *irer*) of the foundations of society and, eventually, to murder. (See Chapter 11 regarding קר, the root of defilement, and קרקר, *kirker*, the power that destroys the foundations of the world.)

The danger inherent in the letters פר can be understood by the words "**per**mit" and "**per**missiveness." Permitting that which should be forbidden leads to רשע (*resha*, wickedness). According to Rabbi Samson Raphael Hirsch, the word רשע (*rasha*, wicked person) is similar to רשה (*rasha*, permitted), which indicates that permitting what is forbidden leads to wickedness, the ע (*ayin*) being a stronger form of the ה (*hei*).

In the positive sense, when the פר is joined to צ (*tzadi*), the word צרף (*tziraf*, refined) is produced. This indicates that when people refine and purify themselves, they produce a world that is צרוף (*tzaruf*, refined), free of פרץ (*peretz*, wickedness), a breach of correct values. צרוף (*tzaruf*) represents harmony and unity in the world; פרץ (*peretz*) leads to a breach of this harmony, both in the individual and in the world. The letters פר used positively produce the English word "PuRe," which is related to the word "fire." Fire can burn the impurity from an object, leaving it refined and pure, which is also related to the "pure," refined soul. Judgment is often passed on a man that he should be "poor," in order to "purify" him (מצרפים, *metzarfim*) from his sins. This can be seen by the fact that the word דך (*dach*, poor) is related to זך (*zach*, pure), for ד and ז are often interchanged in Hebrew and Aramaic.

A word similar to צרף (*tziref*, purify) is שפר (*shiper*, improved, beautified). This is also similar to the word ספיר (*sapir*, sapphire), the basis and source of beauty. The same letters, rearranged, form the words רפש (*refesh*, mud) and פרש (*peresh*, dung, a waste product, something unwanted by its source). This idea is also found in the word "perish" (פריש from פרוש, *parush*, separated), when something becomes unfit for use, dirty. This word is similar to פרץ (*peretz*—פריצות, *pritzut*, immorality), which leads to spiritual defilement. The letters of רפש (*refesh*) or פרש (*peresh*) can be changed, using the rule of איק בכר, to form the word חבל (*chavol*, destroyed or damaged; פרש = 80 + 200 + 300; חבל = 8 + 2 + 30). This is similar to the fact that פרץ (*peretz*, defilement) and רצח (*retzach*, corruption) are the source of destruction and troubles in the world.

If the ש (*shin*) is moved from the beginning of the word to the end, a complete change of meaning occurs. The ש, in the positive sense, expresses power and truth, and when it rules over the פר (*par*), the situation is שפיר (*shapir*, fire). When the פר, rules, however, the situation is רפש (*refesh*, ugly), which is similar in form and meaning to the English words "refuse" and "rubbish."

When the holy letter ה (*hei*, from God's name) is added to the word צר (*tzar*, narrow), it becomes צוהר (*tzohar*, shining and pure). The *Sidduro Shel Shabbat* says that צרה (*tzara*, trouble) leads to צוהר (*tzohar*, refinement of the soul), which leads to רצה (*ratza*, finding favor in God's eyes), both having the same letters. The same idea can be seen if we remove the א (*alef*) from the word ארץ (*aretz*, which means and sounds similar to "earth" in English), leaving צר (*tzar*, trouble). Without the א, the אלוף (*aluf*, master) of the world (i.e., God, who is represented by the letter א, whose numerical value is 1), the world is full of trouble (*Sidduro Shel Shabbat*). The Midrash says that ארץ (*aretz*, earth) is so called because "she wanted" (רצתה, *ratzta*) to do the will of her Creator (Bereishith Rabba 5:8).

The Jewish people repented on purim, the time when the force of the פר (*par*, might) threatened to destroy them because of their sins. These sins caused the negative פר to become פור (*pur*, the ו representing the inclusion of holiness). The holy forces of might, of פר, were transferred to the enemies of the Jewish people (*Bnei Yissachar*, Adar 3).

The red "heifer" (פרה, *parah*) came to "purify" the Israelites from the defilement that resulted from contact with a dead body, and להפר (*lehafer*, to annul), the strict judgment and harsh decree (*Zohar* on Chukat). The letters of הפר (*hefer*) are the same as those of פרה (*parah*). It is interesting to note that a young cow is called a "heifer" in English.

Many English words depicting power and strength begin with the letter "f": "force," "firm," "fruit," "fertility." Fire, as we have seen, is connected to the attribute of power.

The words חם (*cham*, hot) and חת (*chet*, fear) are related, for the מ (*mem*, מ = 40) and the ת (*tav*, ת = 400) are interchangeable according to the key of איק בכר. This is also revealed in English: The word "fire" (פיר), the source of heat, is similar to the word "fear" (פיר). (חת, *chet*, fear, is similar to the English word "heat," חית.) "F" and "R" (פר), in English, are the source of many words meaning stability and form: "firm," "form." The connection of form, צורה (*tzura*, 90 + 6 + 200 + 5 = 301), which is based on the פר (*par*, whose source is in fire (אש, *esh*; 1 + 300 = 301), is revealed by the fact that they possess the same numerical value. Fire (אש, *esh*) is the basis of צורה (*tzura*, shape), which is the opposite of the material. The idea that stability (יציבות, *yetzivut*) and shape (צורה, *tzura*), are connected stems from the idea that the structured man (צורה, *tzura*) is stable (יציב, *yetziv*); a material man is subject to change, while the Creation (יציר, *yetzir*) is stable (יציב, *yetziv*; ב = 2 and ר = 200 are interchangeable according to the rule of איק-בכר).

10

The Positive and Negative Meanings of Words

THE FOUNDATION OF HEAT, the source of fire and strength, is the letter ח (*chet*), which, in the positive sense, represents life (חיים, *chayim*). Negatively, the ח represents חטא (*chet*, sin) (*Letters of Rabbi Akiva*, Letter ח). The idea is that if life is not exploited for the good, it becomes the source of evil. This can also be seen by the English word "live," which, if rearranged, forms the word "evil." An example of positive and negative meanings, according to the order of the letters, can be seen also in the words עשר (*osher*, wealth) and רשע (*resha*, evil). If one uses these powers for the good, on the right side, then one acquires עשר (*osher*, riches), but if the left side prevails, the evil side, the רשע (*resha*, wickedness), dominates.

These concepts can also be understood by the use of the words for the sides, the right side being the straight, good side. In English, "right" means "right side" or "correct"; the German *recht* shares both these meanings. The name of the left, the evil side, is שמאל (*smol*), which is similar to the name of the evil angel, סמאל (Samael). Its name, סמאל, reveals its desire to סם אל (*sam kel*, to blind the eyes of God), to extinguish the spiritual and holy with the "left force." This is the evil force that conceals the Godly light. The same idea can be seen in the Hebrew words עור (*ohr*) and רוע (*roa*). The עור (skin), which is a result of evil (רוע), blinds and hides the internal. In the same way, the word חטא (*chet*, sin) hints at its purpose, which is to טח (*tach*, plaster over), hide, the light of the א, the אלוף (*aluf*, Master of the world), God himself (חטא = א–טח). In English, we can find the same idea in the word "veil" (whose meaning is similar to that of וילון, *vilon*, curtain), which has the same letters as "evil" and "vile."

Deeper analysis of the word "vile" will give us a greater appreciation of the depth of the holy language. "Vile," denoting wickedness and worthlessness, is similar to the Hebrew word בל (*bal*, emptiness and worthlessness; the "b" (ב) and "v" (ב) sounds are the same letter in Hebrew), which, when reversed, spells לב (*lev*, heart). These letters are also the first two letters of the word בלע (*bela*, wickedness). This is apparent from the numerical similarity between the words בלע (2 + 30 + 70) and רשע (*resha*, wickedness; 200 + 300 + 70). We see the same idea in the fact that the word following אפס (*efes*, nothingness) in the alphabet is בצע (*betza*, ill-gotten gains).

The Gemara says (*Shabbat* 104a) that the Hebrew ר (*raish*) suggests a רשע (*rasha*, wicked person). The word רשע contains the same letters as רעש (*raash*, noise), for the רשע (wicked person) causes a great commotion; he becomes agitated in his efforts to satisfy his desires. The English word "rash" means doing something in a rush without giving proper thought. The word "race" also refers to hurrying, and is close in sound and meaning to the Hebrew רץ (*ratz*); the words "rash" and "rush" sound similar to ריש (*raish*). When the letter ר (*raish*) is the initial letter, then "rashness" and rules, and the result is רשע (*resha*, wickedness). However, when the letters of the word רשע are reversed, and the ע (*ayin*, suggesting perception and thought) rules, the result is עשר (*osher*, wealth).

The word "live" (also, "love") is associated with לב (*lev*, heart), and when the heart is corrupted, the letters are reversed, forming the word "evil." The very word אהבה (*ahava*, love) is based on the word הבה (*hava*, giving), which shows that the basis of love is giving to others. Giving is the basis of life; a person who receives and does not give is considered as if dead, as our rabbis say (*Nedarim* 64b): "A poor person is considered as a dead person." It is for this reason that the word for life ("live") is similar to the word that expresses giving ("love").

We can learn from the fact that "live," reversed, is "evil." Being evil or wicked distorts and ruins a person's life; (life used in the sense of happiness and enjoyment). A similar idea can be found in Hebrew by reversing the word בצע (*betza*, ill-gotten gains), forming the words עצב (*etzev*, pain). Ill-gotten gains cause pain to the perpetrator and destroy his purpose in life.

Another example of a word in which reversing the order of the letters reverses its meaning is ענג (*oneg*, delight) and נגע (*nega*, plague).

From this we can learn that having the correct attitude in life brings delight, and having the wrong causes a "plague"—i.e., troubles come about. The English word "agony" (עגוני) is similar in sound and meaning to the Hebrew יגון (*yagon*, sadness), which is the sadness a person feels as a result of pain (נגע, *nega*). The word נגע is the same as the word נגע (*noga*, also meaning pain; the ע and the ה are interchangeable, as both are guttural letters) as can be seen in Lamentations (3:32–33): כי ה׳ הגה על בל חטותי–ה, "Because God caused pain due to her sins." The ע is stronger than the ה; therefore, נגע is a stronger form of pain than נגע.

Words that differ from each other only in the degree of emphasis of a particular sound show a process of change. For example, the words יסר (*yasar*), ישר (*yashar*), and יצר (*yatzar*) differ only in the degree of emphasis of their middle letters, which are all dental. One can see from these differences that the power of יסורים (*yisurim*, suffering) corrects (ליישר, *leyasher*) a person's spiritual standing, and changes (ליצר, *leyatzer*) him into a person of צורה (*tzura*, one who is fully formed, mature).

The action of יסר (*yasor*, to torture, cause suffering), is stronger than that of ישר (*yashar*) or יצר (*yazar*), as can also be seen in נסר (*nasar*, sawed) and נשר (*nashar*, fell out). Sawing wood or iron (נסר, *nasar*) is an action that requires strength and strong tools, while the נשר (*nashar*) refers to shedding hair or wool, not requiring strength. "To saw" has the "s" sound of נסר (*nasar*); "to shear" (as in sheep) has the "sh" sound of נשר (*nashar*). יסר (*yasar*) is similar to נסר (*nasar*) because troubles (יסורים, *yisurim*) "saw" upon the body and soul. Similarly, the words "sore" (סור) and "sorrow" (סורו) (צער, *tzaar*) are connected to יסר (*yasar*) and perhaps to the word "sour," bitter, as well. In a deeper sense, however, "sour" may be connected to שאר (*seor*, yeast), the ingredient that makes dough ferment, i.e., sour. Kabbalah says that the source (ראש, *rosh*—שאר, *seor*, rearranged) of defilement, Amalek, the chief of the other nations, is the "sourness in the dough" that causes troubles and suffering in the world.

The homonyms "saw" (cut with a serrated edge) and "saw" (from the verb "to see") are related. "Saw" (past tense of "to see") is similar to the Hebrew word שור, (*shor*), which means seeing (the שs and שs are interchangeable). We find in Kabbalah that the words שיר (*shir*, song) and זמר (*zemer*, melody) are both connected to the idea of cutting. זמיר (*zamir*, pruning), a form of cutting, is related to שיר (*shir*, from להשיר, *lehashir*, to cut off hair), for both denote the "cutting down" of the barrier of materialism between a man's soul and his Creator. A שיר (*shir*, song) is close to שור (*shor*, seeing) because the removal (השרה, *hashara*) of these barriers opens a person's eyes to a higher degree of perception, as when all the children of Israel sang שירת הים (*Shirat Hayam*, the song they sang at the crossing of the Red Sea).

The Hebrew word שר (*sar*, officer or minister), meaning an important person, is connected to the verb שרר (*sarar*, ruled) and the noun שררה (*serara*, high position). This is, perhaps, the derivation of the word "sir" (סר), a title given to someone of high standing. Kabbalistically, this is also connected to שרר (*sharor*, singing). The power of song refers to the attribute of strength (גבורה, *gevura*), as the *Zohar* says in connection with the word ישרא-ל (Israel, which, if rearranged, spells שיר-א-ל): שיר (*shir*, song, which is related to גבורה, *gevura*, strength); א-ל (*kel*, which is related to חסד, *chesed*, kindness, referring to God of lovingkindness) *Kehillat Yaakov*, Yisrael. Kabbalistically, the Levites, who sang in the Temple, are said to be connected to the attribute of strength.

שרר (*sarar*, 300 + 200 + 200), according to the בכר-איק, has the same numerical value as גבר (*gavar*, 3 + 2 + 200), showing the strength of שר. In this way, שררה (*serara*, high position) and גבורה (*gevura* might) are connected. The English word for שרר and גבר is "govern." According to Kabbalah, the Hebrew letters of the English word "man" (מן), meaning גבר, represent the two most important attributes of might of the five attributes of might represented by the final letters פ, ך, מ, נ, צ (*Kehillat Yaakov*, Man).

The letters of גדר, "guard" (*gader*, enclosure or fence), follow those of גבר (*gever*, man), indicating that a man, גבר, guards himself from evil with the attribute of might (גבורה, *gevura*) through his strength of character. According to the key of איק-בכר, the word גדר (*geder*, 3 + 4 + 200) is connected to the word שמר (*shamar*, 300 + 40 + 200), which also means "to guard."

The English word "sore" sounds like the Hebrew צרה (*tzara*, trouble, or, in Ashkenazic pronunciation, "tzoro"), similar to the English word "sorrow." (The English "s" is interchangeable with the Hebrew צ, *tzadi*.)

An interesting feature of the words עצב (*etzev*) and יגון (*yagon*) is the fact that the letters of each word contain words meaning color: עצב becomes צבע (*tzeva*, color) and יגון contains גון (*gvan*, shade of a color). Just as a color is a covering, so, too, is evil a cover that prevents the light of truth from being revealed. This can also be seen by rearranging the word "evil" into "veil," and רוע (*roa*, evil) into עור (*or*, skin). The word צר (*tzar*, narrow) is an expression of limiting light, because צער (*tzaar*, trouble) and עצב (*etzev*, pain) are related (the ר, *raish*, and ב, *bet*, are interchangeable by the key of איק-בכר).

Hebrew vowels, according to Kabbalah, are very important because they stem from the "counting of high" (ספירת העליונה, *sefira elyona*, the upper spheres). There are nine different vowels, corresponding to nine of the ten attributes. The attribute of majesty has no parallel vowel assigned to it because it is all-inclusive. Because of this, we often find two different Hebrew words made up of identical letters, but different vowel sounds; for example, קדשה (*kedusha*, holiness) has the same letters as קדשה (*kedaisha*, prostitute), indicating that by making a small change from holiness, the complete opposite ensues.

Certain letters are stronger than others, and when comparing words that have similar letters, the one with the stronger letter will show a stronger aspect of that word. This can be seen in the words אור (*ohr*, light) and עור (*or*, skin, or *iver*, blind), both sounding the same except that the ע, which symbolizes materialism, is a stronger letter. Thus, materialism (implied by עור) is a cover, a skin, covering the light (אור). This idea was discussed earlier in this chapter with the words נגה (*noga*) and נגע (*nega*).

The same idea is shown kabbalistically with the words טל (*tal*, dew) and לט (*lat*, enwrap), its reversed form. טל represents the attribute of light: טליך כי טל אורות, "For Your dew is the dew of light" (Isaiah 26:19). This refers to the light that is reserved for the Resurrection after the coming of the Messiah, as stated in the Gemara (*Ketubot* 111b). The color of the crystal of dew is the foundation of light (*Kehillat Yaakov*, Tal).

The connection between טל (*tal*) and light can also be seen by a numerical analysis. The value of טל is 39. The value of the word אהל (*ohel*), suggesting light, is 36 (1 + 5 + 30 = 36, plus 3, one for each of its letters, equaling 39). The three letters of the word אהל suggest the three sources of celestial light from which the thirty-six lights are derived. These thirty-six lights are represented by the word אהל (*ohel*).

לט (*lat*, טל, *tal* reversed) denotes covered and hidden, and is the Aramaic word for "curse." Its numerical value, 39, suggests the thirty-nine forces of defilement that conceal and close up the source of light (*Zohar* 3:194a). From this we understand why the thirty-nine types of creative work prohibited on the Sabbath are of such severity, as the day of שבת (*Shabbat*) is the source of light. Interestingly, the English

word "lot" means "fate," and denotes hidden forces within the Creation, and is thus related to the Hebrew word לט (hidden).

The letters following לט (*lat*) in the alphabet are מי (*mi*, who),
suggesting that לט, concealment of the Divine Presence arising from
the material covering, leads people to ask: מי ("Who is guiding the
world")?

The word חבל (*chavol*, to injure or wound) is the strong form of
the words הבל (*hevel*, nonsense or vanity) and עוול (*avel*, injustice), the
latter similar in meaning and sound to the English word "evil." This
indicates that deeds of injustice and vanity cause wounding and injury
in the world. The curses given to the children of Israel before they entered the land were given on a mountain called Eval, which is similar
to the English word "evil."

11

The Curse of the קר

שקר (*sheker*, FALSEHOOD), SUGGESTING EVIL, leads to מקרקר (*mekar-ker*), undermining of the world's foundations, for both share the letters of the word קר (*kar*), which the *Zohar* explains is the embodiment of the powers of evil.

The English word "curse" (קרס), which is the basis of troubles in this world, is the continuation of the forces of קר (*kar*, evil) with those of Satan, represented by the letter ס (*samech*). The letters following סרק (*srak*, emptiness) in the alphabet spell the word רשע (*resha*, evil), indicating the danger inherent in emptiness and vanity (the רשע—ע-ש-ר denotes poverty—רש—of thought—ע—עיון, which means deep thought).

קסרי (Kisri; today called Kaisari) was the Judean capital of the Roman Empire. The emperor (קסר, *kaisar*, Caesar) ruled over the י (the letter *yud*, which represents God), that which is holy, with the help of the force of evil, the קר (*kar*, emptiness), and Satan, the ס (*samech*).

Chazal say that there are four sins that prevent a person from experiencing the divine Presence, and one of these is שקר (*sheker*, falsehood) (*Sotah* 41b). Those who are involved in materialism are unable to perceive things in perspective, for materialism "blinds the eyes" of man. Another such sin is that of לצנות (*leitzanut*, mockery, scoffing). The word לץ (*letz*), reversed, is צל (*tzel*, shade), which explains how the scoffer is "shaded" from the divine light. Shade (שד) is related to the word "shell" (של), which means קליפה, a covering, signifying the force of defilement, that which covers the light and truth

(ד and ל are interchangeable, as palatal letters). Perhaps the English word "satire," biting wit, is related to the Hebrew סתר (*satar*, cover, as הסתר, *hester*, hidden, stems from the verb להסתיר, *lehastir*, to hide).

Acts of evil form a "skin," a covering, over truth, as can be seen by the word קרום (*krum*, "crust," קרסט); קר (*kar*) represents evil, as we have seen. Crust (קרסט) also contains the letter ס (*samech*), representing Satan, the cover preventing the penetration of the divine light. ס is all "cover" and no content.

Chazal consider anger to be a form of idolatry. The very word כעס (*kaas*, anger, to be "cross") is made up of כס–ע (*kas ayin*, covering the eye), for anger covers up, blinds, the intellect from seeing clearly. Chazal say that when a wise man becomes angry, his wisdom leaves him; the ע (*ayin*; עיון, *iyun*, power of perception) is covered up by his anger. The English word "cross" is similar to "crust," a covering. A person who is cross is blinded.

The evil power of Amalek, whose root is קר (*kar*), as the verse explains (Deuteronomy 25:18): אשר קרך בדרך, "How he chanced upon you on the way," Rashi says (*ibid.*) refers principally to קרי (*keri*, nocturnal defilement). This idea has entered English, with the word "crass" meaning "gross."

The anagrams of the word עמלק (Amalek), מעקל (*makel*, make crooked) and לעקם (*le'akem*, to bend), describe Amalek's cunning, which, like a snake, is crooked and bent. The English word "crooked" is connected to the word "crook," again expressing evil. The word עמלק also includes the word מלק (*malak*, to wring the neck of a living creature); Amalek cruelly wanted to "wring" the necks of the children of Israel and then לוק (*lak*, lick up, from the verb לקק, *lakek*) their blood.

Evil is expressed in the letters קר (*kar*), as can be seen in the words "crook," "cruel," and "crime." It is interesting to note that when the vowels are removed from "**cr**ooK," "cruel," and "crime," and the common "evil" (cr, קר), is eliminated, then the letters k (כ), l (ל), and m (מ) are left—consecutive letters in their respective alphabets. This reveals a connection of ideas and their meaning. We have seen this idea in connection with the letters קרס, which precede the letters that spell רשע (*rasha*, wicked). Interchangeable letters between words also connect ideas, as we have seen in the word חבל (*chavol*, injury), which is intensified by deeds that are עוול (*avel*, evil; ח and ע being guttural letters, and ב and ו having the same sound), which is a result of עוות לב (*ivet lev*, perversion of the heart).

The letters of the word קרס (*karas*, collapse), which precede those of רשע (*rasha*), form the word סקר (*seker*, survey), meaning "curious." From this we learn that curiosity (סקר) is an opening for the forces of evil to enter a person's heart, a heart that is סרק (*srak*, barren), without spiritual content. קר (*kar*), the evil force, combined with the ס (*samech*), the power of Satan, make up the words קרס, collapse, and רסק (*resek*, crushing). Collapse and destruction are a result of defilement caused by evil coupled with the power of Satan. The same idea is found in the English word "crush" (קרש), whereby the evil (קר) allied with Satan's (ש) power causes a breaking into tiny fragments.

When the letter ר (*raish*), suggesting movement and energy, follows another letter, it strengthens the action of that letter. We have already discussed the word קר (*kar*); the word צר (*tzar*, narrow) is similar. When the letter ק (*kof*), in its negative sense, is followed by the ר, it means to utterly destroy the foundations of the world (מקרקר, *mekarker*). The numerical value of קר (100 + 200 = 300) is the same as the value of the letter שין (*shin*, 300), *Kehillat Yaakov*, Shin which, used in the negative sense, refers to the destructive tooth (שן, *shen*) of the wicked and to the destructive aspect of the element of fire.

The total numerical value of the letters ק and ר (קוף = 100 + 6 + 80 = 186; ריש = 200 + 10 + 300 = 510; 186 + 510 = 696) is 696, the value of the word צרות (90 + 200 + 6 + 400 = 696; *tzarot*, troubles), which indicates that these forces lead to troubles. צ precedes ק in the alphabet. The letter צ (*tzadi*) comes from the word צדיה (*tedia*, hunting. *Letters of Rabbi Akiva*, Tzadi). Positively, this suggests the צדיק's (*tzadik*, righteous person), ability to צוד (*tzud*, hunt) the bad ק (*kof*). In the negative sense, it suggests the wicked רשע's (*rasha*, wicked person) power to hunt the souls and powers of the ק, the קדושה (*kedusha*, holiness).

When combined with the "moving" ר (*raish*), the negative aspect of the צ (*tzadi*) produces the words צר (*tzar*, narrow) and צורר (*tzorer*, enemy). The English word "seduce" resembles the Hebrew צד (*tzad*, hunt), suggesting that the seducer ensnares people by enticing them. Perhaps the word "SaDist," one who takes abnormal delight in cruelty, is also related. The English word "side" is also close in pronunciation and meaning to the Hebrew word צד (*tzad*, side, peripheral). The fact that צד means both "side" and "hunt" indicates that the hunter diverts the hunted's attention to peripheral matters in order to capture it.

12

The Constricted *Kaf* and *Samech*

As HAS BEEN EXPLAINED, the letters קר express the strong force of evil. The letter ק (*kof*) represents טומאה (*tuma*, impurity); it tries to imitate קדושה (*kedusha*), which is represented by the letter ה (*hei*). The ק and the ה are similar (*Zohar* 148b), except that the foot of the ק descends below the level of the ה, indicating that it draws its strength from the turbid depths. The letter q corresponds to the letter ק, both are the fourth last letters in their respective alphabets, and it also has a foot that descends beyond the level of its body. (It should be mentioned that the ancient forms of the letters showed that the shape of the letter ק was that part of the body which is the source of טומאיה.) The letter o is related to the letter ס; by adding a "leg," the q is formed, which has a very negative connotation.

The word טמא (*tuma*, defilement), whose main letters are טמ (9 + 40 = 49), suggests the forty-nine degrees of defilement that lead to מט (*mat*, collapse). טמא (defilement) brings about a state of אטם (*atam*, sealed up), whereby the arteries of life are obstructed. It is interesting to note that the English word טמפון (tampon, a plug closing up a passage) has the same idea as אטם.

Integrity (תמימות, *temimut*) and אמת (*emet*, truth), are the basis of existence. The absence of integrity and truth is the root of destruction and death, as can be seen by the reversal of the word תם (*tam*, integrity), which is מת (*met*, death). The letters of *tam*, also the basis of the English word "tame," suggest, in their positive sense, perfection of the four elements in the various worlds; ת = 400 and מ = 40.

A similar idea can be found by removing the א (*alef*) from the word אמת (*emet*, truth), leaving מת (*met*, dead). Truth is the basis of the world, as is indicated by the last letters of the phrase from the Torah: בראשית ברא א-לקים (אמת)—ת—(א; מ, "In the beginning God created" (Baal HaTurim, *ibid.*).

The *Zohar* says (*ibid.*) that the letter ק (*kof*, spelled קוף) suggests the קוף (*kof*, monkey), which tries to imitate man. The monkey, a symbol of טומאה (*tuma*, impurity), attempts to imitate—to "copy"—the force of holiness (the f (פ) and p (פ) are the same letters; thus, קופי and קוף are similar). The word "monkey" (קוף, מונקי, *kof*) is related to מוקיון (*mokion*, a clown), a "mocker," showing that aping and mockery are the root of evil.

The word הקף (*hekef*, surround or encompass) has its root in ק (*Letters of Rabbi Akiva*, Kof). Used negatively, the ק suggests the power of טומאה (*tuma*, defilement), which surrounds the soul, an idea expressed also by the letter ס (*samech*), Satan. This surrounding, or covering, represents externalism and emptiness, which acts as a barrier preventing the light of truth from penetrating. The *Zohar* (*ibid.*) also links the power of טומאה to the characteristics of a snake. The snake, who, according to the *Zohar*, characterizes the power of טומא, the force of Satan, is represented by the letter ס, the sound of the hiss that it makes. In fact, the letters of נחש (*nachash*, **sn**ake) are similar to those of **Satan**, differing only in the ח (*chet*) of נחש, which follows that of the ט (*tet*) of שטן (Satan) in the Hebrew alphabet. The closed, circular shape of the ס suggests the outer shell or cover of the soul, which prevents its light from being revealed. Moreover, the letters that spell סמך (*samech*) also spell מסך (*masach*, screen), a מחיצה (*mechitza*, a barrier; חיץ, *chitz*) resulting from sin. The letters of the word חטא (*chet*, sin) are interchangeable with those of חיץ, according to the key of איק-בכר (חטא = 8 + 9 + 1; חיץ = 8 + 10 + 90 = 8 + 9 + 1).

The hiss of the snake epitomizes its nature, as is true of the sounds made by every other animal (Rabbi Tzadok HaCohen, *Pri Tzadik*, Bechukotai). The word Satan refers to the power that causes a person to turn away, סטה (*sata*, turn away), from the path of truth and righteousness. We have already seen that the letters ט (*tet*; טיט, *taet*, mire), materialism, and נ (*nun*), negatively represent the fifty degrees of defilement. Thus, all the letters of Satan have a connotation of materialism, based on evil stemming from the fifty degrees of defilement. Chazal say that one of the seven names of the evil inclination is אבן (*even*, stone): "And I will remove the stony heart" (Ezekiel 11:19).

This is, perhaps, the derivation of the English word "stone," which is similar to the word Satan, snake, both representing materialism.

The letters סט (st) are also the main letters of the word "stray" and of the name of the planet Saturn, which influences the order of the other planets (*Sefer Yetzira*). The word "Saturn" (סטרן) is made up of the word "star" (סטר) plus a נ (*nun*), the letter representing the source. The stars symbolize the forces of Satan, both of which are based on the letters סט of סטן (Satan), and it is forbidden to worship them. If the ט (*tet*) is replaced with a ת (*tav*), סטה (*sata*, turning aside) becomes סתה (*sata*, seduction), the ט being stronger than the ת. The ט refers to an external action; the ת represents a more internal process, suggesting that seduction by one's desires results in a person's turning away from the true path.

The letters following שטן are סית, the root of להסית (*lehasit*, to corrupt). The English words "incite" and "instigate" also express these concepts. Satan's power in this world is manifested through Esau's power, as is revealed by the fact that the letters of סתה are adjacent to those of עשו, Esau, in the alphabet.

The word מסכה (*masaicha*) and "Mask," its English equivalent, are clearly related. Similarly, the words "smoke," "smog" (a modern word meaning "smoke and fog"), and "smock," a loose garment worn over another as a protection, all represent covering (ק and ג are interchangeable, as both are guttural letters). The meaning of the word מסך (*masach*, a curtain or cover) is further revealed by the fact that the word following it in the alphabet is נעל (*naul*, lock). According to the key of בכר-איק, נעל is related to עשן (*ashan*; נעל = 50 + 70 + 30; עשן = 70 + 300 + 50). If one exchanges the ק (*kof*, surrounding or covering) for a כ (*kaf*; the sounds are similar), many words are formed, like כופר (*kofer*, a person who denies, covers up the truth); כפרת (disbelieved); and the English word "cape." By exchanging the פ for a ב (both are palatal letters), the word "cover" is formed.

From the above, it appears that a monkey and a snake symbolize defilement, an idea manifested in the form and pronunciation of their names. (It is interesting that the English word "snake" (שנק), is related to the Hebrew word נחש, *nachash*: the ש, shin or sin, is parallel to the "s"; the נ, *nun*, "n," is common to both words; and the ק, *kof*, representing the "k," is interchangeable with ח, *chet*, in the key of א"ל ב"ם). Chazal say that the נחש, snake, has its ח, poison, between its teeth, שן (*shen*). Perhaps this is why copper (נחושת, *nechoshet*) is the metal that kabbalistically, is associated with the נחש, snake (*Kehillat Yaakov*;

Nachash). We know that Moses, for example, formed a snake from copper. The English word "CoPPer" (קופר) is related to the word קוף (*kof*, monkey).

The relationship between Amalek and various animals is discussed in the *Zohar* (3:124a). Amalek epitomizes all the negative attributes of the right and the left, נחש (*nachash*, the snake) being related to Ishmael. The letters following קס are רע (*ra*, evil) which shows from whence evil derives its strength. The idea of the English word "case" (קס), a container that conceals its contents, is the same as that expressed by the meaning of its Hebrew letters. The main sounds of קופסא (*kufsa*, box) and "case" are also קס.

The letter ק (*kof*) is articulated by a short, constricted sound at the back of the throat. We can understand, then, why the words קטן (*katan*, small) and קצר (*katzar*, short) both begin with a ק. (It should be mentioned that the three letters that make up the root of a Hebrew word correspond to the three parts of the נפש, *nefesh*, the spirit—נפש, spirit; רוח, *ruach*, breath of life; and נשמה, *neshama*, soul—in reverse order. The main meaning of a word, the נשמה, therefore, lies in the first letter of its root; in this way we can find many non-Hebraic words that resemble their Hebrew counterparts.) The German words קליין, *KleiN* (קטן in Hebrew) and קורץ, *KuRTZ* (קצר in Hebrew) clearly correspond to what has been said. The consonants that differ between קליין and קטן are the ל (*lamed*) and ט (*tet*), which are both palatal sounds. The common letters between the words קורץ and קצר are קצ, which denote cutting short (קצץ, *katzatz*).

The letters of שקר (*sheker*, falsehood) follow those of קצר (*katzar*), suggesting that falsehood develops as a result of a tendency to "cut at the saplings,"—to deny the very basis of our beliefs. Similarly the word קט (*kat*), from קטן (*katan*), is derived from the word קטע (*keta*, section). The letters צ (*tzadi*) and ט (*tet*) are interchangeable, according to the איק בכר (צ = 90 and ט = 9). The English word "cut" is derived from קטע (section) or כת (*kat*, sect). The Hebrew words קפא (*kafa*, froze) and קור (*kor*), which in English mean "cold" (קולד) and in German mean *kalt*, are signified by the letter ק (*kof*), a letter of limitation and pettiness. קדר (*kadar*, gloom) also depicts limitation, as does the English word "daRK," both based on the root קר.

The concepts of surrounding and concentration inherent in the letter ק (*kof*) are parallel to the English prefix "co-," which means partnership or grouping, as in "coalition," resembling the Hebrew word קהל (*kahal*, congregation) in both sound and meaning.

The English word "coat" (a covering or wrapping) derives its meaning from its first letter, the ק (*kof*) sound. The cat, which Chazal say exemplifies modesty, for it conceals its excretion, also derives its name in the same way. Moreover, "cat" sounds similar to "coat," as do חתול (*chatul*, cat) and חתול (*chitul*, diaper, which is wrapped around an infant).

The power of ק (*kof*), when it surrounds ל (*lamed*), the לב (*lev*, heart), gives rise to the word קלף, the basis of the קליפה (*klipa*, covering)—that which brings trouble to man and to the world. This is expressed by the word מצר (*maitzar*, distress), which follows that of קלף.

The power of the letter ק (*kof*), which causes anguish, is expressed by the fact that the word קץ (*kotz*, thorn, representing something negative, like the "snake") is close to that of קוף (*kof*, monkey): Both the monkey and the snake represent evil (*Zohar Chadash* 49a). The thorn (קץ) represents that which is negative. The English verb "cozen," "to cheat," also stems from ק. The main power of the thorn, Amalek, is to cause צוק (קוץ reversed: *tzuk*, a cliff), that which causes difficulties, "rocks and stumbling blocks" to Israel.

13

The Letter *Kaf*: a "Sum" of סמ

THE LETTER ק (*kof*), with a round numerical value of 100, is the "sum" (סמ) of the numerical values of ס (60) and מ (40)—(both of which are round in shape and spell the word "sum"). The English words "some" (a group) and "sum" are similar to the Hebrew word סכם (*sechum*, total). The Greek word for "body," the external covering of the soul, is *soma*. The Hebrew word סם (*sam*, drug, poison) describes its ability to limit thinking. Interestingly, a certain Indian plant called "sioma" is used in drug manufacture. The evil part of the angel Samael, the one who blinds and prevents people from seeing the light of truth, is סם.

By reversing the letters ס (*samech*) and מ (*mem*), the word מס (*mas*, tax), is formed. This is related to משא (*masa*, a heavy burden; ס and ש have the same sound) and "mass" in English. A מס (tax) limits a person's freedom, which, according to our rabbis, is a punishment for idol worship. The Midrash says that סם (*sam*) leads to מס (Midrash Rabba, Lamentations 1:1, on the word למס, *lemas*, tribute).

סמ, the first two letters of the word סמל (*semel*, symbol), rule over the ל (*lamed*), a letter symbolizing the heart (לב, *lev*; *Letters of Rabbi Akiva*) and learning (למוד, *limud*). A symbol is something external and limited. Similarly, the "sm" rules over the "l" (ל, the heart), as in the English word "Simple," which means "confined and closed," something that lacks depth.

The word סמן (*simen*) means "to make a sign," or to limit, as the word contains the letters סמ. The word "small" (שמאל), which is "left" in Hebrew, is associated with the force of evil, סמאל (Samael) a symbol of the evil inclination that is connected with smallness or limitation. (The English word "sign" also begins with the limiting ס.)

"Sm," suggesting periphery and covering, also appears in the words "smear" (to spread something on a surface) and "smattering" (referring to superficial learning). The destructive implication of "sm" appears in the word "smash."

The letter ק (kof, spelled קוף) is the basis of the word פקה (puka, to stumble, to err), a stumbling block. These letters form פקפק (pikpek), which expresses ספק (safek, doubt). The limiting ק leads a man to error and indecision. The ס (samech) at the beginning of the word ספק (safek) expresses סתום (satum) and סגור (sagur), both meaning closed, and being "closed" to the light of truth is the cause of doubt. The word ספק is clearly associated with "skeptic" (recall the connection in Hebrew between the p and f sounds). These are also associated with the words אפיקורס (apikores, heretic) and כופר (kofer, one who denies the truth).

The holy books point out the evil power of doubt. The numerical value of ספק (safek; 60 + 80 + 100 = 240) is the same as that of Amalek (עמלק; 70 + 40 + 30 + 100 = 240), עמל-ק (amal kof), "the work of the ק," the "monkey."

14

The Holiness of *Kaf* and *Samech*

THE LETTER ק (*kof*), in a positive sense, represents קדושה (*kedusha*, holiness) (*Shabbat* 104a). (Negatively, it represents defilement, as previously seen.) This is also seen by the numerical value of its letters (ק = 100; פ = 80), which are connected to the word חי (י = 10; ח = 8; *chai*, life; *Letters of Rabbi Akiva*), showing that holiness is the basis of life. The letter ס (*samech*) suggests סמיכה (*smicha*, support), referring to supporting the poor (*Shabbat, ibid., Letters of Rabbi Akiva*, Samech).

In light of this, we can understand the word פסק (*psak*, decision), the basis of which is the holiness of the ס (*samech*) and ק (*kof*), the source of truth and righteousness. It is also connected to the English word "fix" (פקס).

The positive aspect of the letters ספק (*safek*), with different vowels, forms the word ספוק (*sipuk*, satisfaction), which is related to the word "Suffice" in sound and meaning. The first two letters of ספוק, ספ, spell the word סוף (*sof*, end), which is related to the English word "suffix," "ending" or "stopping." The word עצר (*atzar*, stopped) follows that of ספק in alphabetical order. This shows how the force of עצירה (stopping) is affected by a פסק (*psak*, decision) or ספק (*safek*, doubt).

The letter ע (עין, *ayin*), the sense of sight, follows the ס (*samech*) in the Hebrew alphabet, indicating that the power of sight emanates from the ס, Satan. Satan's power is strengthened by that which the eye (עין, *ayin*) sees, which leads to sin. The letters of the word סטן (Satan) precede those of עין, except for the common נ. Even the shape of the letter ע resembles two eyes attached to a pipe that faces left, to the heart, showing how the eye influences the heart. The English word "eye" sounds similar to the word עין, and even resembles it in the way it is written (the "y" resembles the nose). Kabbalah points out that the shape of the letter ס (*samech*) is also reminiscent of an eye. It is, perhaps, for this reason that the actions of the eye ("seeing," "sight") also start with the same sound.

The letters following עין are פכס, which is כסף, revealing that desires or temptations engendered by what the eye sees lead to כסופים (*kisufim*, yearnings of the heart), which are stirred up by sight (see Chapter 15).

The English word "money" (כסף, *kesef*, related to כסופים) is perhaps rooted in the Hebrew word מנין (*minyan*, counting). כסף (*kesef*) also means "silver" in English, and *zilber* in German (which, interestingly, have the same sounds as the Hebrew word ברזל, *barzel*, iron), and both silver and iron are metals (ב and כ, and "s" and "z," are interchangeable). The word "brass" also a metal, has three sounds in common with ברזל, (*barzel*), as does "brazen," which describes a person with a מצח נחשה (*metzach nechusha*, lit. a "copper forehead"), an impudent person. נחשת (*nechoshet*, copper) is related to נחש (*nachash*, copper).

15

The Four Empires

ACCORDING TO THE MIDRASH (Midrash Rabba, Truma, ר״ש), the four metals: gold; silver; copper and iron, correspond to the four Empires: Babylonian, Persian, Greek, and Roman. Four colors correspond to these Empires: red to gold, Babylon; white to silver, Persia; green to copper, Greece; black to iron, Roman Empire.

The Babylonian Empire symbolizes pride, derived from the element fire (Rabbi Chaim Vital, *Shaarei Kedusha*, 1:2), which rises and is red. The words "fire" and "pride" are connected, and include the letters פר (*par*), representing strength. Strength corresponds to the color red, to fire and to pride, and to the haughty Babylonian Empire. "Fire" (אש, *esh*), whose root is שין (*shin*; 300 + 10 + 50) has, according to the rule of איק-בכר, the same basic numerical value as גאה (*gae*, proud: 3 + 1 + 5), showing their connection.

The word Persia (פרס, Paras; 70 + 200 + 60) is also numerically related to the word silver (כסף, *kesef*; 20 + 60 + 70), according to the key of איק בכר. Persia's trait is to desire and crave (כסופים, *kisufim*, which is similar to כסף). Desire and pleasure are connected to the element water, which is associated with the color white.

The word מים (*mayim*, water) is the plural form of the word המ, (*mah*, what). Just as water lacks color and form, the word "what" express something that has no qualities. Perhaps the letters of the word מים represent the water molecule, which is H_2O (2 atoms of hydrogen, the 2 מms; and 1 oxygen atom, the י). The letter מ (*mem*, which according to the *Sefer Yetzira* suggests the basis of water) therefore represents hydrogen, and the ' (*yud*), the basis of life, represents oxygen. This is the connection between מה (what) and מים (water), a concept that has been carried over into many other languages. The connection is apparent in the words "water" and "what" in English; *wasser* (water) and *wass* (what) in German; and *aqua* (water) and *qua* (what) in Latin.

This analogy is rooted in Kabbalah, according to which there are four numerical combinations of God's name (י-ה-ו-ה): עב, סג, מה, בן. God's name can be spelled in four different ways:

מה = 45 = 1 + 5 + 6 + 1 + 6 + 1 + 5 + 4 + 6 + 10 = יוד הא ואו הא
עב = 72 = 10 + 5 + 6 + 10 + 6 + 10 + 5 + 4 + 6 + 10 = יוד הי ויו הי
בן = 52 = 5 + 5 + 6 + 6 + 5 + 4 + 6 + 10 = יוד הה וו הה עב
סג = 63 = 10 + 5 + 6 + 1 + 6 + 10 + 5 + 4 + 6 + 10 = יוד הי ואו הי

The four elements (fire, wind, water, and earth) were created with these four words, which also correspond to the four worlds: אצילות (*atzilut*, divine emanation); בריאה (*bria*), Creation); יצירה (*yetzira*, formation); עשיה (*asiya*, doing). According to this analogy, water was created through the medium of מה (*ma*, what), having the numerical value of 45, which is the same as God's name, י-ה-ו-ה, spelled out in full (יוד = 10 + 6 + 4 = 20; הא = 5 + 1 = 6; ואו = 6 + 1 + 6 = 13; הא = 5 + 1 = 6; 20 + 6 + 13 + 6 = 45).

The connection between the element רוח (*ruach*, wind or spirit), and the "world of Creation" can be explained in a similar way. בריאה (*bria*, creation) contains the letters איר, the basis of the word אויר (*avir*, air), which means and sounds the same. This is made up of אר (*ohr*, light), and the ' (*yud*) that is added suggests the addition of a specific element, which changes light into air (*Mechilta* of Rabbi Shimon bar Yochai, 16).

The numerical value of God's name, יהוה, when spelled out fully as יוד הה וו הה (*yud hei vav hei*), adds up to 52 (10 + 6 + 4 + 5 + 5 + 6 + 6 + 5 + 5 = 52), the same numerical value as בן. These letters are the root of the word בנין (*binyan*, building), hence referring to the "world of doing" (עשיה-ה, *asiya*). This may be the source of the English word "been" (from the verb "to be," "existing"). This word is represented by the letter ב (*bet*), which is בית (*bayit*), also meaning "house."

Greece is associated with copper, the color green, and the element air. Copper (נחשת, *nechoshet*) symbolizes brazenness, מצח נחשה (*metzach nechusha*), a trait of the Greeks, whose anti-Semitic laws were cruel like a "snake" (נחש, *nachash*). Rusted, oxidized copper is green, showing the connection between this color, copper, and the element air. The early Greek philosophers were gifted with the power of speech, which is associated with the element of air. Perhaps this is why the word "Greek" is similar to the word "green." Greek is considered the most beautiful of the non-Hebraic languages: יפת א–לוקים ליפת; "May God extend (יפת, *yefet*, related to יפה, *yafe*, beautiful) Yefet (which refers to Greece)" (Genesis 9:27).

The color green corresponds to glory; white, to חסד (*chesed*, lovingkindness), from the element water; and red, to strength. Between strength and glory, between red and green, lies the attribute of פאר (*p'er*, beauty), a word similar in sound and meaning to "fair." The letters following ירק (*yarok*, green) spell the word כשר (*kasher*, a proper situation). The letters of יון (Yavan, Greece) suggest the word הונאה (*honaa*, deceit), for deceit's essential quality is dirt and filth (יון means "mud"). The word ירק, rearranged, spells קרי (*keri*, nocturnal emission), suggesting that defilement comes from the force of קר (*kar*, cold). We have already seen that the letter קוף (*kof*) also means "monkey," which attempts to imitate man, as Greece similarly tried to "ape" the culture of Israel.

The English counterpart of נחושת (*nechoshet*, copper, קופר) is also based on the letters קר, referring to defilement. These letters are also the basis of the word פרק (*perek*), which is similar in sound and meaning to the English word "break" (ברק; the ב and פ are interchangeable, as labial letters). פריקת עול (*prikat ol*, throwing off the heavenly yoke) and כפירה (*kefira*, heresy) were the basis of the Greek Empire.

Just as the snake is connected to קר, so, too, is עקרב (*akrav*), the scorpion, which has a deadly sting. עקרב is made up of עקר–ב (*akar bet*), the uprooting of the ב, the house, which reveals its destructive nature. The destructive force of קר is found in the word "crack," which is similar to קרקר (*kirker*, the action of the destruction of foundations).

It is interesting that the English word "crab" is similar to the עקרב (*akrav*, scorpion), which is also the שרטן (*sartan*), similar to the word שטן (Satan), which, in turn, is related to קר. The English word "scorpion" (סקורפיון) is made up of letters indicating destruction: קוף (*kof*, monkey); פרק (*pirek*, broke up); קרס (*karas*, collapsed). עקרב belongs to the three shells (קליפות, *klipot*) of evil (רע, *ra*) mentioned in the Torah (Deuteronomy 8:15): "snakes, serpents, and scorpions"; the scorpion is the main one of these shells (*Kehillat Yaakov*, Akrav). The Midrash Rabba says (Genesis 44) that the scorpion refers to Greece. Several forces are at the root of the Greek Empire, just as green is comprised of two primary colors, and air and נחשת (*nechoshet*, copper) are each made up of several components.

Iron, the metal from which weapons are made, corresponds to the Roman Empire, Edom. Edom (Esau) is associated with this metal, as Esau lives "by the sword." As we have seen, several foreign words for various metals are composed of the letters of the word ברזל (*barzel*, iron). According to Kabbalah, the word ברזל contains the initials of Jacob's four wives Bilhah, Rachel, Zilpah, and Leah, hinting at the attribute of the all-embracing majesty (*Kehillat Yaakov*, Barzel). ברזל is associated with the element earth and the color black, which also have an all-embracing quality. Black is the color produced by the absorption of all the colors, and thus is related to the attribute of majesty, the absorption of all the attributes.

The fourth empire was Edom (Rome), and the Italian flag consists of the colors red, white, and green. These three colors represent the three earlier empires, which the Roman empire conquered and incorporated. The quality of majesty (according to the *Chidushei Bnei Yissachar*, Zayn, in the name of many kabbalistic works) is called זאת (*zot*). זאת (this), denoting a specific thing, expresses majesty, just as majesty is the specific manifestation of the divine in the material world. The English word "that" resembles the Hebrew זאת; "the" sounds like the Hebrew זה (*zeh*). The English word, "the," which expresses something clear and known, is expressed by the prefix ה (*hei*) in Hebrew. The letter ה is the final letter of God's name, יהוה, denoting the attribute of majesty. The word זאת suggests majesty: The numerical value of the letter ז is 7, and majesty is the seventh attribute; א and ת, the remaining letters, are the first and last of the Hebrew alphabet, suggesting its all-embracing quality.

16

The Seven Species
of the Land of Israel

THE SEVEN ATTRIBUTES correspond to the seven species with which the land of Israel was blessed. The תמר (*tamar*, date) corresponds to the attribute of majesty (מלכות, *malchut*), as can be seen by its letters and color. The word תמר has the same letters as the word מרות (*marut*, mastery), which also expresses the power of majesty. The date's dark color is similar to black, the color of majesty. The מ (40) and the ת (400), the first and last letters of these words (מרות and מלכות), are numerically the same (4) on different planes. (The seventh sphere of מלכות is parallel to the number four.) Rome ruled over the four kingdoms, and is, therefore, parallel to the date. The English word "date" transliterated into Hebrew as דת (400 + 4) also suggests majesty, as both letters have the numerical value of 4.

The first of the species is wheat, which is connected to the attribute of lovingkindness and its inherent wisdom. Flour is white, the color of water, and signifies lovingkindness and wisdom. This similarity appears in the other languages, too. In German, "wheat" is *witz*, which is similar to *weiss* (white) and *wasser* (water). *Weiss* and *wasser* sound similar to the English word "wise." "White" has the same sound as the Hebrew equivalent of "wheat" (חיטה, *chita*). The connection between חיטה and דעת (*daat*, knowledge or wisdom) is shown in the rabbinic maxim that an infant does not know how to say "Mommy" and "Daddy" until he has tasted wheat. According to Kabbalah, the word חטה (8 + 9 + 5) is 22, corresponding the number of

letters in the Hebrew alphabet; both חטה and the Hebrew alphabet are
the basis of knowledge.

Wisdom is also represented by the translucent color of the sapphire (ספיר, *sapir*) and of water, both of which suggest clarity. Hence a
ספר (*sefer*, book), clarifies, by either סיפור (*sipur*, relating) or ספירה (*sefira*,
recounting). The importance of the sapphire is deduced from its similarity to the word ספירה, which is the basis of the spherical universe
(*Kehillat Yaakov*, Saphir). The sapphire brick that the elders saw in
heaven is the source of all souls; perhaps this explains the similarity
between the English word "spirit" and ספיר (*sapir*): The spirits come
from the sapphire on High.

Both לספר (*lesaper*, to relate, recount) and מספר (*mispar*, number)
have the same root, ספר. In English, "recount" means to "relate" or
"tell"; "tell" also means "to count" (as in "bank teller"). The numerical
value of ספיר (60 + 80 + 10 + 200 = 350) is the same as the letter שׁ (300
+ 50 = 350), which represents fire and light. The word "spirits" can
also be used to mean alcohol, which is highly combustible—that is,
very sensitive to fire, the element represented by the sapphire. The
initial letter of ספיר is ס, suggesting limitation, which in this case refers
to the fact that the lack of air extinguishes fire.

PART II

REVELATIONS ABOUT MARRIAGE*

Many have supposed that the letters of the Hebrew alphabet are a matter of symbolic convention; that is, that the Sages decided among themselves that certain signs would represent the sounds of speech. For example, it is supposed that they agreed that the sounds made by closing the lips would be represented by the forms of the letters *bet* (ב), *vav* (ו), *mem* (מ), and *peh* (פ)—and likewise for the remaining sounds of the language. Other peoples also have symbolic representations for the sounds of their languages. According to this view, there is no difference between the Hebrew alphabet and the alphabets of other nations. The Hebrew letters are the conventional symbols used by the Israelite nation on the advice of Moses through his prophetic inspiration, and the other alphabets are the conventional symbols of the other nations.

It follows, according to this theory, that the written word is nothing more than a vehicle of making known the speaker's intent. Consider a physician who writes a book about the healing art. He doesn't intend for the book itself to be medicine; rather, he intends the book to make known his thoughts or preferences on the subject of healing. Once the reader understands the principles of the healing art, as written in the book, the book itself is of no importance whatsoever. Thus, if a person studies the book for years on end but fails to learn the principles set forth therein, his study has done nothing for him

*From Rav Moshe Cordovero, *Pardess Rimonim*, Chapter 1, *Shaar Ha-Otiot*

and his soul has not been improved at all, since he still does not understand the requirements of the art. In fact, his study has actually done him harm, since he has wasted time and effort without gaining understanding.

The Torah, according to those who hold this view, is just like our example of the medical textbook. The purpose of the Torah is to reveal the inner meanings and processes necessary for the perfection of the soul. Thus, if one does not master the required knowledge, he gains no benefit from his studies (God forbid).

This theory cannot be true, for undoubtedly the words of Torah "restore the soul" (Psalms 19:8). The proof is that *halacha* obligates us to read the weekly Torah portion "twice in the original Hebrew and once in the Aramaic translation," including even seemingly meaningless place names such as "Atarot" and "Divon" (Numbers 32:3). This teaches us that the Torah is perfect. The words and letters themselves have hidden inner meaning, spiritual power, and vitality.

1

Guidelines to *Gematria*

Throughout this book, we cite various works that discuss *gematria*, the analysis of Hebrew words in terms of their numerical value, arrangement of letters, and so on. Thus, it will be useful to summarize some of the basic principles of *gematria*.

Primary *Gematria*

The thirty-two principles of exegesis used by the Sages to interpret the Torah are set forth in a *braitta* in the name of Rabbi Eliezer the son of Rabbi Jose HaGalili. The twenty-ninth principle is a primary *gematria*. The commentary Midrash Tannaim states that the numerical values of the Hebrew letters were given to Israel at Mount Sinai. The values are as follows:

1 – א	10 – י	100 – ק
2 – ב	20 – כ	200 – ר
3 – ג	30 – ל	300 – ש
4 – ד	40 – מ	400 – ת
5 – ה	50 – נ	500 – ך
6 – ו	60 – ס	600 – ם
7 – ז	70 – ע	700 – ן
8 – ח	80 – פ	800 – ף
9 – ט	90 – צ	900 – ץ

The last five letters listed here (corresponding to the numbers 500 to 900) are the "final" forms of the letters מנצפכ. They are used when the letter comes at the end of a word. Sometimes these letters are assigned the same value as the regular form; for example, ך is counted as 20, as is כ. Sometimes, however, the "final" forms are used as shown above, to represent the multiples of 100 from 500 through 900. For example, the primary *gematria* of "livelihood" (*parnassah*, פרנסה) is 395.

parnassah (פרנסה): 80 + 200 + 50 + 60 + 5 = 395

Reduced *Gematria* or Small Numerical Value

The *mispar katan* is the primary *gematria* with any final zeroes removed. Thus, 10 and 100 are both counted as 1.

This type of *gematria* is basic to the teaching of *Tikunei Zohar*, one of the basic works of Kabbalah. It is connected with what the kabbalistic writings refer to as *olam ha'asiyah*, the world of action. This, the lowest of the worlds, is symbolized by the units; the tens and hundreds symbolize higher worlds (Ramchal, *Adir Bamarom*, 65). Thus, when we reduce a word to its *mispar katan*, we discover how the concept represented by that word relates to *olam ha'assiyah*.

Sometimes, the primary *gematria* or the *mispar katan* is reduced even further by adding together all the digits of the number. For example, we saw that the *gematria* of *parnassah* is 395. This can ultimately be reduced to 8.

$$3 + 9 + 5 = 17$$
$$1 + 7 \quad = 8$$

Full *Gematria*

In this form of *gematria*, each letter of a word is written out in full, and the numerical value of all the resulting letters is counted. For example, by the "full' *gematria*, the value of "cold" (*kar*, קר) is 696.

kar (קר) is spelled קוף ריש:
$$100 + 6 + 80, + 200 + 10 + 300 = 696$$

Interchangeability of Letters Formed in the Same Part of the Mouth

Sefer Yetzira, an ancient kabbalistic work, states that the letters may be divided into five groups, based on the part of the mouth where the letter is produced.

1. אחה"ע. These are the guttural letters, formed in the throat, using the back of the tongue or the pharynx.
2. בומ"פ. These are the labial letters, formed primarily by closing the lips.
3. גכ"ק. These are the palatal letters, formed mainly by contact between the palate and the back third of the tongue.
4. דטלנ"ת. These letters are produced with the tip of the tongue against the front of the palate just behind the teeth.
5. זסשר"ץ. These are the sibilants, produced by expelling air between the teeth with the tongue held flat.

Thus, for example, "seven" (*sheva*, שבע) and "abundance" (*shefa*, שפע) are closely related, for ב and פ are interchangeable.

The *Atbash* Transformation

According to Midrash Tannaim, this type of equivalence was also given with the Torah on Mount Sinai. Therefore, examples of it are found in the Talmud and Midrash. In the *Atbash* transformation, the first letter of the alphabet is interchangeable with the last, the second with the next-to-last, and so on. This results in the following table of equivalences.

ז – ע	ד – ק	א – ת
ח – ס	ה – צ	ב – ש
ט – נ	ו – פ	ג – ר
	כ – ל	י – מ

The *Albam* Transformation

This type of equivalence was also given with the Torah at Mount Sinai, according to the Midrash Tannaim. According to the *Albam* transformation, the letters of the alphabet are divided into two groups. The first letter of the first group is interchangeable with the first letter of the second group, and so on.

א – ל	ה – ע	ר – ט
ב – ם	ו – פ	י – ש
ג – נ	ז – צ	כ – ת
ד – ס	ח – ק	

The *Ik-Bechar* Transformation

According to the Midrash Tannaim, the twenty-seven letters of the Hebrew alphabet are divided into three groups, whereby each of the letters in the same group have the same small *gematria*. (The final letters are included in the *Ik-Bechar* transformation.)

א – י – ק	ד – מ – ת	ז–ע–ן
ב – כ – ר	ה – נ – ך	ח–פ–ף
ג – ל – ש	ו – ס – ם	ט–צ–ץ

Addition of the *Kollel*

Sometimes, in finding the numerical equivalent (*gematria*) of a word, we increase the total by one. Rabbi Y. A. Chaver, in *Pitchei Shaarim* (252), explains that in such cases the root (*shoresh*) of a word is still attached to the upper world.

An example is the word "covenant" (*brit*, ברית). Its numerical equivalent, including the *kollel*, is 613.

brit (ברית): 2 + 200 + 10 + 400 = 612
plus the *kollel*:   612 + 1 = 613

There is a total of 613 scriptural *mitzvot*. Thus, this *gematria* teaches us that the concept of covenant (*brit*) is attached to, and cleaves to, the 613 *mitzvot*.

A related practice in *gematria* is to find the total numerical value of a word, and then add the number of letters of the word. By this method, the word, "flag" (*degel*, דגל) has the numerical value of 40.

degel (דגל):   4 + 3 + 30 = 37
plus the number of letters: 3 + 37 = 40

The Baal HaTurim finds a scriptural basis for the practice of adding the *kollel* to a *gematria*. In the verse "Ephraim and Menashe will be the same as Reuben and Simon" (Genesis 48:5), the words "Ephraim, Menashe" have the numerical value of 726, and "Simon, Reuben" have the numerical value of 725. Thus, when we add the *kollel* to the second pair of words, the values are equal. And the Torah itself testifies that they are "the same." This is a hint that sometimes it is necessary to add the *kollel*.

Ephraim, Menashe (אפרים מנשה):
1 + 80 + 200 + 10 + 40 + 40, + 50 + 300 + 5   = 726
Reuben, Simon (ראובן שמעון):
200 + 1 + 6 + 2 + 50, + 300 + 40 + 70 + 6 + 50 = 725
plus the *kollel*:   1 + 725 = 726

Rabbi Yaakov Emden, in his commentary on *Pirkei Avot* titled *Lechem Shamayim* (end of Ch. 3), sets forth basic principles for the use of *gematria*.

One cannot use *gematria* . . . to introduce into the Torah innovations which are not confirmed by our early forefathers, who had direct and trustworthy traditions. However, one may use *gematria* to uphold the teachings of our Sages and the traditions of our forefathers, and whoever originates such *gematriot*—more power to him, and his reward will be great. For this purpose, the scholar is allowed to search tirelessly for a *gematria* with which to support the words of truth.

It is in this spirit that I have not only cited many *gematriot* and related exegeses from other authorities, but have also included some that do not appear elsewhere.

2

Marriage and "Modern" Society

THE BASIS OF MARRIAGE, in many homes throughout the world and in Israel, is progressively crumbling. This is one of the symptoms of sickness of the society we call "modern." This English word has been adopted by the Hebrew language as well: By a slight rearrangement of letters, the Hebrew word for "modern" (*modernit*, מדרנית) becomes "rebellious" (*mardanit*, מרדנית). Indeed, rebelliousness is one of the main characteristics of present-day civilization.

Modern man's rebelliousness, as an accepted axiom of social life sanctioned by the intellectual elite of the generation, shows itself at every level, from the lowliest stratum right up to the very top, where we witness leaders who are unwilling to accept anything that does not fit their will and whim. This same spirit of rebelliousness is splitting the protective walls of the home and bringing it to collapse. This phenomenon was foreseen by the prophets. The Sages of the Talmud expanded on the same theme when they spoke of the disturbances that would characterize the present era, the "heel of *Mashiach*," which immediately precedes the Messianic Age.

Evidence of this situation is the constantly rising divorce rate, which has reached alarming proportions. A statistical study recently undertaken in the state of Israel revealed that one out of every three marriages will end in divorce. Many other couples find themselves with serious marital problems, but do not resort to divorce for various reasons, primarily for the sake of the children. The ideal situation of marital peace and harmony, however, is almost nowhere to be found.

This dismal picture has dire consequences for today's youth, a large portion of whom come from broken homes. The psychological condition of these young people is precarious because they have had to experience the divorce of their parents.

The plague seems to have struck especially hard among the student body of upper-class schools. Yosef Kolonder, head of Psychological Services for Israel's Department of Education, presented a report showing that among schools in well-to-do neighborhoods of Tel Aviv and Ramat Hasharon, the proportion of students living in one-parent homes has reached fifty percent (Nitzah Aviram, *Yediot Acharonot*, 1984).

The disintegration of the family unit is the source of many of the problems of Israeli society, for a broken home is a natural breeding ground for crime and antisocial behavior. Recent years have seen an increase in cases of murder and suicide against a background of family problems.

In our age, we have witnessed the dismantling of the moral framework that has been sanctified since time immemorial and has always guarded the existence of the Jewish people. Hand-in-hand with the weakening of this framework has gone the rise of a permissive atmosphere that is gnawing away at everything good in Israeli society. In the words of Shmuel Shnitzer, writing for the newspaper *Maariv*:

> The philosophy of permissiveness is rapidly dismantling the family unit. . . . People have become so "advanced" that the basis has been undermined for such elementary values as respect for religion, love of country, simple honesty, and consideration of others.

Against the background of family problems, the suicide rate among young people who have failed to find contentment and meaning in their lives has reached an all-time high. The brains of the very best psychologists and various educational specialists have grappled with this phenomenon, but they have not arrived at a clear and definite solution. It is almost certain that they will not arrive at one, for the roots of these problems reach into the profound depths of the Jewish soul. The essence and special nature of the Jewish soul remains a closed book to these experts, whose secular intellectual background feeds from cultural roots that are divorced from Torah and render them incapable of solving problems whose essence is bound up with the sanctity of the Jewish soul.

The Sages of Kabbalah see the structure of the soul as a many-colored mosaic of lights intimately connected with the system of letters of Hebrew, the holy tongue. These lights illumine in various ways, depending on the spiritual level a person has reached in the fulfillment of Torah and *mitzvot*. The Torah and the soul are both woven from the same threads—the letters of the holy tongue. When the "letters" of the soul are in harmony with the letters of the Torah and its commandments, the result is wholeness, happiness, and serenity. By the same token, any injury to the Torah and to its holy letters is an injury to the structure of the soul of the individual and the nation.

According to the Sages, the universe itself is also built from the letters of the holy tongue, and it is the word of God that maintains the existence of everything. It follows that any injury to the Torah injures not only humankind, but the entire universe.

Contemplation of the root of the ever-growing contemporary struggles over Jewish values reveals that these battles result from the feelings of emptiness and discontent that prevail in the secular camp. In accord with the spirit of rebelliousness that typifies the modern world, the secularists attempt to overthrow increasingly more accepted values in an effort to keep themselves occupied and to avoid facing the underlying source of current problems.

In the view of Kabbalah, the letters of the holy tongue are the fundamental building blocks of the soul, just as atoms are the building blocks of the material world. The unfortunate accident at Chernobyl is a sufficient reminder of the power contained in the tiny atom. Similarly, the letters of the holy tongue contain tremendous power. This power teaches us the importance of seemingly small details that have a profound effect on married life. When we begin to understand the basic principles of marriage hidden within the Hebrew language, this sheds a clear light on those small but vital details. One who contemplates them will discover an unexpected reserve of power and energy with which to conduct his or her married life in the most harmonious manner. This can lead to happiness and to the rectification of the family unit and the whole world.

3

Marriage Elevates and Exalts

MARRIAGE, IN HEBREW, is called *nisuin* (נישואין), from the root נשא, which means to lift up. The essence of marriage is to lift up and exalt the husband and wife. Therefore, at the moment of marriage, the couple merit the forgiveness of their sins. One of the expressions for "forgiveness" is *nesiah* (נשיאה), which also comes from the root נשא. Thus, the Sages say: "When a man marries a woman, his sins are dissolved" (*Yevamot* 63b).

The three-letter root of the word "marriage" (*nisuin*, נישואין), נשא, conceals within it the force that creates a tie between man and woman. From it we can learn the exalted status and the importance of marriage.

From the roots of נשא grows a rich harvest of spiritual and material treasure, as can be seen by considering each of these three letters.

The letter נ has the numerical value of 50. This number symbolizes the perfection of the quality of purity, for it represents the last and highest of the fifty gates of purification (*tahara*). Similarly, it represents the highest of the fifty gates of *binah* (understanding).

Two words that mean "soul," *neshama* (נשמה) and *nefesh* (נפש), both begin with נ. The perfection of the soul depends upon the special qualities of this letter.

The next letter, ש, is the letter of truth (*emet*). According to the *Zohar*, the letter ש is the root of such words as serenity (*shalva*, שלוה); peace (*shalom*, שלום); tranquility (*shanenut*, שאננות); quiet (*sheket*, שקט); joy (*simcha*, שמחה); and jubilation (*sasson*, ששון). Words whose foundations partake of the special quality of the letter ש are the source of the holy Divine Presence (*Shechinah*, שכינה). "Song" (*shira*, שירה) is derived from heavenly wellsprings.

The last letter of the root נשא is א. This letter hints at exalted concepts of which it is the initial letter: faith (*emunah*, אמונה), unity (*achdut*, אחדות), love (*ahava*, אהבה), godliness (*elokut*, אלקות), and others.

These holy and noble concepts are embodied in the root נשא, which is the central theme binding husband and wife.

According to Rabbi Avraham, the Admor of Trisk, in his work *Magen Avraham*, the root נשא indicates completion and perfection, for these three letters are the initials of the four images included in the divine chariot (see Ezekiel, ch. 1). The letter נ stands for "eagle" (*nesher*, נשר); the letter ש stands for "ox" (*shor*, שור); the letter א stands for "lion" (*aryeh*, אריה) and "man" (*adam*, אדם).

In Kabbalah, these four images are the root of the four elements of the world—fire, air, water, and earth, which correspond to the four letters of the divine Name: יהוה.

These four elements are the foundation of "mankind" (*enosh*, אנש), a word spelled with the same three letters, נשא. Through these elements the world reaches perfection.

Through the marriage of man and woman, the four-letter name of God, יהוה, is brought to completion. Man (*ish*, איש) and woman (*ishah*, אשה) are both spelled with the letters of "fire" (*esh*, אש). "Man" (איש) adds the letter י to these letters; "woman" (אשה) adds the letter ה. This gives us the first two letters of the four-letter Name: יה. An integral part of the marriage rite is the giving of the marriage contract, or *ketubah* (כתובה). This word can be analyzed into "writ" (*ketav*, כתב) and the letters ה and ו. This completes the divine Name: יהוה.

4

The Letters נשׁא Symbolize and Unify All the Worlds

KABBALAH SPEAKS OF ten spiritual worlds through which the creative emanation of *Hashem* successively descends. These ten levels are referred to as the ten *sefirot* or *midot*: *chochma* (חכמה, wisdom), *binah* (בינה, understanding), and *daat* (דעת, knowledge). The letter א represents *Chochma* (wisdom) because the very name of this letter, *alef* (אלף), comes from a root that means to learn, as in the verse, "I shall teach you (*aalefcha*, אאלפך) wisdom" (Job 33:33).

The letter נ whose numerical value is 50, corresponds to the fifty gates of *binah* (understanding).

The world of *Chochma* (wisdom) is known as the "father," and *binah* (understanding) is known as the "mother." *Daat* (knowledge) is thought of as the child because it unites the forces of the "father" and the "mother," the two uppermost *midot*. The letter ש with its three branches united in one letter, symbolizes *daat*. Thus, the letters נשׁא stand for *Chochma*, *binah*, and *daat*.

The seven lower worlds, or *midot*, are divided into three realms. The upper three of the seven constitute the realm of *bria* (Creation). The next three worlds constitute the realm of *Yetzira* (formation), and the lowest world constitutes the realm of *asiyah* (action). The Hebrew alphabet is also divided into three parts according to the numerical values of the letters. Some represent units, some represent multiples of ten, and some represent multiples of one hundred. The units correspond to the realm of *asiyah* (action), the tens correspond to the realm of *yetzira* (formation), and the hundreds correspond to the realm of *bria* (Creation). The letters of נשא represent all three of these realms. The letter א, whose numerical value is 1, represents the units; נ, whose numerical value is 50, represents the tens; and ש, whose numerical value is 300, represents the hundreds.

Thus, the root נשא unites within it all the worlds in their various groupings.

Some Hebrew letters are indivisible, and others can be analyzed into component letters. For example, נ is an indivisible unit, but א consists of a slanting central ו with two יs—one above the ו, and one below it. The letter ש consists of a baseline to which are attached the letters ויו. If we analyze the root, נשא, into all its component letters, we get נ, ז, ו, and י. If we add the compound letter, א, these letters spell זו and אני, which may be translated "she, I." The word "I" (*ani*, אני), with its letters rearranged, spells "nothing" (*ayin*, אין), alluding to the state of self-abnegation that makes communication and unity possible. The word translated "she" (*zo*, זו) has the numerical value of 13. This number represents the principle of unity, which corresponds to the basis of the created world—i.e., the lowest of the ten *midot*, known as *malchut* (kingdom). These two concepts, "nothingness" (*ayin*, אין) and "kingdom" (*malchut*, represented by *zo*, זו), combine to produce the linguistic root of the word for marriage: נשא.

5

The Exalted Values
Concealed in נשא

THROUGH THE *Atbash* (א״ת-ב״ש) transformation, the root נשא becomes טבת (*tovot*), which means "good things."

נ becomes ט

ש becomes ב

א becomes ת

This teaches us that a couple's marriage is the source of good things for themselves and for the rest of the world. This is in accordance with the verse, "It is not good for man to be alone" (Genesis 2:18). That is, goodness (*tovot*) comes only when a man is in unity with his wife.

By the *Albam* (א״ל-בם) transformation, the letters נשא become גיל (*gil*), rejoicing.

נ becomes ג

ש becomes י

א becomes ל

Reishit Chochma points out that the souls of man and woman were originally one soul derived from the same root. It is only in this world that they are divided and separated. By means of marriage, the two are reunited and connected to their original supernal source. Thus, each partner discovers the highest spiritual root of his or her soul. That is why marriage, represented by the letters נשא, results in great rejoicing (*gil*, גיל).

According to the *Ik-Bechar* (איק-בכר) transformation, the letters נשא are equivalent to קהל (*kahal*), congregation.

נ becomes ה

ש becomes ל

א becomes ק

The basic concept behind the word *kahal* (congregation) is the unity and harmony that results from being connected to a higher source. This is also the concept embodied in the root נשא, as is hinted at by the *Albam* transformation.

In one type of *gematria*, each letter is assigned a number corresponding to its place in the alphabet. The letter א is 1; ב is 2; and so on. By this method, the root נשא has the numerical value of 36.

נ = 14
ש = + 21
א = + 1
total: 36

According to Kabbalah, thirty-six represents the perfection of holiness and the world of *yesod* (foundation), the sixth of the seven lower worlds, or *midot*. Thus, Joseph, who embodies this *midah*, is the sixth of Israel's seven shepherds: Abraham, Isaac, Jacob, Moses, Aaron, Joseph, and David. When this holy number, 6, is multiplied by itself, the result, 36, symbolizes the perfection of its qualities. This is the numerical value of the root of marriage—נשא.

According to Baal HaRokeach, the number 36 also represents the perfection of the concept of light, because the word "light" (*ohr*, אור), in its various forms, appears 36 times in the Torah.

The Torah contains thirty-six transgressions punishable by *karet*, the destruction of the soul. Most of these sins involve matters of holiness between man and woman. Counterbalancing these sins are the thirty-six *tzadikim*, righteous men, who come into the world in each generation.

Thirty-six is also the numerical value of the word "tent" (*ohel*, אהל).

ohel (אהל): 1 + 5 + 30 = 36

The tent symbolizes woman, as in the verse, "You shall know that peace is (in) your tent" (Job 5:24).

6

נשא: Truth, Eternity, and the Perfection of Man's Stature

THE *mispar katan* OF THE ROOT נשא is 9.

נ = 50 = 5
ש = 300 = 3
א   = 1
total: 9

According to the Maharal, nine is the perfect number. Moreover, nine expresses eternity and truth, for no matter what number it is multiplied by, the resulting number's digits will total nine. For example:

9 × 2 = 18   1 + 8 = 9
9 × 3 = 27   2 + 7 = 9
and so on.

As the symbol of truth and eternity, the number nine connects with the upper worlds, as is hinted at by the circle that forms the upper part of the 9.

According to Kabbalah, when the numerical values of the letters of a word are multiplied by each other, the result indicates the deep significance of the word. When the letters of נשא are multiplied by each other, the result is 15,000.

נ   = 50   ש =   300   א = 1
50 × 300 × 1 = 15,000

The number 15,000 is 15 units of 1000 each. One thousand represents the highest of all the worlds, called *atzilut*. Fifteen indicates the name of God, יה, whose letters have the numerical value of 15.

יה: 10 + 5 = 15

Thus, 15,000 alludes to the highest perfection of this name of God, a level attained by man and woman through marriage, represented by the root נשא.

7

Marriage: Man and Woman Are United by Joining Right and Left

THE BUILDING OF THE HOME is accomplished through the bond of marriage, as is revealed by the numerical value of the words for "the home" (*habayit*, הבית) and "marriage" (*nisuin*, נשואין).

habayit (הבית):   5 + 2 + 10 + 400 = 417
nisuin (נשואין): 50 + 300 + 6 + 1 + 10 + 50 = 417

Man and woman are separate individuals before marriage. Then the Holy One, blessed be he, joins them and they achieve the unity of the home, as the verse says, "He settles individuals in a home" (Psalms 68:7). The word for "home," in this verse, is ביתה (*baytah*) instead of the simpler form, בית (*bayit*). The *Ben Ish Chai, Ben Yehoyada* (Sotah p. 2), explains that the letters of *baytah* (ביתה) can be rearranged to spell *batyah* (בתיה, lit., "daughter of God"), an expression referring to the *Shechinah* or Divine Presence. As we have seen, "man" (איש) and "woman" (אשה) together form the name of God, יה (*Yah*). Thus, when the man and woman are unified through the building of their home, this causes the *Shechinah*, or *Batyah*, to dwell with them.

The first step of married life is the wedding ceremony, or *kiddushin* (קידושין). The basis of *kiddushin* is "holiness" (*kedusha*, קדושה), for this is what upholds a marriage.

The numerical value of the word *kiddushin* is 480, which equals ten times the numerical value of the word "mind" (*moach*, מח).

kiddushin (קידושין): 100 + 10 + 4 + 6 + 300 + 10 + 50 = 480

moach (מח):   40 + 8 =   48

                                                                            48 × 10 = 480

Multiplying the value of a word by ten reveals the aspect of perfection of that word. This teaches us that *kiddushin*, the marriage ceremony, brings perfection to a person's mind (*moach*).

The number 480 is also the numerical value of *talmud* (תלמוד), which means Torah study.

Talmud (תלמוד): 400 + 30 + 40 + 6 + 4 = 480

Torah study (*talmud*) represents the perfection of the quality of *daat* (דעת), which means knowledge—specifically, knowledge of God that is brought down to earth and made a part of one's life. The numerical value of "the knowledge" (*hadaat*, הדעת), with the *kollel*, is also 480.

Hadaat (הדעת): 5 + 4 + 70 + 400 = 479

plus the *kollel*:   479 + 1 = 480

The perfection of a person's knowledge of God (*daat*) and mind (*moach*) depend upon the marriage ceremony (*kiddushin*), which binds man and woman and causes the Divine Presence (*Shechinah*) to dwell with them.

From the time of the Exodus from Egypt until King Solomon built the holy Temple, 480 years passed. This interval of time symbolizes the perfection of the spiritual sanctification (*kiddushin*) that was the necessary foundation for the building of the Temple.

The number 480, with the *kollel* added, is the combined numerical value of the words "right" (*yamin*, ימין) and "left" (*smol*, שמאל).

yamin (ימין): 10 + 40 + 10 + 50 = 110

smol (שמאל): 300 + 40 + 1 + 30 = 371

total: 481

480 plus the *kollel* (1): 480 + 1 = 481

Man represents *chesed* (kindness), symbolized by the right hand. Woman represents *gevura* (restraint), symbolized by the left hand. This *gematria* teaches us that *kiddushin* (which, with the *kollel*, equals 381) unites "right" and "left," whose total is 381.

As the Chazon Ish says in one of his *Igrot*, just as the right hand works in harmonious coordination with the left hand, so should a husband and wife work together and complement each other. Through the sanctity (*kedusha*) of the marriage ceremony (*kiddushin*), man and woman walk hand-in-hand in true friendship and holiness.

9

The Wedding Canopy (*Chupah*) Symbolizes the Perfection of the Quality of *Yesod* (Foundation)

THE SECOND STAGE of the marriage process is bringing the bride under the wedding canopy, the *chupah*. (In modern practice the giving of the wedding ring—*kiddushin*—is performed under the wedding canopy. Originally these were two separate steps, and twelve months passed between *kiddushin*, the giving of the ring, and *nisu'in*, bringing the bride under the *chupah*). The *chupah* completes the process of marriage begun by *kiddushin*. The numerical value of the word *chupah* is 99.

chupah (חופה): 8 + 6 + 80 + 5 = 99

This number, consisting of two nines, alludes to the perfection of the quality of the *tzaddik*. As we saw above, nine is the perfect and eternal number and the *tzaddik* is the person who is perfect in righteousness, and therefore merits eternity. Of the ten worlds or *midot* (qualities) mentioned by the Kabbalah, the one that corresponds to the *tzaddik* is called *Yesod* (Foundation) as in Proverbs 10:25: "The *tzaddik* is the foundation of the world." The *Yesod* is the ninth of the ten *midot*.

When we add the *kollel* (see "Guidelines to Gematria"), the numerical value of *chupah* is 100. This is the value of the letter ק, which stands for *kedushah* (קדושה), holiness. The number 100 is the completion of all the two-digit numbers and represents completion and perfection.

Chupah (חופה) can be divided into חפ, which is in the root of the word cover (חפה), and ו-ה, which is the second half of the name of *HaShem*, י-ה-ו-ה. The *chupah* serves as a protective covering for the holiness represented by the name of *HaShem*.

As seen above, the wedding ceremony is a two-stage process beginning with *kiddushin* and reaching its completion with *nisu'in* under the *chupah*. When we add the numerical values of the words, *kiddushin*, *chupah*, and *kollel*, the result if 580.

> *kiddushin* (קידושין): 100 + 10 + 4 + 6 + 300 + 10 + 50 = 480
> *chupah* (חופה):   8 + 6 + 80 + 5 =   99
> total: 579
> plus *kollel*:   579 + 1 = 580

This is equal to the value of the linguistic root, שפר.

> שפר: 300 + 80 + 200 = 580

This root, which is the basis of words like "improvement" (*shipur*, שיפור) and "beauty" (*shefer*, שפר), hints at the strides towards perfection made by means of *kiddushin* and *chupah*.

The word, *chen* (חן), which means "the grace and radiance which cause a person to find favor in the eyes of all," has the numerical value of 58. Multiplying this by 10 gives 580, demonstrating that the perfection of *chen* is achieved through *kiddushin* and *chupah*.

10

A Man Achieves Complete Unification with His Wife's Help

Esau, the archenemy of Jacob, is also known as Seir, after the name of the land that was given to him (Genesis 36:8). Seir (שעיר) is the source of evil in the world, as indicated by the letters of this name, which, when rearranged, spell יש רע, "There is evil."

"Forcefulness" (tokef, תקף) and "phylacteries" (tefillin, תפילין) stand in opposition to the evil force of Seir. Thus all three of these words are equal in value.

Seir (שעיר):   300 + 70 + 10 + 200 = 580
tokef (תקף):   400 + 100 + 80 = 580
tefillin (תפילין): 400 + 80 + 10 + 30 + 10 + 50 = 580

Tokef, a person's forcefulness in maintaining and increasing his holiness, depends upon his righteousness, and especially upon his ability to gain control over and unify all his midot, the various powers and drives that make up his personality. (Tefillin represent this process: They contain the Shema, which states that "Hashem our God is One," and the tefillin are placed on the head, corresponding to the three highest midot, which reside in the brain. The tefillin are also placed on the arm opposite the heart, which is the site of the remaining seven midot. This symbolizes the determination to unify all ten midot for the service of Hashem. The importance of the ability to control and unify one's midot is revealed by the letters of tokef (תקף). By the Ik-Bechar (איק–בכר) transformation these letters become echad (אחד), which means "one." Complete unification of a man's midot is achieved with the help of his wife. Thus his life gains "forcefulness" (580). Through the forcefulness (580) of *kiddushin* and *chupah* (580), a man is able to wage war and subdue the "evil inclination" (*yetzer hara*, יצר הרע), which also has the numerical equivalent of 580:

hayetzer hara (יצר הרע):
5 + 10 + 90 + 200, + 5 + 200 + 70 = 580

11

The Benefits a Wife Brings Her Husband: The Foundation of a Happy Home

WE LEARN FROM THE TALMUD that when a man gets married, this is the first time he merits the term "man" (*adam*, אדם). He also, for the first time, gains the special benefits (*segulot*) of joy (*simcha*, שמחה), blessing (*berachah*, ברכה), wall (*chomah*, חומה), peace (*shalom*, שלום), Torah (תורה), and goodness (*vetovah*, וטובה). The Chidah points out that the initials of these seven *segulot* spell the expression שבח אשתו, "the benefits (or praises) of his wife."

These seven benefits are referred to in the verse, "Wisdoms built the home, hewing out seven columns" (Proverbs 9:1). The seven *segulot* brought by the wife are the foundation of the home. Thus, the Sages say: "'Home' means 'wife.'"

We find in the Talmud (*Yevamot* 62a): "Rabbi Eliezer said: 'Anyone who has no wife is not a man' (*adam*)." The *Ben Ish Chai* explains this statement as follows. The word "man" (*adam*, אדם) begins with the letter א. This letter is composed of a central diagonal, ו, with two י's, one above the ו and one below. Thus, the form of the, א, represents the process by which a child is produced. The lower י alludes to the seed contributed by the father, and the upper י to the seed contributed by the mother; the central, ו alludes to the child born to them. A man who has not yet married lacks the foundation of the letter א—i.e., the central ו from which the א is built. Thus, the letter א is missing from the word "man" (*adam*, אדם), leaving only the letters דם, which spell "silence" (*dom*, דם) or "blood" (*dam*, דם).

The ten worlds, or *midot*, that constitute Creation correspond to the four-letter name of God. The three upper *midot* correspond to the letters יה; the seven remaining *midot* correspond to the letters וה. According to Kabbalah, the seven special benefits (*segulot*) a wife brings her husband hint at the seven *midot* corresponding to the letters וה. The letter ו corresponds to the first six of these seven *midot*; the letter ה corresponds to the last *midah*, which is called *malchut* (kingdom). *Malchut* represents the establishment of God's kingship on earth, and as the seventh and last *midah*, it includes within it all the others.

The seven *segulot* reach full actualization through the *chupah* (חופה), which can be analyzed as חפ וה, "protects וה." Likewise, they are actualized through the *ketubah*, the marriage contract, which can be analyzed as כתב וה, "the writ of, וה." Finally, the seven *segulot* are actualized through the *sheva brachot*, "seven benedictions," which are recited under the *chupah* and at the Grace After Meals of the subsequent wedding feasts.

12

Marriage: Reaching the Ultimate Perfection of Joy

THE WORDS JOY (*simcha*, שמחה) and soul (*neshama*, נשמה) are closely re-lated. If we replace the ח *simcha* with a נ, we have the letters of *ne-shama*. The letters ח and נ stand for that which is above nature. Nature is symbolized by the number seven. When we go beyond seven we have eight, which is the numerical value of the letter ח. Seven multi-plied by itself yields 49, which represents the perfection of nature. When we go beyond 49, we arrive at 50, the numerical value of נ. Thus, 8 and 50 (ח and נ) both represent dimensions beyond nature. The combination of these two letters is חן (*chen*, grace or charisma), a word that alludes to a force from beyond nature that envelops a per-son or thing, investing it with a special glow.

The letters ח"נ are also the initials of *chachmat nister*, the "hidden wisdom," or Kabbalah. Through marriage, represented by the root נשא, a person's soul (*neshama*) reaches its ultimate perfection. Once the person becomes connected with the root of the *neshama*, the shining sparks of joy, *simcha*, are inevitably aroused.

The fact that *simcha*, (joy) results from marriage is revealed by the numerical values of these words. The three-letter root of *simcha* is, שמח. When we total the numerical value of these letters and add three for the number of letters, we get 351, which is the numerical value of the root of marriage, נשא.

שמח: $300 + 40 + 8 = 348$
plus the number of letters: $348 + 3 = 351$
נשא: $50 + 300 + 1 = 351$

As long as a person remains attached to only the natural world, he is subject to sadness. This is reflected in the similarity of the words nature (*teva*, טבע) and sadness (*etzev*, עצב). According to the *Ik-Bechar* (איק-בכר) transformation, the letter ט is equivalent to צ. If we exchange the ט of *teva* (טבה) for צ we have the letters of *etzev* (עצב). On the other hand, when a person rises above nature by means of holiness and attachment to the *neshama*, he arrives at the source of joy (*simcha*).

13

The Father Has Mercy, the Mother Consoles

KING SOLOMON ADMONISHES: "Hear, my son, the chastisement of your father, and do not abandon the Torah of your mother" (Proverbs 1:8). These two forces, the chastisement given by the father and the Torah wisdom instilled by the mother, together have the power to annul the strength of Satan, the accuser of evil inclination.

The nature of the father is to have mercy on his children, as in Psalms 103:13: "as a father has mercy on his children." The nature of the mother is to console her children, as in Isaiah 66:13: "like a man whose mother consoles him."

The expression "has mercy" (*rachem*, רחם) begins with the letter *raish* (ר), hinting at the function of the father, which is to act as the "head" (*rosh*, ראש) of his children and grandchildren, chastising them and instilling in them knowledge of the Torah. His task is to pass along the wisdom and perfection of the "mind" (*moach*, מח). Thus, "has mercy" (*rachem*, רחם) can be analyzed as ר, head, and מח (*moach*), mind.

Similarly, according to Midrash Shochar Tov, the function of the male (*zachar*, זכר) is to remember. The words "male" and "remember" come from the same three-letter root: זכר. The Midrash analyzes this into זך (*zach*, pure) and ר, which indicates the head. By maintaining a pure head, the male remembers.

The word "consoles" (*nachem*, נחם) can be analyzed into the letters נ—which stands for the fifty gates of *binah* (understanding)—and חם (*chom*, warmth). To console means to inculcate faith and constructive feelings in the hearts of children. The task of the mother is to surround her children with warm-heartedness through the power of her *binah*, (understanding and intuition).

The word Satan can be spelled either שטן or סטן. According to the *Ben Ish Chai*, when we look at the letters that alphabetically precede the letters of a word, we find the entity that has the power to annul that word. The letters preceding Satan (שטן) are רחם (*rachem*, has mercy); those preceding Satan (סטן) are נחם (*nachem*, consoles).

ר precedes ש		נ precedes ס	
ח precedes ט		ח precedes ט	
מ precedes נ		מ precedes נ	

The father's mercy (רחם) has the power to annul Satan (שטן), and the mother's consolation (נחם) has strength to annul Satan (סטן).

14

The Characteristics of
Man and Woman

THE WORDS "MAN" (*ish*, איש) and "woman" (*ishah*, אשה) both contain
the word "fire" (*esh*, אש). The fire of the stove heats water to the boil-
ing point so that we can use it for our purposes; the fire of the sun
heats plants so that they can sprout and grow. Similarly, the fire (*esh*,
אש) within the wife (*ishah*, אשה) helps her husband to awaken his latent
potential to benefit the world.

Although man and woman both contain fire, the two fires are not
the same. According to the Admor, Rabbi Avraham of Trisk, in *Magen
Avraham* (Parshat Behaalotecha), the fire of man is white fire, whose
basis is the quality of mercy (*rachamim*) (the color white symbolizes
mercy); the fire of woman is red fire, whose basis is the quality of strict
judgment (*din*). This gives us insight into the characteristics of the
children, the offspring of the father and mother. According to the Talmud (*Niddah* 31:2), the father's seed produces the bones, which correspond to the color white; the mother's seed produces the flesh, which
corresponds to the color red.

The combination of the qualities of *chesed* (kindness) and *din*
(strict judgment), which are interwoven through the unification of
man and woman, produces the quality of *tiferet* (splendor), which
unites the two qualities of *chesed* and *din*.

The quality *tiferet* (splendor) is the foundation of *Shabbat*. The
Sabbath thus combines the qualities of *Chesed* and *din*. We have just
seen that a person's bones correspond to the quality of *chesed*, while
the flesh corresponds to the quality of *din*. *Bnei Yissachar* (Inyanei

Shabbat) points out that the numerical value of *Shabbat* (שבת) equals the combined numerical value of the words "bone" and "flesh" (עצם, בשר).

> *Shabbat* (שבת): 300 + 2 + 400 = 702
> *etzem, basar* (עצם, בשר):
> 70 + 90 + 40, + 2 + 300 + 200 = 702

The word *Shabbat* (שבת) can be analyzed as the letter ש, which stands for *shoresh* (שורש, root) and בת (*bat*, daughter), which stands for *bat yisrael* (בת ישראל), "daughter of Israel," the Hebrew term meaning "Jewish woman." *Shabbat*, which combines *chesed* (kindness) and *din* (strict judgment), is the root and source from which the Jewish woman draws her strength.

When we numerically combine the word *chesed* (חסד) and *din* (דין), the result is 136. This is also the numerical value of the word "ladder" (*sulam*).

> *chesed* (חסד):   8 + 60 + 4 = 72
> *din* (דין):   4 + 10 + 50 = 64
> total: 136
> *sulam* (סולם): 60 + 6 + 30 + 40 = 136

This teaches us that if a man wishes to ascend the ladder of spiritual growth, he must achieve the right combination of *chesed* (kindness) and *din* (strict judgment) all the days of his life. Similarly, he is urged upward by the combination of *chesed* and *din* he receives from divine Providence (*hashgacha*).

The letters ס and ש are interchangeable. Thus, the letters of "ladder" (*sulam*, סולם) are equivalent to those of "peace" (*shalom*, שלום). The special power of peace is the foundation of the ladder by means of which a person rises upward spiritually and materially.

We have already learned that peace (*shalom*) is one of the seven special benefits a wife brings her husband.

The letters of the word, *shalom* (שלום) are the foundation of the quality of *din* (strict judgment), which is embodied in woman. According to *Kehillat Yaakov* (אשה), this is revealed by the fact that the word "woman" (*ishah*, אשה) forms the initials of three names of God: הויה, שדי, אדני. All three of these names represent the quality of *din*.

The name הויה begins with ה. These same letters, arranged in a different order, form the name יהוה, which indicates the quality of *chesed* (kindness). This name begins with the letter י. We have already noted that the only difference between the words for "man" and "woman" is that man (איש) contains the letter י and woman (אשה) contains the letter ה. Thus, man represents the quality of *chesed*, and woman represents the quality of *din*. The unity of man and woman in marriage represents harmonious cooperation between various names of God, each relating to one of the ten *midot* by which the world was created. Some of these *midot* are from the side of *chesed*, and others from the side of *din*. Their harmonious unification is the foundation of and key to joy (*simcha*).

The idea that joy (*simcha*) results from the harmonious combination of *din* and *chesed* is revealed by the three-letter root of "joy": שמח. By the *Albam* (א″ל-ב″מ) transformation, שמח becomes יבק (Yabok, the name of a river first mentioned in Genesis 32:23). According to Kabbalah, the word Yabok alludes to two names of the Holy One, blessed is he. The name *Elohim* (אלהים) represents the quality of *din*, and the name יהוה represents the quality of *rachamim* (mercy). Their combined numerical value is equal to that of Yabok.

Elohim (אלהים): $1 + 30 + 5 + 10 + 40 = 86$
יהוה: $10 + 5 + 6 + 5 = 26$
total: 112
Yabok (יבק): $10 + 2 + 100 = 112$

Thus, the root of "joy," שמח, which is equivalent to Yabok, expresses the names of God that allude to *din* (strict judgment) and *rachamim* (mercy), the qualities that are unified through the marriage of man and woman.

The ten *sefirot* or *midot* through which the divine light devolves in the process of Creation are divided into groups of three, each group consisting of right, left, and middle. Thus, *chochma* (wisdom) is on the right; *binah* (understanding) is on the left; and *daat* (knowledge), combining the two, is in the middle. *Chesed* (kindness) is on the right; *Gevura* (might) is on the left; and *tiferet* (splendor) is in the middle, combining the two preceding *midot*. *Netzach* (eternity) is on the right; *hod* (glory) is on the left; and *yesod* (foundation), which combines these two, is in the middle. Kabbalah teaches that the three middle *midot*—*daat*, *tiferet*, and *yesod*—correspond to three names of God: אדני, which represents kingship and is related to *din*; יהוה, which represents *rachamim* (mercy); and אהיה, which represents *keter* (crown), the highest of the worlds. The combined numerical value of these three names equals the numerical value of Yabok, 112.

אדני: 1 + 4 + 50 + 10 =   65
יהוה: 10 + 5 + 6 + 5=   26
אהיה: 1 + 5 + 10 + 5=   21
total: 112

The letters of Yabok, corresponding to the root of joy, שמח, form the initials of three basic powers of marriage. Yabok (יבק) stands for:

unification (*yichud*): י חוד
blessing (*berachah*): ב רכה
holiness (*kedusha*): ק דושה

The word Yabok is also the foundation of the name of Yaakov (Jacob), the most complete and perfect of the three Patriarchs. The letters of Jacob (יעקב) are identical to those of Yabok (יבק), with the addition of the letter ע. The numerical value of ע is 70. Jacob brought about the realization of the name Yabok by means of the seventy children of Israel who went down to Egypt and who were the root of the entire Jewish people.

15

The Wife: Source of Her Husband's Sustenance

THE WORD "BREAD" (*lechem*, לחם) comes from a linguistic root meaning to join or connect. The modern verb "to weld" (*lehalchim*, להלחים) is from the same root. The concept of bread is also based on this idea of "connecting." Bread connects and holds together the two basic elements of which man is made—body and soul.

Thus, the wife, whose task is to cleave to her husband and complete him, is sometimes referred to as *lechem*. She, too, connects her husband's spiritual life with his material life.

According to the *Ik-Bechar* (איק-בכר) transformation, "bread" (*lechem*, לחם) becomes "partner" (*shutaf*, שתף). This teaches us that the wife must be a faithful partner to her husband through all life's paths. The husband has a reciprocal obligation to include his wife as a partner in everything he does.

The same letters that spell *lechem* (לחם, bread) also spell מחל (*machal*), the root of the verb "to forgive." When a man acquires a wife, referred to as *lechem*, he also achieves forgiveness. Until now he was alone, and as a result was subject to *tuma*, spiritual impurity. When he marries, his sins are forgiven.

The Torah relates that when Joseph became a slave to Potiphar, he became the chief steward of the Egyptian's household. Potiphar "entrusted everything he had to Joseph's hands, taking account of nothing except the bread (*lechem*) he ate" (Genesis 39:6). When Potiphar's wife repeatedly tried to seduce Joseph, Joseph reproved her: "My master takes account of nothing in the household . . . .

He has held back nothing from me except you" (*ibid.* 8–9). Thus, as the Sages remark on this passage, the word *lechem* referred to Potiphar's wife.

The *Ben Ish Chai, Ben Yehoyada* (*Sotah,* 72), explains the correlation between wife and bread as follows: The "bread" and material prosperity of a household come through the merit of the wife, as the Sages say: "Blessing only comes to a man's household for the sake of his wife" (*Bava Metzia* 59a). That is why the wife is referred to as "bread."

This is also why a man who leaves his wife to pursue an indecent woman (*zonah*) will, in the end, come to beg for a loaf of bread and not find it, as it is written: "For the sake of an indecent woman—to a loaf of bread" (Proverbs 6:26). The wife is the source of a man's daily bread. Whoever betrays his wife (God forbid) ruins his own sustenance.

16

The Shared Powers of Husband and Wife: The Source of Joy

THE WORD "JOY" (*simcha*, שמחה) has the same letters as "five" (*chamisha*, חמשה), a that which alludes to this world. According to the Midrash, the world was created with the letter ה, whose numerical value is 5. As we have seen, the letter ה refers to woman.

The shape of the letter ה is composed of a ד with a י inside it. The ד, whose numerical value is 4, alludes to this world, where everything is made from the four elements. The works of Kabbalah tell us, however, that there is a fifth element, which activates the other four and is referred to as "the image of God." This is symbolized by the י within the ד.

On another level, the ד represents the womb, and the י stands for the life force sheltered therein. By the *Ik-Bechar* (איק-בכר) transformation, the letter ד becomes מ. This letter has two forms: the "open" form (מ), used in the beginning or middle of a word, and the "closed" form (ם), used at the end of a word. These represent the "open" womb (i.e., the womb during menstruation) and the "closed" womb (during the time of menstrual purity).

In fact, the letter י appears in both איש (*ish*, man) and אשה (*ishah*, woman). In the word for "man" it is the central letter; in the word for "woman," it is concealed as a component part of the letter ה.

The letter י in the word for "man" stands for supernal life, and the letter י in the word for "woman" stands for the practical life of this world.

The relationship between these two forms of life, or vitality, is symbolized by the letter א. This letter is composed of an upper י and a lower י, which are joined by a slanting letter ו. The letter ו corresponds to what Kabbalah refers to as the quality of *yesod*, which relates to the cohabitation of man and woman.

The letter י, which is possessed by both man (איש) and woman (אשה), teaches us about the life force contained within them.

In *Ben Yehoyada* (*Yevamot* 62b), the *Ben Ish Chai* draws another connection between the words "five" and "joy." He points out that, according to the Talmud, there are five basic household tasks a wife is obligated to perform for her husband. This is hinted at in the verse, "Go, eat your bread in joy" (Ecclesiastes 9:7). We have seen that the term "bread" sometimes indicates the wife. The word for "joy," with the letters rearranged, spells "five." Thus, the verse suggests that the wife benefits her husband through five basic tasks.

This is one of the reasons why the Grace After Meals recited at a wedding feast contains the special added phrase, "Joy is in His dwelling" (שהשמחה במעונו). The word joy hints at the five tasks. These tasks symbolize the support and aid a wife gives her husband, which constitutes his source of joy.

The root of joy is honesty, as it is written, "The honest-hearted have joy" (Psalms 97:11). Honesty is the state of man in his perfection, as he was originally created. Thus, King Solomon states, "God made man honest, but they sought numerous calculations" (Ecclesiastes 87:29). The calculations that Adam and Eve indulged in ruined the honesty of their souls.

When husband and wife achieve honesty with each other, it causes joy. The three-letter root of "joy" (*simcha*, שמחה) is שמח. The "inner" *gematria* of these three letters is obtained by spelling out the names of the letters and then counting only the "inner" part of the names.

shin (ש) is spelled: שין
mem (מ) is spelled: מם
chet (ח) is spelled: חית

The "inner" letters of these three names, with their numerical equivalents, are:

ין:	60
ם:	40
ית:	410
total:	510

This total equals the numerical equivalent of "honesty" (*yosher*, ישר).

yosher (ישר): 10 + 300 + 200 = 510

This teaches us that the inner meaning of joy is honesty. Joy sprouts and grows from the trait of honesty.

By the same method we can find the "inner" *gematria* of the word "joy" (*simcha*, שמחה). We have just seen that the "inner" *gematria* of the first three letters, שמח, is 510. The remaining letter is ה, whose name is spelled הה. The "inner" part of this name is ה, whose numerical value is 5. Hence, the "inner" *gematria* of joy is 515. This equals the numerical value of the word "prayer" (*tefillah*, תפלה).

tefillah (תפלה): 400 + 80 + 30 + 5 = 515

The perfection of prayer depends upon a person's joy, as indicated by the verse, "Worship *Hashem* with joy" (Psalms 100:3).

The underlying basis of prayer, *tefillah*, is that it unifies husband and wife. This is symbolized by the story of our forebears, Isaac and Rebecca. The Torah relates that they prayed together for a child, and were answered. According to Kabbalah, the power of their prayer is indicated by the fact that the combined numerical value of their names is equal to 515, the numerical value of the word prayer.

Isaac (יצחק):   10 + 90 + 8 + 100 = 208
Rebecca (רבקה): 200 + 2 + 100 + 5 = 307
total: 515

The essence of Isaac and Rebecca was prayer and a state of constant attachment to God.

Isaac and Rebecca also symbolize the foundations of harmony and unification that build marriage. Isaac represents the quality of *din* (strict justice); Rebecca represents *chesed* (kindness). In their marriage, these two opposites joined together in unity.

17

Woman's Understanding Is Greater than Man's

THE LETTER ה has the numerical value of 5. As the second letter in the name of God, יהוה, it represents, according to Kabbalah, the quality of *binah* (understanding). This is the quality with which woman is especially blessed.

Regarding the creation of woman, it is written: "The Lord God built the side (to be woman)" (Genesis 2:22). The word for "built" (ויבן) has the same linguistic root as *binah* (בינה). From this the Talmud (*Niddah* 45b) derives the principle that woman's *binah* (understanding, intuition) is greater than man's. For this reason, the Sages attached special importance to the advice of one's wife in worldly matters.

As mentioned, the numerical value of ה is 5. We have seen that "five" and "joy" are spelled with the same letters in Hebrew. Through her feminine intuition, a woman helps to solve her husband's problems, and thus causes him joy. Another form of the word *binah* is *havanah*. Through the *Ik-Bechar* (איק-בכר) transformation, the word for "understanding" (*havanah*, הבנה) becomes "rejoicing" (*renanah*, רננה). The letter ב (2) is interchanged with ר (200), and the letter ה (5) is interchanged with נ (50). Thus, correct understanding is the foundation of happiness and rejoicing.

According to Kabbalah (as cited by *Kehillat Yaakov*, שמחה), another name for *binah* (understanding) is *simcha* (joy). This is hinted at by the verse, "The mother of the sons is joyous" (Psalms 112:29); Kabbalah refers to the quality of *binah* as the "mother" of the other qualities.

The word *amen* (אמן), which indicates one's acquiescence to a blessing or prayer, comes from the same linguistic root as "faith" (*emunah*, אמונה). *Amen* indicates profound contemplation of the meaning of life. This is the source from which a person is inspired with joy; wherever there is faith and contemplation, there is no room for despair and depression to take hold of a person. The person is fully aware that everything happens by divine Providence and that all is for our good.

The foundation of woman is her power of understanding and intuition—*binah*. Thus, the Sages advise (*Bava Metzia* 59a): "If your wife is small, bend over and whisper to her." *Kehillat Yaakov* explains the reason for this counsel: A God-fearing woman is given control over the processes and conduct of the world. Thus, the numerical value of "woman" (*ishah*, אשה) is equal to that of the sentence, "This is the way; walk in it."

ishah (אשה): $1 + 300 + 5 = 306$
"This is the way; walk in it" (זה הדרך לכו בו):
$7 + 5, + 5 + 4 + 200 + 20, + 30 + 20 + 6, + 2 + 6 = 305$
adding the *kollel*: $305 + 1 = 306$

The ways of this world are given over to the God-fearing woman.

18

Shin: The Central Letter of "Woman"

WHILE MAN'S SPECIAL POWER is wisdom (*chochma*), that of woman is understanding (*binah*). This power of woman's is symbolized by the middle letter of the word "woman" (*ishah*, אשה), the letter ש. The name of this letter (*shin*, שִׁן) hints at the linguistic root, שנן, which indicates "repetition" and "sharpening." The activity of sharpening one's knowledge through diligent repetition leads to the faculty of *binah* (understanding).

The letter ש, whose shape is composed of three evenly spaced branches, also hints at the characteristics of balance and cooperation. These characteristics are symbolized by the shape of the letter, with its three evenly spaced branches, and also by the letter's oral expression, which involves the simultaneous activation of tongue, teeth, and lips. Thus, ש is the initial letter of such words as joy (*simcha*, שמחה); peace (*shalom*, שלום); tranquility (*shalva*, שלוה); quiet (*sheket*, שקט); and serenity (*shanenut*, שאננות).

Woman's *binah* (understanding) has the power to bring joy and peace to the life of her family.

The relatively simple and concentrated nature of man (*ish*, איש) is indicated by the tiny letter י in the center of the word. By contrast, the broad and complex letter ש in the center of woman (*ishah*, אשה) symbolizes the wide scope of her vision. (This idea is also indicated by the letter ה, which, as discussed, is the characteristic letter of woman.)

The letter ש is also the foundation of the word "fire" (*esh*, אש). This teaches us that the woman's function is to enlighten the eyes of her husband, as the Sages say: "She enlightens his eyes" (*Yevamot* 63a). In addition, the wife, with her foundation of fire, provides warmth for her husband when he returns home from his worldly activities, which chill his spirit and cloud the light of his soul.

According to Kabbalah, the three letters of the word "woman" (אשה) correspond to three aspects of the body. The letter א corresponds to the head; ש, to the heart; and ה, to the rest of the body. Thus, the letter ש, which is in the center of the word, represents the heart, which is in the center of the body and coordinates all its activities.

19

Woman's Weaponry

We have seen that the word *chamisha* (חמשה) means "five." This is the numerical value of the letter ה, the letter of the woman. The linguistic root of *chamisha* is חמש. This root, besides referring to the number five, also refers to the concept of armor and weaponry (*chimush*).

The wife's function is to guard and defend her husband. Only with her help can he stand against the forces of Satan, the powers that scheme to overthrow him. Thus, the Sages explain (Bereishith Rabba 17:6) that God waited to create Satan until He had created woman, man's weapon of defense against the Accuser (Satan).

Kehillat Yaakov (שמחה) explains that the trait of *simcha* (joy) stems from that of strength (*gevura*), which is the attribute of woman. This is why woman is the source of joy.

When we write out the names of the letters of שמח, the root of joy (שמחה), add their numerical values, and add the *kollel*, the total is 861.

שמח is spelled: שין, מם, חית.

The numerical value of these letters is:

300 + 10 + 50, + 40 + 40, + 8 + 10 + 400 = 858
adding 1 for each of the three letter names:
858 + 3 = 861

This is also the numerical value of the phrase "holy Temple" (Beit Hamikdash, בית המקדש).

Beit Hamikdash (בית המקדש):
2 + 10 + 400, + 5 + 40 + 100 + 4 + 300 = 861

With the help of his wife, who gives him joy, a man builds his home, which is like a miniature holy Temple.

The words שמח (sameach, joyous) and חמש (chamesh, five), both of which are spelled with the same Hebrew letters, express the perfection of the quality of strict justice (din). This fact can be discovered by numerical analysis (gematria). As we have seen, the numerical value of שמח (or חמש), when the names of the letters are written out in full, is (with the kollel) 861. This is equal to ten times the numerical value of the name of God (Elohim, אלהים), which indicates the quality of strict justice.

Elohim (אלהים): 1 + 30 + 5 + 10 + 40 = 86
10 × 86 = 860
plus the kollel: 860 + 1   = 861

The number 861 is also the numerical value of the one festival that is based on the quality of strict justice: Rosh Hashana.

Rosh Hashana (ראש השנה):
200 + 1 + 300, + 5 + 300 + 50 + 5 = 861

The letters of שמח, "joyousness," symbolize marriage in yet another way. The first letter, ש, represents the quality of din, strict justice. The letter מ represents the quality of rachamim, mercy. The combination of these two qualities through the building of the holy Temple produces the fundamental quality symbolized by the letter ח, which stands for חיים, "life" (chayim).

The foundation of the structure of the holy Temple is created by husband and wife when they establish a life together, in cooperation based on holiness and purity.

We have already seen that the words for "five" (chamisha, חמשה) and "joy" (simcha, שמחה), when the names of their letters are written out in full, have the numerical value of 515, which is equal to the numerical value of the word prayer (tefillah, תפלה).

The word tefillah is linguistically related to another word spelled with the same letters, petillah (פתלה, wick), which is based on the concept of connection and joining. (The wick is the element that connects the flame with the fuel.)

The numerical equivalent of joy (*simcha*), prayer (*tefillah*), and wick (*petillah*) teaches us that joy has the power to connect man to his Creator, and also to his wife.

Another word for happiness is *chedva* (חדוה, contentment). This word also contains a lesson about the power of joy to make a strong bond between husband and wife. חדוה can be analyzed into חד—which means "one" or "unity"—and the letters וה.

The letter ו represents the holiness of the name of God, which is also related to the bridegroom (*chatan*). ו has the numerical value of 6, which corresponds to the six orders of the Mishnah, the Oral Torah.

The letter ה, whose numerical value is 5, corresponds to the holiness of woman, and also represents the Five Books of Moses, the written Torah.

According to *Tanna Devei Eliahu* (beginning of Ch. 3), armor (*chimush*) and strength (*gevura*) are the source of joy (*simcha*), in accordance with the saying, "I felt awe in the midst of my joy" (*ibid.*). The numerical value of the word "awe" (*yirah*) is equal to that of "strength" (*gevura*).

yirah (יראה): $10 + 200 + 1 + 5 = 216$
gevura (גבורה): $3 + 2 + 6 + 200 + 5 = 216$

It is reasonable to assume that awe of God (*yirah*) is the special quality of woman, as King Solomon said: "A God-fearing woman will be praised" (Proverbs 31:30).

The powers of *gevurah* (strength) and *din* (strict justice), which belong to woman, are also revealed through the word "female" (*nekeivah*, נקבה). The basic meaning of this word is to puncture or bore a hole, like one who drives a nail into wood. Thus, *nekeivah* indicates the firmness of *gevura*. That is, the wife firmly drives into reality the basic spiritual material her husband provides her.

20

Blessing Comes from the Wife

"A MAN IS BLESSED only for the sake of his wife," the Talmud tells us (*Bava Metzia* 59a), citing the example of Abraham, who received great wealth because of the merit of his wife, Sarah (Genesis 20:16).

The linguistic root of "blessing" (*berachah*, ברכה) is ברך, whose numerical value is 222. This number, composed entirely of numeral 2s, indicates the "redoubling" of wealth and prosperity that is brought to perfection by the "pair"—husband and wife.

The Torah calls woman a helpmeet (*ezer* עזר) for man (Genesis 2:18). The letters of this word also spell "seed" (*zera*, זרע), teaching us that the seeds of blessing are contained within the essence of woman.

"A man receives money only through the merit of his wife" (*Zohar*, Parshat Tazria, 52a). The thread connecting blessing, sustenance, and woman is revealed by the author of *Ben Yehoyada* (*Bava Metzia* 74a). He points out that the combined numerical values of the words, "blessing" (*berachah*) and "bread" (*lechem*, the symbol of sustenance) equal the numerical value of "woman" (*ishah*).

> *berachah* (ברכה): 2 + 200 + 20 + 5 = 227
> *lechem* (לחם):   30 + 8 + 40 = 78
> total: 305
> adding the *kollel*:
>   305 + 1 = 306
> *ishah* (אשה):   1 + 300 + 5 = 306

This teaches us that blessing and sustenance come in the merit of the wife.

The word "blessing" (*berachah*, ברכה) has the same numerical value as "male" (*zachar*, זכר).

berachah (ברכה): 2 + 200 + 20 + 5 = 227
zachar (זכר):   7 + 20 + 200 = 227

The Talmud (*Niddah* 31a) tells us that male children are derived from the mother, as suggested by the verse, "When a woman conceives and gives birth to a male" (Leviticus 12:2). Thus, we see again that blessing is derived from the woman.

On the other hand, the same Talmud passage tells us that female children are derived from the father. The word "female" (*nekeivah*, נקבה) has the same numerical value as "damage" (*nezek*, נזק).

nekeivah (נקבה): 50 + 100 + 2 + 5 = 157
nezek (נזק): 50 + 7 + 100   = 157

The female child is derived from the man; hence, when she is on her own, she can easily be damaged. Only with the blessing of marriage does she achieve completion. Then the likelihood of damage is removed.

21

Beit: The "House" of Blessing

THE WORD "BLESSING" IS CONNECTED with water, the source of abundance in which all the blessings are stored. This treasure is stored in a "house"—namely, the letter ב, whose name, *bet* (בית), also means house (*bayit*). This "treasure house" merited to be the letter with which the Torah begins: בראשית ברא—"In the beginning God created . . . ."

The letter א, on the other hand, even though it is the first letter of the alphabet, did not merit to begin the Torah, for it is also the initial of the word "cursed" (*arur*, ארור).

א cannot be the letter of blessing: Its numerical value is 1, indicating separateness and isolation. Blessing exists only where there is plurality, and the minimum plurality is 2, the numerical value of the letter ב. This letter symbolizes the couple—husband and wife. Moreover, the letter ב relates primarily to the wife, for she is the mainstay of the home (*bayit*, בית). That is why the Sages customarily referred to their wives as "my home."

The Jewish woman is called *bat Yisrael* (בת ישראל, daughter of Israel). When she receives the special strength (*segulah*) that comes from being married to her husband, the letter, י, which is central to the word "man," (*ish*, איש), is added to her name. Thus, בת (daughter) becomes בית (home).

By the *Atbash* (א״ת-ב״ש) transformation, the letters of בית (*bayit*, "home") are equivalent to the letters אמש. According to *Sefer Yetzira*, these letters represent the three basic elements with which the Holy One, blessed be he, created the world:

א stands for אויר (*avir*, air).

מ stands for מים (*mayim*, water).

ש stands for אש (*esh*, fire).

These three elements symbolize marriage. Air is the combined product of fire and water. Fire corresponds to woman, who embodies the quality of *din* (strict judgment). Water corresponds to man, who embodies the quality of *rachamim* (mercy). The harmonious blending of these opposites constitutes the building of the home, the *bayit*.

According to the *Ik-Bechar* (איק – בכר) transformation, the letters בית become אמר. These letters, too, are the initials of the three elements used to create the world.

א stands for אש (*esh*, fire).

מ stands for מים (*mayim*, water).

ר stands for רוח (*ruach*, wind).

These elements, too, are built by husband and wife, who constitute the foundation of the home.

22

Binah: The Woman's "Home"

THE LETTER ב alludes to woman's characteristic quality of *binah* (understanding). This quality penetrates to the inner meaning of things. The word "home" (*bayit*, בית) also means, "within," as in the verse, "within (*mibeit*, מבית) the curtain" (Exodus 26:33).

Woman, who is endowed with the quality of *binah* (understanding), has the power to perceive the inner nature of things. This enables her to build the home from the vantage point of a profound and penetrating vision.

According to Kabbalah, blessing is connected with the quality of *din* (strict judgment), which draws nourishment from the quality of *binah* (understanding). Thus, Isaac, the paradigm of *din*, was given abundant blessing, as we read: "Isaac sowed in that land, and he found in that year one hundred measures [one hundred times the normal crop]" (Genesis 26:12).

23

The Blessing of the Letter *Hei*

THE QUALITIES OF *din* (strict judgment) and *binah* (understanding) are also hinted at by the letter ה, which, as we have seen, is the letter of woman. According to Kabbalah, the letter ה contains the power of "seed" and "blessing." This is hinted at in the verse, "Here is seed for you" (Genesis 47:22), where the expression for "Here is" (*hei*, הא) is the name of the letter ה.

When ה was added to Sarai's name, she became Sarah, which gave her the power to have seed—i.e., a child.

The *Atbash* (א״ת–ב״ש) transformation reveals the deeper meaning of words and letters. According to this transformation, ה becomes צ, a letter that represents righteousness (*tzidkut*, צדקות). Thus, it was Joseph who was brought down to Egypt, and who, after making the Egyptians circumcise themselves, told them, "Here is seed for you."

According to Kabbalah, the form of the letter צ consists of י, representing *chochma* (wisdom), and נ, representing *binah* (understanding). The combination of *chochma* and *binah* is produced by woman's power of righteousness.

According to Kabbalah, the letters כ and ה, both of which relate to woman, are connected in yet another way. Each is composed of the letters ד and ו. The כ consists of a ד above, and a horizontal ו beneath. The ה, on the other hand, consists of a ד on the right, with an upright ו at its side. This hints that the letter ה is a more advanced and developed stage of the letter כ. It also shows that the husband should stand at his wife's side in building the home.

We have seen that the source of blessing that resides in woman is related to 2, the numerical value of the letter ב. The number two is also contained in the letter ש, the central letter of the word "woman" (*ishah*, אשה).

The name of this letter, *shin* (שין), is spelled with the same letters as the word *sheni* (שני), the adjectival form of the number two. Moreover, by the *Atbash* (א"ת–ב"ש) transformation, the ש is equivalent to the letter ב, the letter of blessing.

24

Goodness (*Tovah*)

REGARDING THE STATE OF MAN before the creation of woman, the Torah states, "It is not good for man to be alone" (Genesis 2:18). Goodness (*tovah*, טובה) is the force that builds and creates in the world, as opposed to the forces of evil, ruin, and destruction.

The letters of the word "evil" (*ra*, רע) are the same as those of ער, the two-letter root of "disrupt" (*mearer*, מערער) and *arar* (ערער), a barren tree. Man, when he is alone, disrupts the foundations of the world and is like a "barren tree" in the wilderness.

From the Torah's definition of "alone" as "not good," Rabbi Samson Raphael Hirsch deduces that in order for "good" to exist, there must be "two." This can be seen in the very structure of the word "good" (*tov*, טוב). The Talmud states, "There is more good (*tov*) in sitting together than in remaining single" (טוב למיתב טן דו מלמיתב ארמלו). The expression for "together" (טן דו) can be seen as a form of the word *tov*, טוב. If the letter ו is lengthened slightly, it becomes ן. Thus, the first two letters of טוב become טן. The letter ב, as we have seen, can be analyzed as a combination of, ד and, ו. Thus, טוב becomes טן דו: "Good" means "together."

The first two letters of טוב—i.e., טו—have the numerical value of 15. This is equivalent to יה, the name of God that forms the bond between man (*ish*, איש) and woman (*ishah*, אשה). The remaining letter, ב, stands for the good home that results when husband and wife join together in holiness.

The numerical value of "good" (*tov*) is 17.

tov (טוב): 9 + 6 + 2 = 17

As the total of ten and seven, the number seventeen represents the combination of the upper and lower worlds. Ten stands for the upper world, and seven, the number of nature, stands for the lower world. The name יה also represents two worlds: The letter י stands for the world-to-come, and ה stands for this world.

When the two worlds are joined through the union of husband and wife, these worlds become perfected with the quality of goodness. This is the blessing of marriage.

We have seen that the first two letters of "good" (*tov*, טוב)—i.e., טו—have the numerical value of 15, equivalent to יה. This hints at the combination of wisdom (*chochma*), symbolized by the letter י, with understanding (*binah*, symbolized by the letter ה. The result of this combination is knowledge (*daat*) of the Divine.

The perfection of a man's *daat* depends on his wife. The Talmud states: "A fitting wife expands a man's *daat*" (*Berachot* 57b). This is also indicated by the numerical value of the word "marriage" (*kiddushin*, קדושין), which is derived from the word "holiness" (*kedusha*, קדושה). *Kiddushin* is numerically equivalent to the term "the *daat*" (*hadaat*), with the addition of the *kollel*.

kiddushin (קדושין): 100 + 10 + 4 + 6 + 300 + 10 + 50 = 480
hadaat (הדעת):   5 + 4 + 70 + 400 = 479
plus the *kollel*:   479 + 1 = 480

The marriage of man and woman is the foundation on which *daat* is built.

The Talmud cites a verse from a work called *Sefer Ben Sira*: "A good wife will be given into the bosom of a God-fearing man" (*Yevamot* 63b). The author of *Ben Ish Chai*, in his work *Ben Yehoyada* (*Yevamot* 62b), discusses this passage. He says that the feminine form of the word "goodness" (*tovah*, טובה) alludes to woman.

The word טובה can be analyzed as טו–בה, which means, "טו is in her." As we have seen, טו has the numerical value of 15, corresponding to the name of God, יה. The letter of woman is ה, and that of man is י. When the woman, through marriage, receives the letter י from her husband, she contains יה, which is the equivalent of טו. This is the meaning of טו–בה, ("טו is within her"). This is why the verse uses the expression "into the bosom." It indicates that the woman receives the letter י, which is in the bosom of the man (ish, איש).

The opposite of goodness (tov, טוב) is evil (ra, רע). As we saw, the letters רע are the root of the word "disrupt" (mearer, מערער). Evil disrupts the word "dispute" (machloket, מחלוקת), dividing its letters into חלק and מות, which spell chelek mavet, "portion of death." When the home is torn by disputes and fighting between husband and wife, it can drive away יה, the name of God that forms the foundations of goodness (tov, טוב). If the letter י is removed from man (ish, איש) and the letter ה is removed from woman (ishah, אשה), what remains is אש (esh, fire). The two fires wage war against each other, which leads (God forbid) to חלק מות, the "portion of death."

25

"Form": The Embodiment of "Goodness"

ACCORDING TO THE *Ik-Bechar* (איק–בכר) transformation, the word "goodness" (*tovah*, טובה) becomes "form" (*tzurah*, צורה). The letter ט is equivalent to צ, and the letter ב is equivalent to ר. The letters ו and ה, which indicate holiness (*kedusha*), are common to both words. This transformation teaches us that, in the sphere of holiness, goodness is the force that leads to the perfection of form.

The wife is the source of goodness. Because of his wife, a man achieves his destined stature, becoming a "well-formed man" (*baal tzurah*).

This can be learned from the manner in which "goodness" (טובה) becomes "form" (צורה). The two transforming letters of טובה are ט and ב. Their combined numerical value is 11. This number, consisting of two numeral 1s, indicates a lowly world, numerically symbolized by the realm of units. When these two letters are transformed into צ (90) and ר (200), we graduate to the realm of tens and hundreds. This symbolizes the higher worlds to which a man rises with the help of his wife.

26

Goodness of the Soul Comes from the Wife

By the *Atbash* (א״ת–ב״ש) transformation, the word "goodness" (*tov*, טוב) becomes "soul" (*nefesh*, נפש). This teaches us that the foundation of good is the soul, which is the source of a person's life force.

Adam realized the power of his soul with the help of his wife, Eve, whom he called "the mother of all living things" (Genesis 3:20). In the same way, each man perfects the goodness of his soul by means of his wife, who represents his life's destiny.

We have seen that the term "good" refers to the wife. It also refers to light, as in the verse, "God saw the light that it was good" (Genesis 1:4). Thus, there is a connection between "wife" and "light." As the Sages say, the wife "enlightens the eyes" of her husband. This concept of the wife as the source of light has already been mentioned in our discussion of the woman's central letter, ש, which stands for fire (*esh*, אש), the foundation of warmth and light.

27

The Goodness of Righteousness

ACCORDING TO THE WORKS OF Kabbalah, we can learn much about the quality of goodness from the letter ט. This is the initial of the word "good" (*tov*, טוב). Moreover, the first appearance of the letter ט in the Torah is in the word טוב.

The creative emanation of God descends through the ten *sefirot*, which correspond to ten basic qualities (*midot*) of mind and heart. The ninth of these *sefirot* is called *yesod* (foundation). It corresponds to the letter ט, whose numerical value is 9.

Yesod is known as the *sefirah* of the righteous one, the *tzadik*, who is symbolized by the letter *tzadi* (צ). This letter has the numerical value of 90, or ten times the numerical value of the letter ט, the initial of "good" (טוב). Multiplying something by ten indicates perfection. Thus, the perfection of the ninth quality, *yesod*, results in the ultimate of righteousness, as it is written (*Isaiah* 3:10): "Say to the *tzadik* that [he did] good."

The wife is the foundation of goodness. She contains the power of the letter ט, representing righteousness.

The letters ט and ת, both pronounced with the same parts of the mouth, are interchangeable. Hence, the name of the letter ט can be written either טית or טיט. The second of these spellings also means "mud" (*teet*, טיט). This indicates that the woman's function is to care for the material needs of her husband. In fact, another word for mud is *chemar* (חמר), from the same linguistic root as "material" (חומר).

Through her concern for her husband's material needs, the wife enables him to devote himself to developing a life of purity, holiness, and spirituality. In this way, the married couple rises to the highest levels of righteousness.

28

"He Who Finds a Wife Finds Goodness"

THE NUMERICAL VALUE of "good" (*tov*) is 17.

tov (טוב): 9 + 6 + 2 = 17

This is also the "small" *gematria* of one of the words for "soul": *neshama*.

neshama (נשמה): 50 + 300 + 40 + 5
reduces to: 5 + 3   + 4   + 5 = 17

With the help of his wife, a man can reach the quality of goodness that is the foundation of the soul (*neshama*), as it is written (Proverbs 18:22): "He who finds a wife finds goodness."

29

The Goodness of Torah, the Goodness of a Wife

THE TERM, "GOOD," which applies to the wife, applies also to the Torah, as it is written, "The Torah of Your mouth is good to me, more than thousands in gold and silver" (Psalms 119:72). The fact that both wife and Torah are particularly referred to by the term "good" teaches us the importance of the wife in the perfection of a man's Torah learning.

For this same reason, the Torah is compared to a woman, as in the passage beginning, "A woman of valor, who can find?" (Proverbs 31:10). According to the Midrash, this passage refers to the Torah, since one's Torah learning depends upon one's wife.

The Talmud, too, compares the Torah to a wife: "How good is a good wife, for the Torah is compared to her!" (*Yevamot* 63b). The Maharal explains this statement as follows: Just as the Torah has the power to bring a man to the ultimate of perfection, so, too, does the wife. And just as a woman becomes united with a man, so, too, does the Torah becomes one with the man.

Through his wife, a man can achieve perfection in Torah and *mitzvot*. This is revealed by the combined numerical value of the words man (*ish*, איש) and wife (*ishah*, אשה), which is equal to the numerical value of the term "the Torah" (*haTorah*, התורה), with the addition of the *kollel*.

ish (איש): $1 + 10 + 300 = 311$
ishah (אשה): $1 + 300 + 5 = \underline{306}$
total: 617
haTorah (התורה): $5 + 400 + 6 + 200 + 5 = 616$
plus the *kollel*: $616 + 1 = 617$

This teaches us that the building of perfection in Torah is revealed through husband and wife.

We find that two things are referred to in the Torah by the feminine pronoun *zot* (זאת), which is translated "this" or "she." One of these is the Torah itself, in the verse, "This (*zot*) is the Torah which Moses placed before the children of Israel" (Deuteronomy 4:44). The other is woman, in the verse, "She (*zot*) was taken from man" (Genesis 2:23).

The word *zot* (זאת) alludes to the unification of this world with the world-to-come. The first letter, ז, whose numerical value is 7, represents this world of nature; the remaining two letters, את, refer to the root of the world-to-come. This is another indication that "Torah" and "wife" are interdependent.

The *Zohar* (Part 2, 42a) explains that woman corresponds to the tenth *sefirah*, which is called *malchut* (kingdom). The word *zot* (זאת) also refers to this *sefirah*, and that is why woman is called *zot*.

Malchut is the lowest world, which receives the emanations of all the other *sefirot*. Hence, it is thought of as a vessel (*kli*). Similarly, woman is compared to a vessel. Her ability to receive abundance from all the upper worlds depends upon her husband, who influences her.

This characteristic of woman is indicated by the word "female" (*nekeivah*, נקבה), which is said to be an acronym (*notarikon*) made up of two words: *nekiah* (נקיה), which means "empty" (lit., clean), and *baah* (באה), which means "she comes." That is, woman is one who "comes empty," like a vessel, requesting to be filled. Thus, the Talmud characterizes woman as one who declares, "Feed me!" She knows how to pray and demand.

30

The Purity of Torah

THE SAGES SAY that the verse, "The fear of *Hashem* is pure, enduring forever" (Psalms 19:10), refers to a man who marries and learns Torah.

The letters ט and ת are interchangeable, being formed with the same parts of the mouth. This means that the word Torah (תורה) is equivalent to the word, purity (*tohar*, טוהר), teaching us that the perfection of Torah study depends upon the degree of purity that a man, with the help of his wife, achieves.

Both phonetically and in terms of the *Ik-Bechar* (איק–בכר) transformation, the letter ט is interchangeable with צ. Thus, "purity" (*tohar*, טוהר) becomes "gleam" (*tzohar*, צוהר). Woman, who is connected with the letter ט, the foundation of goodness (טוב) and purity (טוהר), is the source of gleaming and light, enlightening and clarifying her husband's Torah knowledge and his personality.

31

The Wife: A "Wall"

THE SAGES RELATE THE LETTER ס to woman, pointing out that this letter appears for the first time in the Torah in the verse describing the creation of woman: "And He closed up the flesh" (ויסגר בשר, Genesis 2:21).

The letter ס, with its closed circular shape, symbolizes a wall. The wife is a wall of defense, protecting her husband against the evil winds that are the forces of Satan, the accuser.

By the *Atbash* (א״ת ב״ש) transformation, "woman" (*ishah*, אשה) becomes "tongs" (*tzevat*, צבת), indicating the wife's power of holding and supporting.

The word *tzevat* (צבת, "tongs") is closely related to *tzevet* (צוות), which means a "pair" or "team." Woman's power to hold and support is the foundation of the family's ability to function as an interconnected team.

32

The Wife: A Support to Her Husband

THE NAME OF THE LETTER ס, *samech* (סמך), also means "upholding" and "supporting." This hints at the fact that the wife upholds and supports her husband. We saw previously section that the letter ס refers to the wife.

Samach (סמך, support) is spelled with the same letters as *masach* (מסך), which means "screen." The wife is a screen of defense for her husband.

We have seen that the wife is compared to a "wall" (*chomah*, חמה). Earlier, we learned that she is connected with the number five (*chamesh*, חמש). When we replace the ה of חמה (wall) with ש, it becomes חמש (five). Both the ה and the ש allude to the woman's quality of *din* (strict justice) and *gevura* (strength).

The word "wall" (*chomah*, חמה) is spelled with the same letters as "the warmth" (*hachom*, החם). The warmth with which a woman fills her home, in combination with her powers of *gevura* (strength), form the wall that protects her husband and family.

33

The Wife: A Vessel for the Perfection of Her Husband

THE WIFE IS RELATED to the letter ס. The numerical value of this letter is 60, or 10 × 6. Multiplying by ten indicates perfection. Thus, the letter ס alludes to the perfection of the six qualities (*midot*) of the six secular days of the week. These are the days of activity, as opposed to *Shabbat*, the day of rest.

The woman's sphere of life revolves around these six qualities, whose perfection is symbolized by the letter ס (60). The Oral Torah consists of sixty tractates. By studying them, the husband rises above and sanctifies the material world, with the help of his wife, who upholds and supports him.

Sixty is also the numerical value of the word "vessel" (*kli*, כלי).

kli (כלי): 20 + 30 + 10 = 60

Thus, the Sages say (*Sanhedrin* 22a), "A woman establishes a covenant only with the man who makes her a vessel (*kli*)."

Changing the י of *kli* (כלי) to ה gives us *kallah* (כלה), which means "bride." The bride is the vessel by which a man improves himself in the service of God.

The basic meaning of the word "covenant" (*brit*, ברית) is the joining of two separated halves. *Kehillat Yaakov* (אשה) points out that the matter of the covenant between husband and wife is symbolized by the fact that the numerical value of "wife" (*ishah*) is exactly half that of "covenant" (*brit*).

ishab (אשה):   1 + 300 + 5 = 306
brit (ברית): 2 + 200 + 10 + 400 = 612

The linguistic basis of the word *kli* (כלי, vessel) are the letters, כל. They spell the word "all" (*kol*). According to Kabbalah, this is a name for the quality of *yesod* (foundation), which is connected with purity in marital relations.

According to the *Ik-Bechar* (איק-בכר) transformation, the word "vessel" (*kli*, כלי) becomes "connection" (*kesher*, קשר). The concept of "vessel" expresses the connection between husband and wife.

The numerical value of *kesher* (קשר, connection) is 600.

kesher (קשר): 100 + 300 + 200 = 600

The letter ו, whose numerical value is 6, corresponds to *yesod*, the sixth of the seven lower qualities (*midot*). This is the quality of holiness and connection. Multiplied by ten, this number yields 60, the value of the letter ס. Multiplied by 100, it yields 600, the value of the word *kesher* (קשר, connection). Thus, *kesher* represents the ultimate perfection of holiness and connection in the upper world.

Six hundred is also the numerical value of the letter ם, the "final" form of the letter מ. Thus, the special powers of unity, friendship, connectedness, and perfection are expressed in the letters ו, ס, and ם.

A *kli*, meaning a vessel or implement, connects the spiritual world with the material world, helping a man to put his ideas into action in concrete form. It is a kind of channel (*tzinnor*, צנור) bringing things from the upper world to the lower world, helping a man actualize his will. That is why the word *tzinnor* is spelled with the same letters as "will" (*ratzon*, רצון).

Thus, we learn in *Tanna Devei Eliahu* (Ch. 9): "Who is a proper wife? One who does the will of her husband." The wife is the channel and the vessel through which the potential treasures of the husband are actualized.

When we write out in full the name of the letter ס, the total numerical value is 300.

ס (*samech*) is spelled: סמך, מם, כף
60 + 40 + 20, + 40 + 40, + 20 + 80 = 300

This is also the numerical value of the letter ש, which represents the woman's power of fire (*esh*, אש). The evils that threaten the husband have their source in coldness and depression. Through the wife's fire, which provides the qualities of strict justice (*din*), warmth, and light, she protects her husband against evil.

The letter ש, representing fire, is the center of the word אשה (*ishah*, woman). Through this power, she gives warmth to her husband in time of crisis, and enlightens his eyes. Thus, he can return to a state of psychological balance. This state of equilibrium, too, is symbolized by the letter ש, with its symmetrical, three-branched form.

The circular shape of the letter ס symbolizes the idea of the surrounding or environment. As we have seen, this letter is especially connected with the wife. It is she who is more strongly connected with the surroundings—family, home, social activities. The husband, by nature, is more apt to be involved in his personal, individual principles.

The ring that the groom gives his bride during the wedding ceremony also has the circular shape of the letter ס. This hints at the wife's functions in connection with this letter: support, aid, defense.

While the letter ש symbolizes the equilibrium that the wife contributes to her husband, the letter ס symbolizes the concrete actualization of this quality. This relationship between ש and ס can be heard in the way they are pronounced. The ש has a softer sound ("shhhhh"); the sound of ס is harder ("ssssss"), suggesting a screen of support and solidity.

34

"When Man and Wife (Are in Unity), the Divine Presence Is Between Them"

THE WORD "PEACE" (*shalom*, שלום), like the word "joy" (*simcha*, שמחה), contains the letters ש and מ, representing, respectively, fire (*esh*, אש) and water (*mayim*, מים). Both peace and joy result from the harmonious unification of these two opposing elements.

The letter ל in the center of the word *shalom* (שלום, peace) alludes to the Holy One, blessed be he, because it stands in the center of the alphabet and is taller than all the other letters. This teaches us that true peace exists only when a person places the Holy One, blessed be he, in the center of his life.

The Sages say (*Sotah*, and also the *Zohar* on Bereishith) that when husband and wife are meritorious, the Divine Presence (*Shechinah*) is between them. This can be seen in the fact that the words "man" (*ish*, איש) and "woman" (*ishah*, אשה) are identical except for the letters י and ה, which spell a name of God, יה. This teaches us that only through the power of the Divine can two opposite forces dwell in peace.

In the Morning Prayer, we say that God "produces light and creates darkness, makes peace, and creates everything." After "peace" comes "everything." Peace is the foundation of everything, in both the upper and lower worlds.

As long as a man remains without a wife, he is not complete (*shalem*, שלם); therefore he does not have peace (*shalom*, שלום). Through his wife, he achieves the state of being complete, and thus merits peace.

The linguistic root of *shalom* (שלום, peace) is שלם. The letter ו represents the holiness of the quality of *yesod* (foundation), indicating the purity of marital relations. Through marriage, this quality is perfected. Thus, the letter ו is added to שלם, and the married couple is granted שלום (*shalom*)—peace.

35

The "Ruler" Merits Peace

THE WORDS PEACE (*shalom,* שלום) and ruler (*moshel,* מושל) are spelled with the same letters. Peace results when a man rules over the forces of evil and destruction, thus becoming master of his house—i.e., his own soul. Thus, a man who rules over his evil inclination merits peace. This is accomplished with the help of his wife, who provides her husband with the weapons of self-defense.

If we remove the two central letters of שלום (*shalom,* peace), what remains is שם, which is the linguistic root of the word "desolate" (*shamem,* שמם). As we have seen, ל represents the Holy One, blessed be he, and ו represents the holy quality of *yesod* (foundation). Without these two central elements, marriage is destined to end in desolation and destruction (God forbid).

Without the letters י and ה the words "man" (*ish,* איש) and "woman" (*ishah,* אשה) remain אש and אש, "fire" and "fire," causing ruin and desolation in married life.

The works of Kabbalah point out that the numerical value of *shalom* (שלום, peace), with 4 added for the four letters of the word, equals 380.

> *shalom* (שלום): $300 + 30 + 6 + 40 = 376$
> $6 + 4 = 380$

This same number, 380, results when we take the name of God that represents *Din* (strict justice) and the name that represents *chesed* (kindness), and combine them through multiplication. The name representing *din* is *Adonai*, אדנ-י; that representing *chesed* is יהוה. They are combined as follows:

אדנ-י: 1,   4,   50,   10

יהוה: ×10, × 5, × 6, × 5

Multiplying: 10 + 20 + 300 + 50 = 380

Kabbalah tells us that the husband is from the root of *chesed* (kindness), corresponding to the element of water, and the wife is from the root of *din* (strict justice), corresponding to the element of fire. When the two become connected and unified, they produce true peace.

The Holy One, blessed be he, makes peace on high between the angels of fire and water. Likewise, he makes peace here below between husband and wife, who are derived from these two opposing elements.

36

The Blessings of Marriage: Peace, Goodness, Torah, and Life

Shalom (שלום, peace) IS ONE OF THE NAMES of the Holy One, blessed be he. Kabbalah tells us that this name is connected with the holy quality of *yesod* (foundation). Another characteristic connected with *yesod* is goodness (*tov*, טוב), and this, too, is one of the names of the Holy One, blessed be he. Through marriage, a man can achieve these two blessings: peace and goodness.

The word *shalom* is also used to refer to the Torah, as in the verse, "All its pathways are peace (*shalom*)" (Proverbs 2:17). After marriage, through the merit of his wife, a man is able to plumb the profound depths of the Torah and discover its secrets.

In describing the curses of Exile, the Torah uses the expression, "lacking everything" (Deuteronomy 28:48). The Sages tell us that the word "everything" (*kol*, כל), in this verse, means a wife.

Kol (כל, everything) is another word that Kabbalah connects with the quality of *yesod* (foundation). It is written, "Everything (*kol*) is in the heavens and the earth" (1 Chronicles 29:11). The heavens and the earth are the foundation of the world. Thus, *kol* refers to foundation.

The heavens correspond to the quality of *din* (strict judgment), and the earth corresponds to the quality of *rachamim* (mercy). *Kol* (כל), which includes these two foundations, corresponds to the wife. Through the wife, a man receives the foundations of goodness and peace.

Peace between a husband and wife is not just a personal matter; it has an effect on the Jewish people as a whole. The Sages say in *Avot d'Rabbi Natan*: "When a person establishes peace in his home, Scripture accounts it to him as if he had established peace among the Jewish people."

The Sages say, "Everything (*hakol*, הכל) is from the wife" (Bereishith Rabba, parshah 17). This implies that the word *kol* is a way of referring to the quality of *yesod*, which is intimately connected with *shalom*, peace.

The six special advantages that result from marriage are:

1. joy (*simcha*, שמחה)
2. blessing (*berachah*, ברכה)
3. goodness (*tovah*, טובה)
4. torah (*Torah*, תורה)
5. wall (*chomah*, חומה)
6. peace (*shalom*, שלום)

All of these are united with the seventh advantage, which is life (*chayim*, חיים), as it is written, "See life with your wife whom you love" (Ecclesiastes 9:9). A full and satisfying life depends upon being married. The Sages say (*Nedarim* 64b), "A childless person is considered as if dead."

We saw earlier that both the words איש (*ish*, man) and אשה (*ishah*, woman) contain the letter י. The יי in the middle of the word חיים (*chayim*, life) stand for these two letters.

The letter א also contains two יs, one above and one below the diagonal line. This hints at the importance of married life, which is symbolized by this letter of primary importance, א.

37

"Be Fruitful and Multiply": The Foundation of the World

THE PRIME PURPOSE of getting married is to obey the commandment, "Be fruitful and multiply." This is the first *mitzvah* mentioned in the Torah, and on it depends the existence of the world, as Scripture states: "He did not create it to be a void; he created it to be settled and populated" (*Isaiah* 45:18).

The *mitzvah* of having children, the first *mitzvah* in the Torah, corresponds to the letter א, the first letter in the alphabet. This is one reason why the letter א appears in words that are basic to the existence of a settled and populated world:

ארץ (*aretz*, earth)

אדם (*adam*, man)

איש (*ish*, also man)

אשה (*ishah*, woman)

The numerical value of the phrase "Be fruitful and multiply" is 500.

"Be fruitful and multiply" (פרו ורבו):
80 + 200 + 6, + 6 + 200 + 2 + 6 = 500

According to Kabbalah, this equals the sum of the number of body parts of man (248) and woman (252). Thus, 500 represents the combination of man and woman.

In this lower world, things are represented by their "small" *gematria*. The small *gematria* of 500 is 5, the numerical value of the letter ה, with which the world was created. Thus, five hundred symbolizes the "beginning of the building"—i.e., the beginning of the process of the world's Creation.

Five hundred divided by two is 250, the numerical value of the word "candle" (*ner*).

ner (נר): 50 + 200 = 250

Thus, "two candles" equal five hundred. The light of the upper world shines down into this world by means of the two candles that are lit on Friday night in honor of the holy Sabbath. These two candles correspond to the two commandments to "remember" and to "guard" the Sabbath (see Exodus 20:8 and Deuteronomy 5:12). "Remember" corresponds to man, and "guard" corresponds to woman.

38

God's Name Revealed Through Husband and Wife

The "small" *gematria* of the word "candle" (*ner,* נר) is 7.

ner (נר):   50 + 200
small *gematria*: 5 + 2 = 7

Thus, the small *gematria* of two "candles" is 14. This is also the numerical value of the letters די, which spell "enough" (*dai*).

dai (די): 4 + 10 = 14

The letters ד and י together compose the letter ה, which consists of a ד on the right and a י on the left, beneath the roof of the ד. The world was created with the letter ה.

The letters די are connected with the Creation of the world and with one of the names of the Holy One, blessed be he: שדי (*Shaddai*). The Talmud (*Chaggigah* 12a) tells us that this name refers to the One who (at the time of Creation) said to his world: "Enough!" That is, God set limits to the world he created.

The letters די represent the source of the existence of the world. The linguistic root of "existence" (*kiyum,* קיום) is קם. These letters have ten times the numerical value of די.

ק (100) is ten times י (10)

מ (40) is ten times ד (4)

The "inner" *gematria* of the name שדי (*Shaddai*) is found by writing out the names of its letters, and then removing the outer (i.e., initial) letters.

Shaddai (שדי) is spelled: שין, דלת, יוד
removing the outer letters leaves: ין, לת, וד:
10 + 50, + 30 + 400, + 6 + 4 = 500

We have seen that 500 is the combined number of man and woman. Thus, the unity of husband and wife brings about the continuing revelation of *Shaddai* (שדי), he who "controls" (*meshadded*, משדד) all the forces of the world.

39

The Wife Is "Everything"

THE TALMUD SAYS that the phrase "lacking everything" means "lacking a wife." The word "everything" (*kol*, כל) refers to the wife, since she completes her husband and perfects his independent form. This wifely function begins at the wedding, when she is the bride (כלה, *kallah*) of her bridegroom (*chatan*, חתן).

The word "bridegroom" (*chatan*, חתן) is spelled with the same letters as "piece" (*netach*, נתח). Without his *kallah*, the *chatan* is only a "piece," lacking wholeness.

The numerical value of "wedding" (*chatunah*), with the *kollel*, is equal to that of "season" (*eit*, עת).

chatunah (חתונה): 8 + 400 + 6 + 50 + 5 = 469
plus the *kollel*: 469 + 1 = 470
eit (עת): 70 + 400 = 470

According to Kabbalah (see *Kehillat Yaakov*, עת), *eit* (עת) alludes to the tenth and final quality, *malchut* (kingdom), which represents the Messianic Age, when the kingship of God will be universally accepted on earth. This is expressed by the fact that 470, the numerical value of *eit*, equals ten times forty-seven, the combined numerical value of two of God's names.

The divine Name אהיה alludes to *keter* (crown), the highest and most ineffable manifestation of God. The name יהוה alludes to the qualities of *tiferet* (splendor) and *rachamim* (mercy). The combined value of these two names is 47.

אהיה: 1 + 5 + 10 + 5 = 21
יהוה: 10 + 5 + 6 + 5 = 26
Total: 47

Multiplying by ten indicates perfection. Thus, the word *eit* (470) indicates perfection of these two holy names of God, which are joined together by the wedding (470) of husband and wife.

Combining the words "bridegroom" and "bride" (*chatan* and *kallah*) with the *kollel* of both words yields 515, the numerical value of "prayer" (*tefillah*).

chatan (חתן):   8 + 400 + 50 = 458
kallah (כלה):   20 + 30 + 5 = 55
plus 2 for the two words: 2
total: 515
tefillah (תפילה): 400 + 80 + 30 + 5 = 515

The perfection of prayer comes about when man is connected with the upper worlds through the joining of bridegroom and bride.

The numerical value of "bride" (*kallah*, כלה) is 55. This number consists of fifty and five. Fifty alludes to the upper realm, which embodies the perfection of the five basic elements of which the world is built. Five is the numerical value of the letter ה, which stands for woman. Thus, *kallah* (bride) indicates the perfection of the upper realm, brought down into this world through woman.

From another viewpoint, 55 consists of two numeral fives, whose total is ten. This refers to *malchut* (kingdom), the tenth of the kabbalistic qualities. The final ה of God's name, יהוה, also alludes to *malchut*.

The quality of *malchut* (kingdom) reaches perfection through the bride. Thus, she is also referred to as "queen" (*malkah*, מלכה), as in the verse (Psalms 45:14) that characterizes the Jewish woman: "All the honor of the princess is within" (כל כבודה בת מלך פנימה).

The *Zohar* teaches that the perfection of husband and wife through the observance of Torah and *mitzvot* is indicated by the verse, "A *mitzvah* is a candle, and the Torah is light" (Proverbs 6:23). The wife is symbolized by a candle; she is the vessel that makes it possible for the husband to kindle the light of Torah.

40

The Wife: A Help to Her Husband

THE TORAH TELLS US (Genesis 2:18) that Eve was created for the purpose of being a helpmeet (*ezer*, עזר) to Adam. This is the task of the wife: to fulfill her husband's needs.

The letters ע and א, both formed in the same part of the mouth, are interchangeable. In the same way, the letters צ, ז, and ש are interchangeable. Thus, the word עזר (*ezer*, help) is closely related to the following words:

אזר (*azar*, gird)

עצר (*atzar*, stop)

אצר (*otzar*, storehouse)

עשר (*osher*, wealth)

All these words express the special functions of the wife.

The word *adam* (אדם, man) is related to *adameh* (אדמה, "I resemble"). His basic characteristic is expressed by the verse, "I resemble the supernal" (Isaiah 14:14). It is proper for him to devote himself with his whole being to the spiritual mission of his life, for this is the foundation of his nature. Hence, the wife must fulfill her role within the yoke of material life. The four words we have listed explain how she does this.

אזר (*azar*, **gird**): The wife girds her husband with might. She supplies him with the forces of *din* (strict judgment) and *gevura* (strength), which he needs in order to cope with the difficulties of life.

Thus, she serves as a "strengthening belt" around his waist, supporting him upright on his two feet and helping him to stand firm. As we read in Proverbs (31:17), "She girds her waist with might, tightening her arms."

עצר (*atzar*, stop): This word expresses the wife's function of closing off and blocking the forces of evil that threaten her husband. She stops these forces and prevents them from penetrating the boundaries of the home.

The wife also stops her husband from overreaching himself. The man lives in a complex world, and tends to rush forward headlong, without sufficient pause for reflection. He may try to achieve goals that are beyond his powers, taking off into the stratosphere of his aspirations while neglecting his basic obligations and his life's purpose. The wife's function is to restrain him, holding him within the accepted framework of his place in life.

Finally, the word עצר (*atzar*, stop) alludes to the quality of *malchut* in woman. She stops herself from being exposed to public view: "All the honor of the princess is within."

אצר (*otzar*, storehouse): By his wife's merit, a man stores up his powers and accomplishments, so that they are not dissipated on empty vanities.

עשר (*osher*, wealth): Blessing and riches depend upon the wife. Rava says: "Honor your wives, so that you will become wealthy" (*Bava Metzia* 59a). The main wealth is spiritual, not material, as the Sages say: "Who is wealthy? He who has a wife whose deeds are praiseworthy."

41

"Female": Shield of Her Husband

WE HAVE SEEN that the wife screens out the forces of evil, preventing them from penetrating the home. This function is expressed by the fact that the letters of the word *soger* (סוגר), meaning to close off or shield, directly follow the letters of "female" (*nekeivah*, נקבה).

ס follows נ

ו follows ה

ג follows ב

ר follows ק

The Torah tells us that woman was created from the *tzela* (צלע) of man. This word means "side" (*tzad*, צד). This teaches us that the wife's task is to stand at her husband's side, supporting and upholding him, acting as a shield that surrounds him. Thus, the letters מקף, which form the linguistic root of the word "surround" (*mekif*, מקיף), follow directly after the letters of *tzela*.

מ follows ל

ק follows צ

פ follows ע

Tzela (צלע) and *tzad* (צד) refer to the "side" from which woman was created. The root of these two words is their initial letter, צ (*tzadi*). This letter stands for "righteousness" (*tzidkut*, צדקות), which is the special power of woman, since the wife has the ability to make her husband righteous.

The female (*nekeivah*, נקבה) is the source of righteousness. This is revealed by the fact that the numerical value of "female" is the same as that of the words Zion (ציון) and Joseph (יוסף), with the addition of the *kollel*.

nekeivah (נקבה): 50 + 100 + 2 + 5 = 157
Zion (ציון):   90 + 10 + 6 + 50 = 156
plus the *kollel*:   156 + 1 = 157
Joseph (יוסף): 10 + 6 + 60 + 80 = 156
plus the *kollel*:   156 + 1 = 157

The words, Zion and Joseph, symbolize the perfection of righteousness. Both of them (without the *kollel*) have the numerical value of 156. This number is six times twenty-six, the numerical value of the name of *Hashem*.

Hashem (יהוה): 10 + 5 + 6 + 5 = 26
Multiplying by six: 6 × 26 = 156

The number six refers, in Kabbalah, to the sixth quality, *yesod* (foundation). Multiplying by 26, the numerical value of *Hashem*, indicates the perfection of *yesod*. Joseph, who corresponds to the quality of *yesod*, alludes to peace (*Shalom*).

Zion (ציון) indicates the building of the holy city, Jerusalem, which is referred to by that name. The word Zion is derived from a linguistic root meaning "to distinguish," because Zion is distinguished (*metzuyenet*, מצוינת) for holiness.

Zion and Joseph both symbolize concentration, gathering, and brotherhood. By the *Ik-Bechar* (איק–בכר) transformation, the word "together" (*yachad*, יחד) is equivalent to the root of "surround" (מקף).

Thus, the brotherhood and togetherness of the Jewish family are brought about through the wife, whose task is to surround and defend the family.

42

Woman: The Inner Essence of Man

MAN, WHO WAS CREATED in the image of God, is "a part of the supernal God" (חלק אלוקה׳ ממעל). This concept is reflected in the numerical value of the word "man" (*adam*, אדם), which equals the numerical
value of the name of *Hashem* spelled out in full.

> *Hashem* (יהוה) is spelled יוד, הא, ואו, הא:
> $10 + 6 + 4, + 5 + 1, + 6 + 1 + 6, + 5 + 1 = 45$
> *adam* (אדם): $\qquad\qquad 1 + 4 + 40 = 45$

On the other hand, the "inner" *gematria* of God's name, found
by removing the outer (initial) letters, is 19, equal to the numerical
value of Eve (חוה).

> The inner spelling of יהוה is וד, א, או, א:
> $10 + 6 + 4, + 1, + 1 + 6, + 1 = 19$
> Eve (חוה): $\qquad 8 + 6 + 5 = 19$

This teaches us that woman is part of the inner essence of man, as it is
written, "She . . . is the essence of my essence" (Genesis 2:23). Only
through woman, and with her help, can man fulfill his destined role
on earth.

Adding up the digits of the number 19 (the numerical value of
Eve) yields ten ($1 + 9 = 10$). Thus, Eve (חוה) alludes to *malchut* (kingdom), the tenth of the kabbalistic qualities. As we have already seen,
woman is especially connected with *malchut*.

In the chain of divine emanation described by Kabbalah, each quality (*midah*) receives influence from the one above it. *Malchut*, the tenth *midah*, receives influence from *yesod*, the ninth. Just as woman is connected with *malchut*, man is connected with *yesod*. As we saw, the numerical value of "man" (*adam*, אדם) is 45. The sum of its digits is nine (4 + 5 = 9), corresponding to *yesod*, the ninth quality.

Just as *malchut*, the tenth quality, receives influence from *yesod*, the ninth, woman (Eve, 10) receives influence from man (Adam, 9).

The Torah calls Eve "the mother of all living things" (Genesis 2:20). She draws down into the world and actualizes the potential for life. This power is indicated by her name, Chava (Eve, חוה), which is identical to the word "alive" (*chaya*, חיה), except that the letter י is replaced by ו. The י is central to the word "man" (*ish*, איש). In the name Chava (חוה, Eve), this letter is lengthened and brought down to earth, becoming ו.

43

Adam and Eve: The Root of the World

THE PHRASE "ADAM AND EVE" (*Adam veChava*, אדם וחוה) has the numerical value of 70.

Adam veChava (אדם וחוה): 1 + 4 + 40, + 6 + 8 + 6 + 5 = 70

This number stands for the ultimate perfection that can be achieved in this world, as indicated by the saying: "There are seventy facets to the Torah."

The revelation of this perfection is built on the seven lower *midot*, or qualities, mentioned by Kabbalah. When seven is multiplied by ten, the number of perfection, we have seventy. This is revealed through husband and wife, "Adam and Eve" (70).

Likewise, Jacob's family numbered seventy when he went down to Egypt. This was the basic nucleus with which the children of Israel confronted the seventy nations of the world.

"Male" (*zachar*, זכר) has the numerical value 227, and "female" (*nekeivah*, נקבה) totals 157. The difference between them is 70.

zachar (זכר):   7 + 20 + 200 = 227
nekeivah (נקבה): 50 + 100 + 2 + 5 = 157
the difference: 70

This teaches us that, through his wife, the male causes the revelations of the foundation of the number seventy, representing the seventy facets of the Torah and the entirety of life in this world.

Eve (Chava, חוה) is the root of life, the mother of all mothers. This fact is hinted at by the numerical value of her name, which is 19. This number can be analyzed as 1 + 18.

Eighteen is the numerical value of "alive" (*chai*, חי), which refers to the root of life. One corresponds to the letter א, which symbolizes the supernal Source from which all other forces derive. This is the force embodied in woman, as represented by Eve (19).

Eve came from the *tzela* (צלע, side) of Adam. The numerical value of this word is 190, which is also the numerical value of the word "end" (*ketz*, קץ).

tzela (צלע): 90 ¦30 + 70 = 190
ketz (קץ):   100 + 90 = 190

The wife is the "side" (*tzela*) of her husband. If he acts with undue urgency, without exercising the proper restraint, she is there to put a boundary and an end (*ketz*) to his excesses.

The fact that man (*ish*) and woman (*ishah*) are the source of life is revealed by the "inner" *gematria* of these two words. Both words have the inner value of 180.

ish (איש) is spelled שין, יוד, אלף
The inner letters are לף, וד, ין:
30 + 80, + 6 + 4, + 10 + 50 = 180
ishah (אשה) is spelled אלף, שין, הי
The inner letters are לף, ין, י:
30 + 80, + 10 + 50, + 10 = 180

The number 180 is ten times the numerical value of "alive" (*chai*, חי).

chai (חי): 8 + 10 =   18
10 × 18   = 180

Thus, we learn that the foundations of life and vitality are contained in husband and wife together.

That husband and wife together constitute the complete life is also symbolized by the letter א, the only letter shared in common by איש (*ish*, man) and אשה (*ishah*, wife). Contained within the א are two י's, one above the diagonal line and one below. The upper י symbolizes the spiritual life of the upper worlds, which is the arena of the husband's activity. The lower י symbolizes the life of this world, which is given over to woman.

The fundamental concept of "life" joins husband and wife in a process of healthy and well-ordered development. The concept of life is also expressed in the age at which the Talmud recommends marriage. The Sages say, in *Pirkei Avot*, "At eighteen—the wedding canopy." We have already seen that 18 is the numerical value of life. Thus, eighteen is the right age for the fulfillment of a young man's life by uniting with his bride.

When the names of the letters that spell "bride" (*kallah*) are written out in full, their total numerical value is 180.

kallah (כלה) is spelled כף, למד, הא:
20 + 80, + 30 + 40 + 4, + 5 + 1 = 180

The number 180 is eighteen multiplied by ten (the number of perfection). The perfection of being alive (*chai*, חי = 18) comes about through marriage with one's bride (*kallah*, כלה = 180).

44

Husband and Wife:
The Crown of Creation

OF THE VARIOUS HEBREW terms for "man," *adam* (אדם) signifies man in his complete state—that is, husband and wife together. Thus, when Adam and Eve were first created, the Torah says, "He called *their* name Adam" (Genesis 5:2). Only after the first man had taken a wife was he fit to be called *adam*.

When we write out in full the names of the letters that spell *adam* (אדם), their total numerical value is 625, which equals the numerical value of the term "the crown" (*haketer*, הכתר).

adam (אדם) is spelled אלף, דלת, מם:
1 + 30 + 80, + 4 + 30 + 400, + 40 + 40 = 625
haketer (הכתר):   5 + 20 + 400 + 200 = 625

In Kabbalah, *keter* (crown) is the highest of all the ten stages (*sefirot*) of Creation. *Keter* is the height (*si*, שיא) of Creation. The letters of "height" (שיא) are the same as those of "man" (*ish*, איש). Just as *keter* (crown, 625) is the height of perfection, so *adam* (man, 625), once he is married, is also the height of perfection. Husband and wife complete each other, and this produces between them a strong and indomitable love. Rabbi Eliahu Dessler writes that "the Holy One, blessed be he, incorporated this force in the very nature of man" (*Michtav MiEliahu*, 3:38).

The Sages say, "Whoever does not have a wife is not a complete man" (*Yevamot* 63a). A man in isolation is lacking, and cannot fulfill his proper role in life. Therefore, when husband and wife are united, they love each other.

Love (*ahava*, אהבה) can be analyzed as א–הבה. It is based on *hava* (הבה), which signifies "giving." This giving is grounded in א (*alef*), a letter that symbolizes the lofty values connected with the Holy One, blessed by he, the *Aluf* (chief) of the universe.

The word "love" (*ahava*, אהבה) alludes to the perfected connection of husband and wife to their spiritual roots. The root of man is *chochma* (wisdom); that of woman is *binah* (understanding). Kabbalah refers to these two qualities as "father" (*chochma*) and "mother" (*binah*).

The word *ahava* (love, אהבה) results from the connection between the letters א and ב, which are found in this word. These, the first two letters of the alphabet, represent *chochma* and *binah*, the first two *sefirot*. The remaining letters are ה and ה, which come from the name of God, יהוה.

The four letters of the word אהבה (*ahava*, love) are closely connected with the four letters of the name of God, יהוה. Both words have ה as their second and fourth letters. The remaining two letters of אהבה, א and ב, are interchangeable with the remaining two letters of God's name, ו and י. By the *Ik-Bechar* (איק–בכר) transformation, א (1) is equivalent to י (10). ב and ו are both pronounced with the same parts of the mouth; in fact, they are pronounced identically. Thus, the love (*ahava*, אהבה) between husband and wife completes, as it were, the name of God.

The souls of man and woman were created from a single source. It is only in this world that they were split apart. Through marriage (*kiddushin*, lit., sanctification), they again become connected to their supernal source. This is the reason for the spiritual love between husband and wife.

The numerical value of the word *keter* (כתר, crown) is 620.

keter (כתר): $20 + 400 + 200 = 620$

The Ten Commandments, as recorded in Exodus, contain 620 letters. These correspond to the 613 Scriptural *mitzvot*, plus the seven Rabbinic *mitzvot*. By the merit of observing the 613 *mitzvot*, one also merits the crown (*keter*) of the world to come.

Half the numerical value of *keter* (כתר, crown) is 310, which is the numerical value of the word שי (*shai*, gift). Proverbs (8:21) says, " . . . to cause those who love Me to inherit substance (*yaish*, יש)." Reversing the letters of *yaish* (יש) gives *shai* (שי). The Sages derive from this verse that those who love God will inherit the gift of 310 worlds.

If both husband and wife love God, each will inherit 310 worlds. Together, they will inherit 620 worlds, i.e., the crown (*keter*, 620) that represents completeness in the world-to-come.

"Your God will rejoice over you as the bridegroom rejoices over the bride" (ישיש עליך אלקיך כמשוש חתן על כלה). The word "rejoice" (*yasis*, ישיש) has the numerical value of 620. The numerical value of "the bridegroom . . . over the bride" (חתן על כלה) is 613.

> *yasis* (ישיש):   10 + 400 + 10 + 400 = 620
> חתן על כלה: 8 + 400 + 50, + 70 + 30, + 20 + 30 + 5 = 613

Husband and wife together create the crown (*keter*, כתר), the highest level of perfection. This is revealed by the combined numerical value of man (*ish*, איש) and woman (*ishah*, אשה). Their total, when we add 2 for the two words and 1 for the *kollel*, is 620, the numerical value of *keter*, crown.

> *ish* (איש):   1 + 10 + 300 = 311
> *ishah* (אשה):   1 + 300 + 5 = 306
> plus 2 for the number of words: 2
> plus 1 for the *kollel*:   1
> total: 620

45

The Wife:
The Foundation of Peace

WE HAVE SEEN THAT THE "inner" *gematria* of both "man" and "woman" is 180. Together, they total 360.

In Kabbalah, the first six of the lower *midot* (qualities) are known as the foundation of this world. The number 360 (6 × 60) alludes to the perfection of these six *midot*.

Sixty is the numerical value of the round-shaped letter ס. Thus, sixty stands for the "small circle." On the other hand, 360, the number of degrees in a full circle, stands for the "large," or complete, circle.

The "small" *gematria* relates to this lower world. The small *gematria* of 360 is 36, the numerical value of the letters לו. These are the letters that stand in the center of, and complete, the word "peace" (*shalom*, שלום). Without לו, what remains of שלום are the letters ש and מ, which stand for the desolation (*shemamah*, שממה) caused by the strife between two diametrically opposed forces, fire (אש) and water (מים). In other words, the letters לו build peace (*shalom*, שלום).

Fire corresponds to woman, and water to man. Thus, לו (36) is the medium that joins husband and wife in peace. This number also alludes to the thirty-six hidden righteous ones (*tzadikim*) who uphold the world in each generation.

The number thirty-six, which joins husband and wife in peace, is the holy channel (*tzinnor*) through which a man receives abundance. On the other hand, the Torah mentions a total of thirty-six sins for which the punishment is *karet*, the cutting off of the soul. These represent the destructive forces that oppose the holy aspects of thirty-six.

The peace that exists between husband and wife forms a shield against the thirty-six negative "cutting off" sins (*kritot*) mentioned in the Torah. Thus, it is written (Isaiah 30:11), "Fortunate is he who works for Him," where the term "for him" (*lo*) is spelled לו, 36.

The name of the letter ש (*shin*) also has the numerical value of 360.

shin (ש) is spelled שין: 300 + 10 + 50 = 360

This letter, which is common to both man (*ish*, איש) and woman (*ishah*, אשה), thus represents peaceful cooperation and mutual understanding between husband and wife.

Peace (*shalom*, שלום) unites husband and wife. This can be seen from the "inner" *gematria* of "man and woman" (*ish veishah*, איש ואשה) when the names of the letters are written out in full. It equals the numerical value of "peace" (*shalom*).

"man and woman" (איש ואשה) is spelled:
אלף ,יוד ,שין ,ויו ,אלף, שין ,יה
The inner letters are: לף ,וד, ין, יו, לף, ין, י
30 + 80, + 6 + 4, + 10 + 50, + 10 + 6, + 30 + 80, +

10 + 50, + 10 = 376

shalom (שלום):   300 + 30 + 6 + 40 = 376

By themselves, the words, "man" and "woman" (איש, אשה) total only 360. In the above calculation, it is the letter ו (signifying "and") that fills out the number to 376, equaling "peace." In this sense, the letter ו makes the necessary connection between husband and wife, producing a situation of peace.

This function of ו as a connector between husband and wife can be seen in the structure of the letter א. This letter consists of an upper י, representing man, and a lower י, representing woman. The connection between them is a diagonal letter ו.

46

Modesty:
The Symbol of Woman

THE LETTER ש symbolizes woman. By the *Ik-Bechar* (איק-בכר) transformation, the name of this letter, *shin* (שין), becomes "home" (*ohel*, אהל, lit., tent). This teaches us that the wife's place is in the home, as can be seen from the Sages' dictum: "A man's home is his wife" (*Yoma* 2a).

The symbol of the wife is modesty. Thus, Abraham said of Sarah, "Behold, she is within the tent" (Genesis 18:9).

Again, by the *Ik-Bechar* transformation, the name Eve (חוה) becomes ספן, a linguistic root meaning "to hide." This indicates the modest, hidden world to which the wife belongs.

It is the way of the world that women, by nature, love privacy and domestic life. Therefore, their tendency is to set limits. This is a corollary of the quality of *gevura* (discipline), which characterizes woman. As the Sages observed, "The wife tends to be stingy toward guests" (*Bava Metzia* 87a).

The basic quality of the husband, on the other hand, is *chesed* (kindness). Hence, he tends more toward openhandedness; he is also more drawn to the open social arena outside the home.

In relation to the husband, the wife leans more toward strictness (*din*) and limitations (*tzimtzum*). Thus, the wife gives attention to every detail of the home, as opposed to the husband, who does not attach importance to these things.

47

Husband and Wife: The Foundation of Righteousness

THE PHRASE "HUSBAND AND WIFE" (*ish veishah*, איש ואשה), when the names of the letters are written out in full, has the numerical value of 999.

איש ואשה is spelled: אלף, יוד, שין, ויו, אלף, שין, הי
1 + 30 + 80, + 10 + 6 + 4, + 300 + 10 + 50, + 6 + 10 + 6,
+ 1 + 30 + 80, + 300 + 10 + 50, + 5 + 10   = 999

This number, composed all of nines, alludes in Kabbalah to the quality of *yesod* (foundation), which is the ninth of the ten *sefirot*, or stages of divine creative emanation.

The ten *sefirot* are divided into four worlds. From lowest to highest, these are:

1. *Asiya* (action)
2. *Yetzira* (production)
3. *Bria* (Creation)
4. *Atzilut* (effluence)

Above all these worlds is *keter*, crown.

In numerical values (*gematriot*), the units correspond to the world of *asiya*; the tens, to *yetzira*; the hundreds, to *bria*; and the thousands, to *atzilut*.

Thus, the number 999 alludes to the quality of *yesod* (foundation, 9) in the worlds of *asiya*, *yetzira*, and *bria*. If we add 1 for the *kollel* we have 1000, which alludes to the world of *atzilut* and, beyond it, the world of *keter.*

The word "one thousand" (*elef,* אלף), with different vocalization, becomes the name of the letter א (*alef,* אלף). This letter represents the perfection of husband and wife, and stabilizes their life.

The word *matzav* (מצב, situation) comes from the linguistic root meaning "to be upright, stable." Its letters come directly after the letters of *alef* (אלף) in the alphabet.

מ follows ל

צ follows פ

ב follows א

This teaches us that the letter א represents the concept of stability in life.

48

God's Names Contained Within Husband and Wife

EACH LETTER IN THE WORDS "man" (*ish*, איש) and "woman" (*ishah*, אשה) is the initial of a name of the Holy One, blessed be he.

א	*Adonai*	אדני
י	*Hashem*	יהוה
ש	*Shaddai*	שדי
א	*Adonai*	אדני
ש	*Shaddai*	שדי
ה	*Hoyah*	הויה

The name יהוה alludes to the quality of mercy (*rachamim*). The same letters, almost exactly reversed, spell the name *Hoyah* (הויה), alluding to the quality of strictness (*din*), which is the fundamental quality of woman. These two names, spelled with the same letters, can be counted as one for our present purpose. Thus, the words "man" and "woman" contain three holy names. Their total numerical value, plus the *kollel* for each name, is 408, which equals the numerical value of the feminine pronoun *zot* (זאת), meaning "this" or "she."

Hashem (יהוה), or its reverse, *Hoyah* (הויה):

$$10 + 5 + 6 + 5 = 26$$

Adonai (אדני): $1 + 4 + 50 + 10 = 65$

Shaddai (שדי): $300 + 4 + 10 = 314$

plus 3 for the three names: $\underline{3}$

$$408$$

zot (זאת): $7 + 1 + 400 = 408$

As we have seen, the word *zot* (זאת) refers, in Kabbalah, to the quality of *malchut* (kingdom).

49

The Wife's Function: Expressing Her Opinion to Her Husband and Children

THE FIRST MOTHER mentioned in the Torah, the "mother of all living things" (Genesis 3:21) is named not *chaya* (חיה, alive), but Chava (חוה, Eve). These letters are the linguistic root meaning "to express an opinion."

The wife is the one who must be concerned with passing on the traditions of Judaism to her children, as it is written, "Do not abandon the Torah of your mother" (Proverbs 6:20).

This task of the wife is revealed by the fact that the letters of the word "son" (*ben*, בן) come directly after those of the word "mother" (*em*, אם) in the alphabet.

ב follows א

נ follows מ

This means that in the spiritual as well as the physical sense, the son draws nourishment from the mother. Thus, according to *halacha*, the question whether or not a child is Jewish depends exclusively on whether the mother is Jewish.

This special connection between mother and son is expressed in Psalms (113:9): "The mother of the sons is happy."

50

Woman's Adaptability

THE LINGUISTIC ROOT of the word "women" (*nashim*, נשים) is נשה. These are the same letters as שנה, a root meaning "to change." This indicates woman's natural ability to change and adapt to the various situations she must cope with, as in the education of her children or her relationship with her husband. The Sages say, "Women are easily influenced," נשים דעתן קלה (*Avodah Zarah* 17b). This is so that they can mold and devote themselves with undaunted determination to their husbands and children.

The wife has powers of change and adaptability because she is to her husband as material is to form. The material is more given to change than the form. For this reason, the Sages warned husbands to be careful not to speak harshly to their wives, since "her tears come easily" (*Bava Metzia* 59a). The word for "tears" (*dima*, דמע) has the same letters as מעד (*maad*), which means to totter or slip. That is, a woman's tears come easily because she is easily influenced and her position is easily made to totter.

It is true that the wife also provides form for her husband, helping him to become a "well-formed" man, for her basic element is fire.

The words "form" (*tzura*, צורה) and "fire" (*esh*, אש) share the numerical value of 301.

tzura (צורה): 90 + 6 + 200 + 5 = 301
esh (אש):   1 + 300 = 301

Nevertheless, the wife remains connected to the concept of materiality, for her main task concerns the material world.

The combined numerical value of the words "material" and "form" (*chomer, tzura*; צורה, חמר) is 550, including the *kollel*.

chomer (חמר):   8 + 40 + 200 = 248
tzura (צורה): 90 + 6 + 200 + 5 = 301
Plus the *kollel*:   1
Total: —
                                 550

The number 550 is composed of 50 and 500. The number 50 represents the fifty gates of understanding (*binah*), which are the root of this world.

The number 500 also relates to this world, which was created with the letter ה, whose numerical value is 5. Multiplying by 100 indicates perfection; thus, 500 represents the perfection of this world. This is also the total number of body parts of man and woman.

Man and woman (500) act together for the perfection of this world (500) through the fifty gates of understanding (50). They are able to accomplish this because together they constitute material and form (550).

The word "women" (*nashim*, נשים) has the same letters as *shanim* (שנים), a type of red cloth, as in the verse, "Her whole family is dressed in red cloth" (Proverbs 31:21).

The Talmud (*Niddah* 31a) tells us that in the conception of a child, the mother contributes the basis for the flesh, whose color is red. The man (who corresponds to the element of water) contributes the basis of the bones, whose color is white. White symbolizes the man's basic characteristic of *chesed* (kindness).

Another word spelled with the same letters as *nashim* (נשים, women) is *shnayim* (שנים), which means "two." This number is connected with the quality of *din* (strictness): On the second day of Creation, the sky was created to separate the upper waters from the lower waters. This separation is based on the force of *din*. The sky sets limits for the upper and lower waters, telling them, as it were, "Enough" (*dai*, די), a word that is included in the word *din* (דין). Strictness (*din*) is the basic quality of woman.

51

Matches and Marriages

THE WORD *kiddushin* (קידושין) means marriage. It comes from the linguistic root קדש, which means "holy." Holiness protects the connection between man and wife. The letter א, which is common to both איש (*ish*, man) and אשה (*ishah*, woman), symbolizes holiness because it unites within it the upper י and the lower י on a basis of ו, the letter of holiness.

Since they are both palatal letters, כ and ק are interchangeable. Thus, the linguistic root of "match" (*shidduch*, שידוך), שדך, is closely related to the root of "marriage" (*kiddushin*, קידושין), קדש.

"Matchmaking" (*shidduchin*, שידוכין) comes before the marriage, and constitutes a preparation for the principle of holiness (*kedusha*).

The letters שדך form the linguistic root of the word "match" (*shidduch*, שידוך). In Aramaic (a language closely related to Hebrew), the letters שדך spell "quiet." This alludes to the completeness and tranquility achieved through the holiness of *shidduchin*, the match, which leads to *kiddushin*, marriage.

Through *kiddushin*, marriage, the letters יה shine forth from husband and wife. When the *ketubah*, or marriage contract, is given to the bride under the wedding canopy (*chupa*), this adds the letters וה, thus completing the holiness of God's name, יהוה, which protectively envelops the married couple.

52

Man and Woman:
Completed Through Holiness

HOLINESS (*kedusha*, קדושה) BRINGS COMPLETION to the bridegroom and the bride. This is revealed in the numerical value of these words.

"Bridegroom" and "bride" (*chatan, kallah*; חתן, כלה) have the numerical value of 513.

chatan (חתן): 8 + 400 + 50 = 458
kallah (כלה): 20 + 30 + 5 = 55
Total: 513

The symbol of *kedusha* (קדושה, holiness) is its initial letter, ק, whose numerical value is 100.

When we add holiness (100) to bridegroom and bride (513), the sum is 613. This, the number of *mitzvot* in the Torah, signifies completeness. It also symbolizes a different kind of completeness: the total number of limbs (248) and sinews (365) in the human body.

Thus, when the bridegroom and the bride (*chatan* and *kallah*) add to themselves the principle of ק, i.e., holiness (*kedusha*), they bring completion to both their spiritual and physical essences.

At their wedding, the bridegroom and the bride become husband (*ish*, איש) and wife (*ishah*, אשה). The numerical value of these two words together equals that of crown (*keter*, כתר). The ultimate goal of the life of husband and wife is to reach the crown of Torah and holiness.

The letter ק, with its numerical value of 100, symbolizes not only holiness (*kedusha*), but also the unity that results from *kedusha*; 100 is a complete group of numerical units, with none missing.

The unity brought about by marriage is also symbolized by the word "couple" (*zug*, זג), which at the next level of the alphabet becomes "one" (*chad*, חד).

ז is followed by ח

ג is followed by ד

A closely related idea is seen in the word "half" (*plag*, פלג), which at the next level of the alphabet becomes "pair" (*tzemed*, צמד).

פ is followed by צ

ל is followed by מ

ג is followed by ד

Man, who before marriage was half of the original whole, becomes, after marriage, a pair of mates.

When the names of the letters that spell "bride" (*kallah*, כלה) are written out in full, their numerical value totals 180. This equals the numerical value of the name of the letter of holiness, ק (*kof*, קוף).

kof (קוף): 100 + 80 = 180

The number 180 also symbolizes the perfection of life, for the numerical value of "alive" (*chai*, חי) is 18. Multiplying this by ten, the number of perfection, yields 180.

Thus, we learn that the perfection of the fundamental value, life, depends upon holiness and purity, which in turn stem primarily from the will of the wife, the bride (*kallah*).

53

Atonement and Life
Through the Wife's Influence

THE TALMUD STATES (*Yevamot* 62b): "Whoever lacks a wife remains without atonement and without life." The Sages tell many stories of husbands who changed for the better on account of their wives, as it is written, "Everything comes from the wife" (Bereishith Rabba 17).

This matter of achieving atonement through one's wife is reflected in the numerical value of the letters כפר, the linguistic root of the word "atonement" (*kaparah*, כפרה). Its numerical value is 300.

כפר: 20 + 80 + 200 = 300

This equals the numerical value of the letter ש. As we have seen, ש, the central letter of the word "woman" (*ishah*, אשה), represents the wife and symbolizes her basic element, fire (*esh*, אש). This letter indicates forces in the wife that help the husband to purify and refine himself and achieve atonement.

Thus, on the verse "The fear of *Hashem* is pure" (Psalms 19:10), the Sages comment (*Yoma* 72b): "This refers to one who marries and studies Torah."

The connection between wife (*ishah*, אשה) and atonement (*kaparah*, כפרה) is further highlighted by the fact that these two words have equivalent numerical values.

ishah (אשה):   1 + 300 + 5 = 306
kaparah (כפרה): 20 + 80 + 200 + 5 = 305
plus the *kollel*:   305 + 1 = 306

Nine indicates everlastingness, purity, and connection with the upper worlds. The *Zohar* (*Bereishith* 39) states that woman is connected with the holy *Shechinah*, the Divine Presence.

The element of fire (*esh*, אש), which constitutes the essence of woman, appears while she is still a girl (*bat*, בת). This is evident from the fact that the letters of *bat* follow immediately after those of *esh* in the alphabet.

ב follows א

ת follows ש

In marriage, the בת (*bat*, girl) receives the letter י from the center of her husband (*ish*, איש). Thus, בת becomes בית (*bayit*, home). As Rabbi Jose said: "I never called my wife, 'my wife' but 'my home'" (*Shabbat* 113b).

We also find halachic expression of the fact that man's atonement depends upon his wife. Regarding the service performed in the holy Temple by the *Kohen Hagadol*, the High Priest, the Torah writes: "He shall atone for himself and for his family" (lit., "his home," ביתו; Leviticus 16:6). From this verse, the Talmud derives the *halacha* that as long as the High Priest has a wife, he can achieve atonement for himself and for the whole Jewish people. If he does not have a wife, he cannot achieve atonement (*Yevamot*).

The strong element of fire in the basic constitution of woman explains the Sages' statement that a woman's anger is slow to die down, and women are hard to appease. Fire, by nature, is not easily extinguished. (Man, on the other hand, comes from the root of *chesed*, kindness, and is easier to appease.) For this reason, the Sages emphasized that a man must be careful not to hurt his wife's feelings.

Moreover, woman was created from bone, as it is written: "She . . . is bone of my bone" (Genesis 2:23). Bone is not a soft substance, and woman is not "soft" in being appeased.

According to Kabbalah, woman's basis of fire explains the Torah's insistence that she should not belong to the army or bear arms.

54

The Connection Between Husband and Wife

THE STRONG CONNECTION between husband and wife is revealed by the verse, "Therefore a man shall leave his father and his mother and cleave to his wife, and they shall become one flesh" (Genesis 2:24).

From this verse the commentators conclude that the word "women" (*nashim*, נשים) is related to the root נשה, meaning "to forget." The wife has the power to make her husband forget his original home, and to engrave his new home upon his heart. This also explains why a man's connection with his parents and family is not as strong as the woman's connection with her parents and family, a connection that remains even after marriage.

The plain meaning of the word "holy" (*kodesh*, קדש) is "separated from materialism." According to the *Atbash* (א″ת-ב″ש) transformation, קדש (*kodesh*, holy) becomes דבק, a linguistic root indicating the concept of cleaving or sticking to something. This teaches us that being holy—i.e., removed from materialistic drives—brings about a mighty cleaving and connection between husband and wife.

Because the letters ד and ר are similar, the word קדש is closely related to קרש (*keresh*), a "board," a thing whose hardness makes it endure for a long time. These letters also spell קשר (*kesher*), "connection." Through the principle of holiness, the connection between husband and wife is made firm and enduring.

55

Revelation of the Divine Presence Through "Male" and "Female"

THE UNIFICATION IN HOLINESS of man and woman leads to the revelation of the *Shechinah*, the Divine Presence. This is reflected in the combined numerical values of the words "male" and "female" (*zachar, nekeivah*; זכר, נקבה), with the *kollel*. This total, 385, equals the numerical value of *Shechinah*.

zachar (זכר):	7 + 20 + 200 = 227
nekeivah (נקבה):	50 + 100 + 2 + 5 = 157
Plus the *kollel*:	1
Total:	385
Shechinah (שכינה):	300 + 20 + 10 + 50 + 5 = 385

This numerical equivalence teaches us that when the male, the influencer, joins in holiness with the female, the receiver, they merit the revelation of the *Shechinah* in their lifetime.

If we add 1 to each of its digits, the number 385 becomes 496. This is the numerical value of the quality referred to in Kabbalah as *malchut* (kingdom), which alludes to the revelation of God's kingship in the Messianic Age.

malchut (מלכות): 40 + 30 + 20 + 6 + 400 = 496

By means of the male and female, the quality of *malchut* is perfected through the revelation of the *Shechinah*.

Mathematicians call 496 a "perfect" number because it is equal to the sum of all its factors. Another example of a perfect number is 6, whose factors are 1, 2, and 3 ($1 \times 6 = 6$; $2 \times 3 = 6$; $3 \times 2 = 6$; $1 + 2 + 3 = 6$).

Similarly, the factors of 496 are 1, 2, 4, 8, 16, 31, 62, 124, and 248 ($1 \times 496 = 496$; $2 \times 248 = 496$; $4 \times 124 = 496$; etc.; $1 + 2 + 4 + 8 + 16 + 31 + 62 + 124 + 248 = 496$).

The quality of perfection that applies to the numbers 6 and 496 expresses, on the spiritual level, the concept of perfection. Perfection depends on holiness (*kedusha*), which is symbolized by the number six. Perfection is also the root of *malchut* (kingdom), whose numerical value is 496.

The rectification of the *Shechinah* through the unity of husband and wife builds the quality of *malchut* (kingdom). It also builds the holy city of Jerusalem, as the Sages declare: "Whoever marries is as if he had rebuilt one of the ruins of Jerusalem" (*Berachot* 7a).

The connection between the Divine Presence (*Shechinah*) and Jerusalem is revealed by the numerical value of these words. When we write out the names of the letters that spell *Shechinah*, their total numerical value is 596, which is precisely the numerical value of Jerusalem.

Shechinah (שכינה) is spelled שין, כף, יוד, נון, הה:
$300 + 10 + 50, + 20 + 80, + 10 + 6 + 4, + 50 + 6 + 50, + 5 + 5 = 596$
Jerusalem (ירושלים):
$$10 + 200 + 6 + 300 + 30 + 10 + 40 = 596$$

56

The Function of Man: To Conquer

THE FUNCTION OF THE MAN is to go out and conquer, achieving things in the world and storing them in his memory in order to pass them on to future generations. Thus, the Torah says (in a verse addressed to men): "Fill the earth and conquer it" (Genesis 1:28).

The linguistic root of "conquer" is כבש. These letters are closely related to the word איש (*ish*, man). Both words share the letter ש. Moreover, the first two letters of כבש follow immediately after the first two letters of איש in the alphabet.

כ follows י

ב follows א

The propensity of man to conquer is further revealed by the linguistic root חלש, meaning "to weaken." The letters of this root follow directly after those of זכר (*zachar*, male) in the alphabet.

ח follows ז

ל follows כ

ש follows ר

The special power of the male (זכר) is expressed by the fact that he weakens (חלש) the forces of evil.

Moreover, if we advance one step in the alphabet, changing ח to ט, the linguistic root חלש becomes שלט, a root meaning "to govern." This represents a further step in the male's task of conquest.

Likewise, it is the husband's task to rule over his wife, as it is written concerning woman: "Your desire will be for your husband, and he will rule over you" (Genesis 3:16). The husband should provide spiritual direction for his home by acting as the ruler (*moshel*). In this way he brings peace (*shalom*) to the home, as can be seen from the fact that *moshel* and *shalom* are spelled with the same letters in Hebrew: שלום מושל.

This explains the importance of the respect and admiration the wife should have for her husband. The author of *Menorat Hamaor* quotes a wise mother who told her daughter: "Stand before him as you would before a king, and he will honor you like royalty."

57

"A Time of Finding": The Wife

THE WIFE IS AN INTEGRAL part of the husband. Therefore, until a man finds his mate, a woman is regarded as a "lost" item, as indicated by the verse, "He who *finds* a wife finds good" (Proverbs 18:22).

In order to find this lost item, a man must pray. It is written, "For this (*zot*, lit., "her") every zealous man must pray to You for a time of finding" (Psalms 32:6). The Sages comment: "'A time of finding' means 'a wife.'"

If we regard the Hebrew alphabet as a circle, where א follows after ת, we may observe that the letters of "finding" (*metzo*, מצוא) follow directly after those of "prayer" (*tefillah*, תפלה).

מ follows ל

צ follows פ

ו follows ה

א follows ת

This teaches us that finding the right woman requires prayer on the part of the man, who is like one seeking a lost part of himself.

58

Love: The Basis of Marriage

SUCCESS IN MARRIAGE depends on cooperation between husband and wife in all areas of life, each partner being willing to give to the other.

By the *Ik-Bechar* (בכר–איק) transformation, the linguistic root אהב, which means to love, is equivalent to קרן, which means to beam forth. This hints that love results in a supernal light that beams forth, permeating the couple's life.

Love (*ahava*, אהבה) unifies two people, making them one (*echad*, אחד). This is expressed in the fact that both these words have the same numerical value: 13.

ahava (אהבה): 1 + 5 + 2 + 5 = 13
echad (אחד): 1 + 8 + 4 = 13

Together, these two words have the numerical value of 26, just like the name of God, יהוה. This teaches us that oneness and love between husband and wife have their root in the name of God.

Among the good things mentioned in the blessings recited at a wedding are peace (*shalom*, שלום) and friendship (*reut*, רעות). The second word comes from the same linguistic root as "shepherd" (*roeh*, רועה). The verb "to shepherd" (*lirot*, לרעות) is almost identical to the verb "to see" (*lirot*, לראות). To shepherd a flock means to watchfully observe the creatures that have been given into one's charge.

Peace and friendship (*reut*, רעות) are built upon the couple's watchful concern for each other, like the concern of a shepherd (*roeh*, רעוה) for his flock.

59

The Dangers of a
Life Based on Emotions

MARRIED LIFE IS BASED ON EMOTIONS. For this reason, it obligates us to exercise intellectual contemplation and a large measure of calm judgment.

A life based purely on feelings (*regesh*, רגש), devoid of intellectual values, is bound to end (God forbid) in banality (*shigrah*, שגרה), which can lead ultimately to divorce (*gerushin*, גרושין). The roots of all three of these words—רגש, שגר, and גרש—are spelled with the same letters.

These same three letters, however, also spell גשר (*gesher*), which means "bridge." By contemplating each other's positive intellectual qualities, a husband and wife draw close to each other and build the bridge of communication. Thus, in the alphabet, the letters of the linguistic root of "bridge," גשר, follow directly after those of the root of "close," קרב.

ג follows ב

ש follows ר

ר follows ק

A strong bridge (*gesher*, גשר) of closeness on the intellectual level prevents divorce (*gerushin*, גרושין), for the danger of divorce stems mainly from the life of steadily hardening banality (*shigrah*, שגרה) that can develop after marriage.

By the *Ik-Bechar* (איק-בכר) transformation, the letter ש is interchangeable with ל. Thus, the word "banality" (*shigrah*, שגרה) becomes "habit" (*hergel*, הרגל).

Banality results from living purely according to habit. That is why it is important to continually refresh daily married life through intellectual contemplation of the process of living. Such contemplation ensures the shared spiritual growth of husband and wife.

60

Married Happiness Depends upon the Enlightenment of the "Head"

HAPPINESS (*osher*) in marriage depends, to a large extent, on the enlightenment of the "head" (*rosh*). In fact, these two words are spelled with the same letters: *osher* (אשר) and *rosh* (ראש).

On the other hand, life based on a mixture of emotions can cause (God forbid) irritability (*atzbanut*, עצבנות) and anger. Intellectual enlightenment and contemplation eliminate *atzbanut*. The linguistic root of this word is עצב, whose letters can be analyzed as עב (*av*), a "thick cloud" that surrounds and obscures the essence of the צ (*tzadik*), the righteous person.

By the *Ik-Bechar* (איק-בכר) transformation, the letter ד is interchangeable with מ. Thus, the word "new" (*chadash*, חדש) is equivalent to "happy" (*sameach*, שמח). A spirit of innovation and renewal in life causes happiness and leads to cooperative effort between husband and wife.

Thus, by the *Ik-Bechar* transformation, the letters חד become פת. חד are the two main letters of "new" (*chadash*, חדש), and תפ are the two main letters of "cooperation" (*shituf*, שיתוף). By working for a life that is constantly new, the married couple builds a spirit of cooperation.

61

Gentle Speech: The Foundation of the Home

A GOOD RELATIONSHIP between husband and wife is essential to a peaceful home. Therefore, each must be careful not to speak harshly to the other, but to adopt a pleasant and gracious tone.

Interpersonal tension in the home is fundamentally negative. It results when one of the partners has an attitude of impatience and intolerance (*hakpadah*, הקפדה). Excessive impatience in married life causes alienation between husband and wife, which destroys the peace of the home. Thus, the verbs "to be impatient" (*makpid*, מקפיד) and "to cut off, destroy" (*mekaped*, מקפד) come from the same linguistic root: קפד.

The letters of this root, קפד, are immediately adjacent to the letters of צרה (*tzara*, calamity) in the alphabet.

ק is adjacent to ר

פ is adjacent to צ

ד is adjacent to ה

Intolerance and impatience in the home cuts off the thread of life and is the source of domestic calamity.

62

Truth: The Basis of Marriage

TRUTH IS THE QUALITY that joins opposites, creating unity and solidarity between them.

Jacob represents the quality of truth (*emet*, אמת), as it is written, "You give truth to Jacob" (Michah 7:20). Thus Jacob is the one who unified within himself the opposing traits of Abraham (*chesed*, kindness) and Isaac (*gevura*, discipline). This intermediate, unifying trait of Jacob is called *tiferet* (splendor).

The quality of truth is inherent in the very Creation of the world. The opening words of the Torah are: "In the beginning, God created. . . ." (בראשית ברא אלקים) (Genesis 1:1). The final letters of these words spell אמת (*emet*, truth).

The word "falsehood" (*sheker*, שקר) can be analyzed as ש-קר: Falsehood is the symbol of destructive forces, and has the power to "shake apart" (*lekarker*, לקרקר) the foundations of the home.

The letter ש represents the root (*shoresh*, שרש) of things. In the word *sheker* (שקר, falsehood), it stands for the root of the qualities symbolized by the letters קר. These letters spell "coldness" (*kor*, קר); reversed they spell "empty" (*reik*, רק). *Sheker* produces coldness in the home, destroying family life and emptying it of meaning.

According to the *Ik-Bechar* (איק-בכר) transformation, the word "truth" (*emet*, אמת) is equivalent to the word, *yated* (יתד), which means a "peg" that holds firm. Truth is the basis for the development of the home, the peg that holds firm the structure of family life.

The long-term stability engendered by truth, as opposed to the instability of falsehood, is symbolized by the forms of the letters that spell these two words. All three letters of "truth" (*emet*, אמת) stand on a broad, firm base; they are not easily toppled. The letters of "falsehood" (*sheker*, שקר), on the other hand, all stand on a single point, and hence can fall easily.

The importance of truth (*emet*, אמת) in building a firm structure is further indicated by another transformation. The letter מ can be exchanged for ב, for both are labials. Similarly, ת can be exchanged for נ; both letters are pronounced by placing the tip of the tongue against the front of the palate, just behind the teeth. Thus, אמת (*emet*, truth) becomes אבן (*even*, stone). Truth is the stone from which the home is built.

The foundation of the home built by husband and wife is the embodiment of man's perfection, and this depends upon the basic principle of truth in their lives.

The perfection of man depends upon the basic principle of truth. Thus, by the *Ik-Bechar* (איק–בכר) transformation, the last two letters of truth (*emet*, אמת) are equivalent to the last two letters of man (*adam*, אדם).

Truth, the foundation of man, must be expressed by full coordination of husband and wife in every area of activity. The words truth (*emet*, אמת) and coordination (*teum*, תאם) are spelled with the same letters.

The fundamental principle of truth has the power to unify the opposing forces of man and woman. Through this unification of opposites, the offspring can become leaders on the highest material and spiritual levels.

We see this process in the Patriarchs and Matriarchs of the Jewish people. Abraham, the symbol of *chesed* (kindness), was married to Sarah, the symbol of *gevura* (discipline). (Sarah's name comes from the same linguistic root as "domination," *serarah*, שררה.) Likewise, Isaac, the symbol of *din* (strict justice), was married to Rebecca, who is characterized by acts of kind giving (*gemilut chasadim*). From these marriages of opposites came the house of Israel.

Regarding the verse "Buy truth and don't sell" (Proverbs 23:23), the Sages expound: "Truth means Torah." The basic quality of holiness (*kedusha*) that exists between the marriage partners depends upon the foundation of the Torah. This is emphasized by the fact that the letters of "the Torah" (*hatorah*, התורה), in the alphabet, follow directly after those of "holiness" (*kedusha*, קדושה).

ה follows ד

ת follows ש

ו follows ה

ר follows ק

ה follows ו

The quality of truth is hidden and contained within the letters יה, the letters that bind husband and wife in holiness. When we write out in full the names of these letters, the total numerical value is 26, the same as that of the name of God, יהוה.

yud, hei (הא, יוד): 10 + 6 + 4, + 5 + 1 = 26

י–ה–ו–ה: 10 + 5 + 6 + 5 = 26

This name of God is related to the special quality of Jacob, which is the quality of truth.

63

Man and Woman: The Sun and Moon

"BRIDE" (*kallah*, כלה) contains the letters כל. By the *Ik- Bechar* (איק-בכר) transformation, כ is equivalent to ב. Thus, כל becomes לב (*lev*), which means "heart." The bride (wife) is particularly connected to the realm of the heart.

The wife corresponds to the moon (*levanah*, לבנה), another word that contains the word לב (*lev*, heart). The husband, on the other hand, is particularly connected to the realm of the mind (*moach*, מח). He corresponds to the sun (*chamah*, חמה), a word that contains the letters מח.

Sun (*chamah*, חמה) and moon (*levanah*, לבנה) have the combined numerical value of 140, which is also the combined numerical value of the words "wisdom" (*chochma*, חכמה) and "understanding" (*binah*, בינה).

chamah, levanah (חמה, לבנה):
 8 + 40 + 5, + 30 + 2 + 50 + 5 = 140
chochma, binah (חכמה, בינה):
 8 + 20 + 40 + 5, + 2 + 10 + 50 + 5 = 140

The qualities of *chochma* (wisdom) and *binah* (understanding), which belong to husband and wife, respectively, illuminate family life like the sun and the moon.

The comparison of the wife to the moon, which reflects the light of the sun, symbolizes a basic principle mentioned by the Chidah (*Midbar Kadmut*, נשים): The behavior of the wife reflects the essential nature of the husband.

Similarly, the wife's exalted function is to develop and give direction to the rich potential hidden within her husband.

The number 140 is also the value of the verb *kam* (קם), which means "to stand firm, to rise up."

kam: 100 + 4 = 140

This teaches us that cooperation between husband and wife, each with his or her special qualities and abilities, results in a relationship that is enduring and elevated.

64

The Interdependence of Self-restraint and Modesty

THE ABILITY TO BE SATISFIED with what one has, and modesty—i.e., proper behavior in male–female relationships—are two qualities that go together. Together, they form one of the foundations of married life.

The letters of "satisfaction" (*sipuk*, ספק) come immediately before those of "stop" (*atzar*, עצר) in the alphabet.

ס precedes ע

פ precedes צ

ק precedes ר

The fact that the couple feels satisfaction with their portion has the power to stop improper appetites and exaggerated aspirations that otherwise would pose a danger to married life.

Moreover, the letters of "satisfaction" (*sipuk*, ספק) come immediately after the letters of "modest" (*tzanua*, צנע) in the alphabet.

ס follows נ

פ follows ע

ק follows צ

This teaches us that after a person acquires the quality of modesty (*tzniut*), he finds himself in a position to be continually satisfied and happy.

The quality of modesty is a shield that prevents the forces of evil from penetrating the home. The letters of "modest" (*tzanua*, צנע) are close to those of "side" (*tzela*, צלע), a word that alludes to woman, as in the verse: "And the Lord God built the side (*tzela*) that he had taken from man to (be) woman" (Genesis 2:22). This teaches us that the quality of modesty relates primarily to the wife, who is the buttressing side (*tzela*) of the home.

The word "modest" (*tzanua*, צנע) can be analyzed into two parts: צנ and ע. The first part, צנ, forms the basis of the word "shield" (*tzinna*, צנה); the second part, the ע (*ayin*), stands for the "eye" (*ayin*). Modesty is a shield that guards the eye from gazing in the wrong direction.

The letters צ and ש are interchangeable, for both are formed by the same parts of the mouth. Thus, the word "stop" (*atzar*, עצר) becomes "wealth" (*osher*, עשר). The ability to stop one's appetite leads to a feeling of wealth in life, as the Sages say: "Who is wealthy? He who is happy with his portion" (Avot 4:1).

The great importance of modesty (*tzniut*) is indicated by the fact that the numerical value of this word, with the addition of the *kollel*, is equal to that of "the crown" (*haketer*), the name of the highest of the worlds mentioned in Kabbalah.

tzniut (צניעות): 90 + 50 + 10 + 70 + 6 + 400 = 626
haketer (הכתר):   5 + 20 + 400 + 200 = 625
plus the *kollel*:   625 + 1 = 626

Modesty (*tzniut*) has the power to elevate a person to the lofty worlds connected with the crown (*haketer*), which is the foundation of kingship (*malchut*).

65

Controlling Urges Makes for a Secure Home

ONE CONDITION FOR PRESERVING the completeness of married life is the power to control urges and to prevent inappropriate outbursts. This can be achieved through observance of the laws and *mitzvot* the Torah has prescribed for the regulation of family life. To achieve this completeness, it is necessary for the couple to exercise a high level of self-control (*hitapkut*, התאפקות). The linguistic root of this word is אפק. In the alphabet, these letters immediately precede those of בצר, a root meaning "to fortify."

א precedes ב

פ precedes צ

ק precedes ר

This teaches us that the fortification and security of family life depends upon the powers of self-control exercised by the husband and wife.

This lesson can be deduced from the verse, "The counsel of *Hashem* will stand forever" (Psalms 33:11). The letters אפק, the root indicating self-control, immediately follow the letters of "counsel" (עצת), as found in this verse.

א follows ת (viewing the alphabet as a cycle)

פ follows ע

ק follows צ

The couple that follows the counsel of God will be able to achieve the necessary powers of self-control. The counsel (*eitzah*, עצה) of the Holy One, blessed be he, is the means by which the tree (*eitz*, עץ) of marriage flourishes.

The letters of the word "secure" (*betach*, בטח) form the initials of blessing (*berachah*, ברכה), goodness (*tovah*, טובה), and life (*chayim*, חיים). The inner nature of these concepts is shown by the "inner" letters of their names.

ב is spelled בית

ט is spelled טית

ח is spelled חית

After the first, or "outer," letter is removed, the inner letters of all three names are ית. The numerical value of ית is 410, which is also the numerical value of "holy" (*kadosh*, קדוש).

kadosh (קדוש): 100 + 4 + 6 + 300 = 410

This teaches us that the fundamental qualities of blessing, goodness, and life depend upon holiness, which is the guarantor of a home that is secure (*betach*, בטח).

The quality of patience is the basis of self-control and the reining in of blind urges. This achievement means that the married partners can be flexible and adapt to each other. The linguistic root of "patience" (*savlanut*, סבלנות) is סבל. These letters are very close to סגל, the root of "adaptability" (*histaglut*, הסתגלות). Patience and adaptability are interdependent.

Adaptability is the fundamental quality that sets married life on its proper footing. This is revealed by the fact that the letters סגל, the root of "adaptability" (*histaglut*, הסתגלות) directly precede the root of "stand," עמד.

ס precedes ע

ג precedes ד

ל precedes מ

By means of mutual adaptability, the married couple is able to stand together through all the changing conditions of their married life.

This stability is also symbolized by the vocalization mark whose name, *segol* (סגול), is also based on the linguistic root סגל. The *segol* consists of three dots that form an equilateral triangle. No matter which way the triangle is turned, it always has a firm base.

The system of equivalence known as *Ik-Bechar* (איק–בכר) reveals that happiness (*osher*, אשר) in married life depends upon the strong connection (*kesher*, קשר) between husband and wife and upon the honesty (*yosher*, יושר) of their relationship. These three words all end in the letters שר. Their initial letters have the numerical values 1 (א), 10 (י), and 100 (ק). Thus, they represent the full range of the numerical values of the alphabet, from the units to the tens to the hundreds.

Since the letters formed at the back of the palate are interchangeable, it makes sense that by means of the *kesher* (connection, קשר) between husband and wife, the couple forms a *gesher* (bridge, גשר) between them through strong mutual bonds of *regesh* (feeling, רגש).

66

The Impurity of Illicit Relations Damages the Married Couple

MARRIED HAPPINESS FLOWS from the holiness of the couple. By the same token, the impurity (*tuma*) of forbidden relations damages the couple and shakes the foundation of their life. This is reflected in the structure of the word *erva* (ערוה), "illicit relations." This word can be analyzed as ער, a root meaning to shake, challenge or disturb, plus the letters וה.

The letters וה are holy because they are the last two letters of the name of God, יהוה. In married life, this holiness manifests itself in the word *chupah* (marriage canopy, חופה), which can be analyzed as the protection of holiness, and the word *ketubah* (marriage contract, כתובה), which can be analyzed as the "writ of holiness."

The holiness of the first two letters of God's name, יה, is extended and is brought down into the world through the last two letters, וה, as embodied in the *chupah* and *ketubah*. As we have seen, the letters יה are contained in the union of man (*ish*, איש) and woman (*ishah*, אשה).

Thus, the letters וה represent the essence of the holiness of marriage. The sin of *erva* (ערוה, illicit relations), which we have analyzed as ער וה, shakes and disrupts the foundations of this holiness.

67

"Illicit Relations" and "Badness": Spelled with the Same Letters

THE VARIOUS SINS of illicit relations (*erva*) are the source of evil in the family, and also in the world-at-large. The same letters that spell "illicit relations" (*erva*, ערוה) also spell "badness" (*roa*, רועה).

The pursuit of "appetite" is an evil root from which sprout all kinds of bitter outgrowths, including the sins of *erva*, illicit relations. These, in turn, lead to "abomination" (*toevah*, תעבה).

The letters pronounced with the same parts of the mouth are considered interchangeable. When the weakly pronounced letters א and ו are interchanged with their more strongly pronounced counterparts, ע and ב, the result is that appetite (*taavah*, תאוה) becomes abomination (*toevah*, תעבה).

Excessive appetite and the consequent increase in sins of *erva*, illicit relations, are the source of evil and wickedness. The numerical value of "evil" (*ra*, רע) is 270.

ra (רע): 200 + 7 = 270

This is ten times the number associated with the word *zav* (זב), which means an exudation resulting from venereal disease. The letters of this word have the numerical values 2 and 7, which together form the number 27. Ten times twenty-seven is 270, the numerical value of evil.

The impurity of *zav* results from excessive appetite, which is the source of evil (*ra*, רע) that shakes (*meareret*, מערערת) the foundations of the world.

Appetite (*taavah*, תאוה) is the source of all the perversities (*ivutim*, עיוותים) of the world. The roots of these two words are interchangeable. The letter ע is a stronger form of the letter א; thus, אוה, the linguistic root of "appetite," is equivalent to עוה, the root of "perversity." From the same linguistic root, עוה, come the words "sin" (*avon*, עוון) and "outrage" (*avel*, עוול), referring to something that distorts (*meavettet*, מעוותת) the life of the individual and the society.

"Illicit relations" (*erva*) has the same numerical value as *pere* (פרא), which means "wild, lawless."

erva (ערוה): $70 + 200 + 6 + 5 = 281$
pere (פרא): $80 + 200 + 1 = 281$

This teaches us that defective observance of the laws of *erva* brings a person to wildness and lawlessness, and to lack of control over one's urges in married life. This, in turn, shakes and ruins the proper regulation of the home.

We have learned that the letters יה, the first two letters of the God's name, יהוה, symbolize the holy unity of man (*ish*, איש) and woman (*ishah*, אשה). The departure from the holy ways of God, with regard to man and woman, is represented by the expression *surya* (סוריה), which means, literally, "to depart from יה." One who goes on this errant path is destined to cause himself to reach an even lower stage.

The same letters, slightly rearranged, spell *rusya* (רוסיה), meaning "to destroy יה," a further stage of moral degeneration involving the destruction of the basic holiness of the male–female relationship. (In Hebrew, these two expressions are spelled like the names of the countries Syria and Russia.)

Both of these expressions have the same numerical value as *erva* (illicit relations) and *pere* (wild, lawless).

surya or *rusya* (סוריה or רוסיה):
$200 + 6 + 60 + 10 + 5 = 281$

The reverse of this degenerative process is symbolized by another transformation that also depends upon the equivalence of the letters א and ע. Given this equivalence, badness (*roa*, רוע) becomes light (*ohr*, אור). The light of Torah and holiness in a home annuls the badness that otherwise would cover up and soil married life.

The impurity of *erva* (illicit relations) has the power to blind a person from seeing the light of truth. *Erva* is spelled with the same letters as "the blindness" (*haivur*, העור). Tradition tells us that sins of *erva*, in the past, caused God to "hide his face" from the Jewish people—i.e., to treat them as if he were "blind" to their needs; this led to severe calamities.

If a couple lives together in impurity, they cause the closing and blockage of their feelings for each other. Thus, the letters of "impure" (*tameh*, טמא) are the same as those of "blockage" (*itum*, אטם).

As a consequence of transgressions, a person's heart becomes closed and blocked. The brain, too, experiences difficulty in understanding simple, straightforward matters.

68

"Menstrual Impurity" and "Judgment": Spelled with the Same Letters

WHEN ADAM AND EVE SINNED, damaging their souls by eating from the tree of knowledge, they brought into the world the severe form of impurity (*tuma*) known as *niddah* (menstrual impurity). *Niddah* comes from the forces of *din* (strict judgment).

On the interpersonal level, strict judgment (*din*) means that people are critical and unforgiving. This force causes quarrels between husband and wife. The resulting psychological unease and lack of harmony between the partners can lead (God forbid) to divorce.

The force of *din* (strict judgment) resulting from the failure to observe the laws of family purity creates a wall, erecting a mountainous barrier between husband and wife. It robs the couple of mutual understanding.

Thus, the letters of the word *sukkah* (סוכה), indicating a screen or barrier, immediately follow, in the alphabet, those of *niddah* (menstrual impurity), which are also the letters of "the judgment" (*hadin*, הדין).

ס follows נ

ו follows ה

כ follows י

ה follows ד

The linguistic root of "barrier" (*sukkah*, סוכה) is the same as that of "quarrel" (*sichsuch*, סכסוך) and "screen" (*masach*, מסך). The screen and the quarrels that arise between husband and wife develop out of sins regarding menstrual impurity (*niddah*).

It is not just the couple that suffers from these transgressions; the Jewish people as a whole suffers from the violations of individual Jews. The prohibition against relations with one's wife when she is a *niddah* is included by the Torah with the other prohibitions of *erva*, illicit relations. (See Leviticus, Ch. 18.) The influence of individual transgressions upon the people as a whole can be exemplified by the destruction of the First Temple. The main reason for that destruction was the impurity of illicit relations.

In order to emphasize the seriousness of the sin of having marital relations with a *niddah*, a transgression that brings harsh judgment upon the world, let us examine passages from the *Zohar* (Parshat Shemot).

> There are three who push the Divine Presence (*Shechinah*) out of the world, bringing it about that the dwelling of the Holy One, blessed be he, should not be in the world, and that people cry out in prayer, but their voice is not heard. These (three) are: He who lies down with a *niddah*; for there is no stronger impurity (*tuma*) in the world than that of *niddah*. He who lies down (with her) becomes contaminated, and anyone who touches him (lit., "comes close to him") becomes contaminated with him. Wherever they go, the *Shechinah* is pushed away from before them. And not only that, but he brings evil diseases upon himself and upon the children to whom he gives birth.

The *Zohar* discusses with similar severity a Jew who has marital relations with a non-Jew. This sin arouses a very strong force of *din* (strict judgment) against the Jewish people, as happened to the children of Israel in the wilderness, when the people became involved with the women of Moab and Midian, bringing down the wrath of God upon the Jewish people.

Calamities and particularly harsh judgments are aroused in the world because of abortions, as can be seen from this next passage in the *Zohar*:

> He does three evils which the entire world cannot tolerate, and hence the world falls apart little by little, and no one perceives why it is happening. And the Holy One, blessed be he, departs from the world, and war, famine, and death come upon the world.
>
> And these are the three evils that he does: He kills his children; he demolishes the building of the King (i.e., he terminates the fetus, which

is a building made by the Holy One, blessed be he); and he pushes away the *Shechinah* and goes wandering in the world, and finds no rest in the world. For these things the Holy Spirit weeps, and the world is judged with all these judgments. Woe unto that person (who does these evils)—woe unto him; it would be better if he had not been created.

69

The Ritual Bath

Purification in the *mikveh* (ritual bath) creates hope for a bright new future. This is reflected in the close relationship between the words *mikveh* (מקוה) and "hope" (*tikvah*, תקוה). The only difference between these words is the initial letter, which changes from מ to ת; these two letters, with their respective values of 40 and 400, are equivalent, according to the *Ik-Bechar* (איק–בכר) transformation.

Through immersion in the *mikveh*, a person subjugates himself to the Holy One, blessed be he, and removes from himself the shell of physicality and materiality.

The initials of the first three words of the verse, "Create for me, o God, a pure heart" (לב טהור ברא לי אלקים) (Psalms 51:12) are the letters of the word "immersed" (*taval*, טבל).

Through the *mikveh*, as represented by the word "immersed" (*taval*, טבל), a person acquires a good heart. In fact, the expression, "good-heartedness" (*tov-lev*, טב–לב) is made up of the letters of "immersed" (טבל).

According to the Tannaitic work, *Otiot d'Rabbi Akiva*, the letter ל stands for the heart. Again, we see that "immersed" (*taval*, טבל) can be analyzed into טב (*tov*, good) and ל, heart.

By a slight rearrangement of its letters, *taval* (טבל, immersed) becomes *batel* (בטל), meaning "to be annulled" or "to be subordinate, subservient." This word can be analyzed into בל and ט. The letters בל are the linguistic base of the word *bilui* (בילוי), which means "wearing away," and the letter ט stands for the word "mud" (*teet*, טיט),

symbolizing that which is physical and material. Thus, through immersion in the *mikveh*, one annuls and wears away the materialistic side of his nature.

Through immersion in the *mikveh*, a person acquires the trait of goodness and purity of heart. In this way, the foundation is laid for spiritual productivity and future fruitfulness.

The words "immersed" (*taval*) and "mother" (*em*) have the same numerical value.

> *taval* (טבל): 9 + 2 + 30 = 41
> *em* (אם):   1 + 40 = 41

This number, 41, consists of two elements, 40 and 1. The number forty corresponding to the מ, stands for the *mikveh*, which, according to Jewish law, must contain a minimum of 40 *sea* (volumetric measure) of water. The number one corresponds to the א (*alef*), which stands for the Holy One, blessed be he, the Chief (*aluf*) of the universe, who is One.

The word *em* (אם) is sometimes used to refer to the womb, the primal source where physicality is formed. In Hebrew, this source is linked with the concepts of purity and immersion in the *mikveh*.

When the letters of the name of God, אהיה, are written out in full, the total numerical value is equal to that of *mikveh*.

> אהיה is spelled אלף, הה, יוד, הה:
> 1 + 30 + 80, + 5 + 5, + 10 + 6 + 4, + 5 + 5 = 151
> *mikveh* (מקוה):   40 + 100 + 6 + 5 = 151

This equivalence teaches us that through immersion in the *mikveh*, a person connects with the root of this name of the Holy One, blessed be he, אהיה, which corresponds to the highest of the kabbalistic worlds, the world of *keter* (crown), and to the quality of *binah* (understanding). In this way, the person who immerses is prepared for a new level of existence.

The number 151 is also the numerical value of נקא. In Aramaic, the language of the Gemara, this three-letter root means "to cleanse." The purification of the *mikveh* is a cleansing of the mind, heart, and soul.

These three letters, in a different order, spell קנא, the root of the Hebrew word for "zealous," as in the verse about Pinchas, who was "zealous (קנא) for his God" (Numbers 25:13). Zeal for the sake of holiness is the outcome of purification.

When we add up the digits of the number 151, the result, 7, is the "small" *gematria* of the word *mikveh*. Seven stands for the perfection of the quality of *malchut* (kingship, which relates to the complete revelation of God's kingship, which will occur in the Messianic Age). In Kabbalah, *malchut* is the seventh of the lower worlds, or *sefirot*.

By the same token, *mikveh* is related to *Shabbat*, the seventh day of the week.

Mikveh (מקוה) is spelled with the same letters as "stature" (*komah*, קומה). The perfection of a person's stature is achieved by means of purification in the *mikveh*.

The numerical value of *mikveh* (מקוה) is 151. When we add 4 for the number of letters in the word, the total is 156. This number alludes to the perfection of the quality of purity because it is a multiple of 26, the numerical value of the name of God, יהוה.

יהוה: 10 + 5 + 6 + 5 = 26
26 × 6 = 156

Purity is the sixth rung in the ladder of spiritual accomplishment. It is achieved through immersion in the *mikveh*. The tradition of *gematria* informs us that when the numerical value of a word includes the number of letters (as when we added 4 to the value of *mikveh*, 151, to make 156), the result indicates the means to an end. Thus, in our case, the *mikveh* is the means by which we achieve purity.

The number 156 is also the value of the following four terms, all of which symbolize the perfection of purity and holiness: Joseph; Zion; zeal (*kinah*); and the Tent of Meeting (*ohel moed*).

Joseph (יוסף):   10 + 6 + 60 + 80 = 156
Zion (ציון):   90 + 10 + 6 + 50 = 156
kinah (קנאה):   100 + 50 + 1 + 5 = 156
ohel moed (אהל מועד): 1 + 5 + 30, + 40 + 6 + 70 + 4 = 156

The letters in the alphabet that come after those of *mikveh* (מקוה) spell *rozen* (רוזן, nobleman).

ר follows ק

ו follows ה

ז follows ו

נ follows מ

Thus, the purification of the *mikveh* ennobles.

The word *rozen* (רוזן, nobleman) can be analyzed as נזר and ו. The first part, נזר (*nezer*), means a diadem. The second part, ו, is the letter of holiness. The *mikveh* makes a person noble, crowning him with a diadem of holiness.

Mikveh (מקוה) can be analyzed as קם and וה. The first part, קם, is the linguistic root of the word *mekayem* (מקיים), which means to establish something, to make it endure. The second part, וה, is part of the name of God, יהוה. The letters וה also represent the holiness of marriage. This suggests that the *mikveh*, קם וה, helps to establish the holiness of marriage and make it endure.

When we write out in full the names of the letters, the numerical value of *mikveh* totals 298. This is also the numerical value of the word "bathe" (*rachatz*) and "shine" (*tzochar*).

> *mikveh* (מקוה) is spelled מם, קוף, ואו, הי:
>
> 40 + 40, + 100 + 6 + 80, + 6 + 1 + 6, + 5 + 10 = 294
>
> Plus 4 for the four letters: 294 + 4 = 298
>
> *rachatz* (רחץ):   200 + 8 + 90 = 298
>
> *tzochar* (צחר):   90 + 8 + 200 = 298

Through bathing in the *mikveh*, the soul becomes shining white.

Writing out in full the names of the letters of *mikveh*, and then taking the "inner" letters, yields the numerical value of 143, which is the value of the inner letters of the name of God, אהיה.

The inner letters of *mikveh* (מקוה) are מ, וף, או, י:

$$40, + 6 + 80, + 1 + 6, + 10 = 143$$

The name אהיה is spelled אלף, הא, יוד, הא:

$$1 + 30 + 80, + 5 + 1, + 10 + 6 + 4, + 5 + 1 = 143$$

This is another hint that the hidden meaning of the *mikveh* is connected with the supernal world of *keter* (crown), which Kabbalah associates with the name אהיה. This name is considered the source of the name of God, יהוה, as can be seen from the close relationship between the letters of these two names. Both names contain the letter ה twice; the remaining two letters are interchangeable. The letter א becomes י by the *Ik-Bechar* (איק-בכר) transformation; and י, when lengthened, becomes ו.

PART III

RICHES AND RIGHTEOUSNESS

IT USED TO BE THAT almost every Jew was Torah-observant. In those days, if (God forbid) some disaster befell the people, the judges of the Torah court (*beit din*) would exert themselves to discover what transgression had brought about the punishment. The Sages say that when suffering comes upon a person, he must examine his deeds and discover what sin he committed with the afflicted part of the body (see Midrash Tanchuma, Parshat Tazria, sec. 8, and Parshat Metzora, sec. 4). The same principle applies to the Jewish people as a whole. The *beit din* would probe and investigate the moral cause of the calamities that the people suffered. Thus, the Rambam writes (Taaniot 1:2,3):

> When trouble comes, and the people cry out in prayer and sound the *shofar*, everyone realizes that the evil befell them because of their bad deeds, as it is written, "Your sins brought about these things" (Jeremiah 5:25). And this is what causes the trouble to be taken away from them. But if they do not cry out in prayer and do not sound the *shofar*; if instead they say, "This thing is just a natural occurrence; this trouble only happened by chance," such a response constitutes hard-heartedness and causes them to cleave to their bad deeds. In that case, the trouble will bring other troubles in its wake. This is what is written in the Torah: "If you go with Me by accident, I shall go with you by fierce accident." That is to say, "When He brings trouble upon you so that you will repent, if you say that it is an accident, we shall multiply that same 'accident.'"

The *beit din* did not always succeed in discovering the exact source of the trouble. Sometimes they were aided by dreams sent from heaven to answer their questions.

Just as the individual must examine the deeds of a specific organ or limb of his body, so, too, the nation as a whole must examine its various parts. Concerning the individual, the Sages state, "If he does not find the cause, he may assume it is neglect of Torah study" (*Berachot* 5a). The same holds for the nation as a whole.

The Vilna Gaon explains the Sages' last statement as follows. If one fails to find the true cause of suffering, one may assume that the reason for this failure is neglect of Torah study. By the merit of Torah study, Divine Providence enlightens a person and reveals to him the cause of his affliction.

Moreover, Torah is like the soul and the blood of a person and of the world. Just as defective blood can adversely affect the whole body, so neglect can of Torah study cause all kinds of maladies in the body or in the world.

In the past, the *beit din*'s investigation of the cause of the disaster that had befallen the people led to the isolation of wicked and dishonest people. The Rambam states (*ibid., halacha* 17):

> They (the *beit din*) remove the causes of the sins; they warn and probe and investigate dishonest and sinful people, and isolate them, and (they warn, probe, and investigate) people who use force to get their way, and they subdue such people.

Unfortunately, in our time, which is plagued by all kinds of problems and troubles, it is very difficult to determine the specific cause of each disaster. However, just as defective blood can cause all kinds of diseases in the body, likewise certain *mitzvot* are like the soul and the blood of the nation. Examples are *Shabbat*, sexual morality, and Torah study.

Rabbi Yosef Chaim, the spiritual shepherd of the Jews of Iraq in the second half of the nineteenth century, writes in his classic work, *Ben Ish Chai* (Drushim, Parshat Pinchas):

> When economic difficulty afflicts a generation, the first step should be to investigate the sin of promiscuity (*znut*); for this sin, more than all others, reduces prosperity.

Here, we shall examine some of the statements of the Sages in the Talmud, Midrash, and Kabbalah that explain the source of economic troubles for the individual and for society as a whole. Such troubles, according to the Sages in Tractates *Sanhedrin* 97a and *Sotah* 49b, will be prominent in the period just before the Messiah, the era known as the "heel of *Mashiach*." Our Torah leaders inform us that this is the present era.

A Jew is obliged to contemplate current events and study how these events reveal Divine Providence, just as he is obliged to study Torah in depth. Rabbi Elchanan Wasserman states (*Kovetz Maamarim*, Maamar Zechor Yemot Olam):

> Just as one must understand the teachings of the Torah, and study it in depth, likewise one must contemplate all the events which happen in the world, and find their underlying basis in the laws of the holy Torah.

Thus, Rabbi Wasserman endeavors to explain the developments that led to the Holocaust. He directs his attention primarily to the plagues of the *Haskalah* and Reform movements, parallel to which the Nazi movement arose measure for measure.

Rabbi Eliahu Dessler attributes particular importance to the work of understanding the providence of God in our generation, the period of the "heel of *Mashiach*." In *Michtav MiEliahu* (Part 3, 283), he writes:

> Even in an orphaned generation like ours, a person can raise the level of his perception of the Providence of *Hashem*, blessed be he, from the spiritual viewpoint of the Torah. With this true outlook, even if he adds only one small point to the perception of *Hashem*'s ways, he will thereby achieve a merit which is beyond estimation. For by so doing, he repairs all the spiritual pollution and degradation of the generation.

The Sages long ago foresaw that our generation, the time of the "heel of *Mashiach*," would be a time of rebellion and permissiveness, when perversity and falsehood would show their face in every aspect of Jewish life. In this generation, we are witnessing the last death pangs of the forces of *tuma*, spiritual impurity. The many ideologies that drew their nourishment from that *tuma* have bankrupted themselves. A guttering fire casts long flames in every direction just before it finally goes out; a person who is breathing his last tries to squeeze the most out of every moment. In the same way, *tuma*, sensing that its end is drawing near, shoots its arrows in every direction, with no control or restraint.

This rampage is evident wherever we look. It instills dread throughout Orthodox Jewry. These facts double and redouble our obligation to discover and acknowledge the Divine Providence that is shaping events.

The contemplation of current problems in the light of the Torah is especially important in the month of Elul, the season of repentance. This is hinted at in Parshat Reh, the Torah portion that is read at the beginning of Elul. The opening verses of the parshah call upon each individual to study and contemplate the events that befall the whole people.

> Behold, I put before you today a blessing and a curse: the blessing, if you obey the *mitzvot* of *Hashem* your God which I command you today; and the curse, if you do not obey (Deuteronomy 11:26–27).

The main lesson of these verses for the Jewish people, according to the commentary of Seforno, is that there is no compromise for the Jewish nation in history. Its situation is either one extreme or the other, either blessing or curse, depending on whether the people fulfill the *mitzvot* of the Torah. A "middle" way does not exist.

The recent history of the state of Israel certainly furnishes much material for contemplation of the ways of Divine Providence. Such contemplation will lead to the realization that the existence and fulfillment of the Jewish nation depends upon the Holy One, blessed be he.

Revealing the ways of Divine Providence to the rest of the nations is one of the important functions of the Jewish people. When they fail to fulfill this task, the strength of the other nations is aroused, as is their desire to influence the Jewish people and permeate them with *tuma*. Rabbi Eliahu Dessler writes (*op. cit.*, Part 2, 114):

> Part of the Jewish people's task is to teach the entire world the ways of *Hashem*, and to reveal his kingship, blessed be his name. . . . But for every good force, God created a corresponding force of evil. Thus the nations, on their part, wish to influence the Jewish people to follow their way. This *tuma* can take hold only if the Jewish people are lacking in their aspiration to influence the other nations.

When the troubles and calamities that befall the Jewish people go unexplained, this leaves an opening for the forces of *tuma* of Christianity and other religions, which explain these troubles and calamities as a curse upon the Jews for not converting to their religion. Unfortunately, innocent Jews, mainly in the Diaspora, are snared by these arguments. It is distressing to observe that these arguments are now being used in our own land as well, primarily by the Mormons, who have gained a foothold in Israel in order to trap Jews in their net. As Rabbi Dessler points out (*ibid.*), the very act of revealing the light of *Hashem*'s providence through the words of our Sages will drive the darkness of *tuma* out of our land.

1

The Obligation to Acknowledge God's Providence in Our Time

RABBI ELIAHU DESSLER writes about the great importance of studying and understanding all the exiles that the Jewish people have undergone among the nations ever since the children of Israel became a people. The events of exile come to teach us and to help us repair what is needed so that we can arrive at perfection. One who does not understand the exiles is lacking fundamental knowledge about the service of God (*op. cit.*, Part 3, 207).

This obligation is all the more urgent in our day. As Rabbi Dessler writes (*Michtau mi Eliyahu*, Part 3, p. 207):

> We are all the more obliged to study the meaning of the exile in which we now live. According to all the signs that the Sages have given us (see *Sotah* 49b), we have arrived at the time just before the coming of the righteous redeemer. It will be a great loss if we do not learn to understand the way in which heaven is directing the events of our time, and if we do not know how to estimate correctly the urgent duties that have been placed upon us.

In this light, Rabbi Dessler explains the various types of suffering that have afflicted our people in the different exiles. He states (*ibid.*, 210): The particular exile reflects the nature of the sins that the Jews committed.

Through this effort to understand the types of troubles that have befallen the Jewish people, a person comes to perceive his sins, and repents.

The destruction of the First and Second Temples serve as a classic example of the relationship between the sin and the punishment. Rabbi Dessler writes (*ibid.*, 214):

> The First Temple was destroyed because of the sins of idol worship, promiscuity, and murder. The root of all these sins was unbridled appetite. . . . Therefore, when the people arrived at the point where they had to be punished, they were given over into the hands of Babylonia, whose basic characteristic is unbridled appetite. . . .
>
> When the people returned to *Eretz Yisrael*, they were still subjugated to Persia, because they were still spiritually lacking. This continued until the Men of the Great Assembly buttressed and reinforced Torah observance by means of enactments and preventive decrees (*takanot* and *siyagim*) and built up the study of Torah by raising up many disciples and students.
>
> Later, when the people again became negligent in Torah observance, the Greek exile came upon them . . . the Greek philosophy, which conquered the world and darkened the eyes of Israel. The Greeks imposed decrees against Torah study, *Shabbat*, and circumcision. Only when the Hasmoneans aroused and strengthened themselves and put their lives at stake for Torah study and observance, did the people overcome this exile. Thus was the rule of Torah fortified in that era.

At the end of the Second Temple period, strife and mutual hatred became prevalent among the Jewish people. As the Sages state, "Why was the Second Temple destroyed? Because there was causeless hatred there" (*Yoma* 9b). The root of these sins was pride, impudence, and lack of a sense of shame, as well as the refusal to listen to reproof. Therefore, when the trait of pride spread and gained control among the Jewish people, reaching the point where punishment had to come, the Temple was destroyed and the Jews were given into the hands of the fourth kingdom (i.e., the last of the four kingdoms who were destined to hold Israel in exile): Edom, or Rome. The basic characteristic of that nation is arrogance and atheism, their slogans being "My strength and the might of my arm" (Deuteronomy 8:17), and "I and nothing else" (Isaiah 47:8).

Ever since the destruction of the Second Temple, the forces of arrogance of the fourth kingdom have been constantly increasing. In this exile, the darkness and the concealment of divinity grow continually. The materialistic philosophies gain control and cast a dark pall over spirituality.

Rabbi Dessler continues his analysis of our present era (*ibid.*, 217):

> The end of this exile is the era described by the Sages as "the heels of *Mashiach*," a time in which "arrogance will increase" (*Sotah* 49b). In that time, the exile of the Divine Presence (the *Shechinah*) is in the hands of the arrogant members of the Jewish people. These are the souls of the mixed multitude (*eruv rav*, people who were not descended from Jacob but who accompanied the people of Israel when they left Egyptian bondage). The main source of *tuma* (spiritual impurity) of the *eruv rav*, who are mixed in among the Jewish people, is arrogance toward heaven, which is the trait of Amalek.
>
> The Gra states (in his commentary on *Tikunei Zohar Chadash*, 27b): "The *eruv rav* among Israel are the Amalekites. As the *Zohar* explains, the *eruv rav* includes five nations, the initials of whose names spell out the Hebrew words ערב רב, *eruv rav*. The main one of these is Amalek (עמלק), whose initial, ע, is the first of the five initials. Governance over the holy people has been given into the hands of the *eruv rav*, who are "the head of the holy people in the final exile," as it is said, "Her enemies have become the head" (Lamentations 1:5). It is written in *Raaya Mehemna* that by the force of their pride and governance they attempt to introduce polluted philosophies and cynical principles (*apikorsis*). Their motto is "My strength and the might of my arm" (Deuteronomy 8:17), and they rise up arrogantly and brazenly against faith, Torah, and the service of *Hashem*."
>
> The task of the Jewish people in this era is to withstand the difficult test presented by the false philosophies, whose motto is, "My strength and the might of my arm," to oppose them unflinchingly and with spiritual heroism; not to be awed or influenced by the brazenness of those who deny God and his Torah. The Jew today must not feel overwhelmed by these forces. On the contrary, he must strengthen his faith, not budging one inch from the viewpoint of the Torah and the Sages. He must dedicate himself completely to the inner work of Torah study, prayer, and fear of heaven. "These are the ones who will merit complete redemption by our righteous *Mashiach*, quickly, in our day" (*ibid.*, 218).

The words of Rabbi Eliahu Dessler, written decades ago, cast an invaluable light on the events of our time. Today, the basic values of the Jewish people and their religion are encountering an opposition and an attack that go beyond the limits of reason and intelligence. We see Jews who exhibit profound hatred toward everything that is holy in the Jewish nation. The only fitting explanation is that given by

Rabbi Dessler on the basis of the *Zohar* and Kabbalah: that souls from the root of Amalek are intermingled among the leaders of this era of the "heel of *Mashiach*." This is why reasonableness and intelligence have no effect whatsoever.

Rabbi Eliahu Lopian, *zatzal*, used to say that even the most orthodox newspaper, in describing world news, damages faith in Divine Providence. The various news reports are presented as mere happenings, without any kind of commentary that would relate each event to the providence of the Holy one, blessed be he.

It is true that people of flesh and blood cannot point unmistakably to the exact cause of a particular event: nevertheless, the Sages have given us a general rule (*Yevamot* 63a): "Rabbi Elazar ben Avina said: Disasters come upon the world only for the sake of instructing Israel, as it is said (*Zephaniah* 3:6–7): "I have cut off nations, their leaders have been desolated. . . . I said: Just fear Me, o Israel; learn a lesson . . .'"

The purpose of these world events is to arouse awe and fear in the Jewish people. The Ran states in his *Drashot* (sixth *drush*):

> Sometimes events erupt at great distances and in far-away continents in order that Israel should be aroused to repentance and should experience awe and fear lest these disasters strike them. This is the meaning of the prophecy, "I have cut off nations. . . . I said: Just fear Me; learn a lesson. . . . " And when the Jewish people do not learn a lesson from the troubles of others, the disasters begin moving closer and closer. . . . Therefore, there is no doubt that at such times it is proper to search painstakingly for a remedy for the soul; and this takes priority over a remedy for the body.

Comments of this sort, if they were printed in newspapers preceding reports of events and catastrophes that befall the world, would arouse people to recognize and believe in the providence of God. Likewise, any events that highlight the fact that we are now in the period of the "heel of *Mashiach*" (as the Torah leaders of recent times have indicated) would make a strong impression. A comment of this sort, preceding an article reporting the relevant event, would sharpen the Jewish reader's awareness of the importance of the era in which he lives, and would add to his faith.

As we have seen, Rabbi Eliahu Dessler explains that the troubles that affect the Jewish people match the sins that they have committed. In this light, some explain the sufferings of our own time. The Sages state (*Sotah, loc. cit.*) that the most prevalent sins in the period just before the coming of the Messiah are promiscuity and pride. Promiscuity—i.e., unbridled appetite—is the basic characteristic of the Ishmaelite nation; pride is the basic characteristic of Edom (Rome). Hence, the representatives of these two negative forces, in particular, cause the main sorrows and sufferings of the Jewish people in the time of the "heel of *Mashiach.*"

The ways of God's providence are revealed not only by the nature of the Jewish people's enemies at a given time, but also by the specific location where the troubles begin. The Gaon Rabbi Yaakov Kanyevsky, *zatzal*, writes in his work *Chayei Olam:*

> We see in this the finger of God. Organized rebellion against the Torah first began in Germany, and from there spread to other countries. Likewise, the decree to kill and destroy the Jews came from that wicked land. Thus the fact that the punishment fits the crime is clearly revealed.

According to the Maggid of Kelem, *zatzal*, it was also revealed by the whole set of new laws instituted by the German Nazis against the Jewish people. These new laws appeared because of the new laws instituted by the Reform movement, which struck at and uprooted the foundations of the *halacha* and statutes of Israel. It is mentioned in *Sefer Hazichronot* of Rabbi Mazah of Moscow that because of the sin of the new *Shulchan Aruch* written by Geiger (of the Reform movement), another new Shulchan Aruch, German-style, would arise against the Jewish people.

Rabbi Chaim Ozer Grodzinsky, writing in 1939, also explains the Nazi persecutions as an outcome of rebellion against the Torah of Israel. In his introduction to Part 3 of his responsa work, *Achiezer*, he states:

> Due to our many sins, faith has weakened, and in Western countries the Reform movement has struck at the roots . . . and as a result many Jews have been completely assimilated and lost among the gentiles. And now, from that same area, the evil has gone forth, pursuing them with wrath and destroying them from the earth.

If the connection between these kinds of sins and the resulting punishment were more clearly emphasized, this would greatly help restore to the Jew a sense of responsibility for his actions. In our time, a widespread indifference toward violation of religious principles is evident in every aspect of political and military life. An outstanding example was the war in Lebanon. It began and concluded on the Sabbath, in total disregard of the opinions of the army's rabbinate and the feelings of Torah-observant soldiers. After the fact, too, the voices of protest were very weak. If religious people had a deeper awareness of the connection, explained by the Sages, between desecration of the Sabbath and the failure of military plans that were formulated on *Shabbat*, public reaction would have been much different.

The holy Torah also makes clear that desecration of the Sabbath and looseness in male–female relations has far-reaching consequences affecting the danger that soldiers undergo in battle. If the public had a deep awareness of this fact, its reaction to the neglect of these basic Jewish values would be much stronger and more vigorous than at present.

Similarly, the events of our time clearly reveal the righteousness of great leaders of our people, such as the Rav of Brisk and the Chazon Ish, *zatzal*, who foresaw with their spiritual vision that the clash between observant and non-observant Jews held great danger, and could even lead to bloodshed. If the words of such great Torah leaders were used to preface news reports about the events of our time, it would strengthen faith in the wisdom of our leaders.

Weakness and slackness among the Jewish people, and the lack of dedication to the fulfillment of Torah and *mitzvot*, strengthens the enemies of the Jewish people. The enemy uses these traits against the nation.

The concept that the weaknesses of Israel become the strengths of our enemies has many applications. The Sefat Emmet uses it to explain a Midrash on the Scroll of Esther. Midrash Rabbah relates that the angels asked the Holy One, blessed be he, why Israel suffered cruel and painful decrees, while the nations of the world reveled in pleasures and luxuries of every sort. The Holy One, blessed be he, replied that the cause of this situation was desecration of the Sabbath. The Sefat Emmet explains that the ability to enjoy this world was originally given to Israel; this pleasure is the basis of *Shabbat*. When Israel desecrates the Sabbath, the quality of pleasure is desecrated and devolves upon the enemies of Israel.

A number of passages in Scripture also reflect the fact that the special qualities of Israel can sometimes be transferred to its enemies. Thus, when the Jewish nation went out of Egypt and the Egyptian army pursued them, the quality of unity, which is the particular gift of

Israel, passed to the Egyptians. This explains the Torah's use of the singular form of the verb "to drive" in the verse, "And behold, Egypt was driving after them" (Exodus 11:10).

The children of Israel were afraid—not of the Egyptians, but of the strength of unity that they were suddenly seen to have. When the children of Israel saw this mighty strength in the Egyptians, they realized that their own traits (*midot*) were defective. This brought them to complete repentance.

Similarly, the power of self-sacrifice (*mesirat nefesh*) is granted especially to Israel. When the Jewish people fail to use this power for Torah and *mitzvot*, it is seen to have passed to Israel's enemies and to the religion of those enemies, who exhibit self-sacrifice, even to the point of suicide, for their anti-Jewish and anti-Torah principles.

Economics is one area in which it is possible to perceive the open providence of God. About the verse "You shall surely tithe your produce," עשר תעשר (Deuteronomy 14:22), the Sages explain the double form of the Torah's expression with an exegesis that capitalize on the similarity of the words for "tithe" (עשר) and "wealth" (עשר). They interpret the verse as hinting: "Tithe, so that you shall become wealthy" (*Taanit* 9a).

In the area of economics, one is permitted to test God's word and prove to oneself that by giving *maaser* (tithes), one will achieve economic success. This is the meaning of the verse (Malachi 3:10):

> Bring all the *maaser* to the storehouse, and please test Me in this . . .
> and I shall pour out for you unlimited blessing.

May God grant that we merit to perceive the ways of his providence in our world. May we proudly raise high the banner of faith in reward and punishment. May our indifference and our fear of the non-religious world vanish, and the will of the Torah be exalted over all.

2

Sexual Purity

A CAREFUL EXAMINATION of the words of the Sages in the Talmud, the Midrash, and Kabbalah clearly reveals that looseness in sexual morality is closely connected with a very shaky economic situation. We will discuss this cause-and-effect relationship in detail.

The spiritual state of the Jewish people just before the destruction of the Second Temple can teach us something about our own era as well. In *Gittin* 57a, the Talmud relates:

> It once happened that the price of grain stood at forty measures per dinar. The price went up, so that a dinar now bought one measure less. The Torah court (*beit din*) investigated and discovered that a father and son had had relations with a married woman on Yom Kippur. They brought them to trial, and the price was restored.

Rabbi Yosef Chaim explains this phenomenon in his work, *Ben Ish Chai* (Drashot Al Hatorah, Parshat Pinchas, 193):

> It is known that no sin damages the economic prosperity of the Jewish people as much as the sin of sexual misconduct (*znut*). This is why the verse says, "For the sake of an immoral woman until a loaf of bread" (Proverbs 6:26). That is to say, the sin which involves an immoral woman damages the "loaf of bread," the abundance of livelihood.
>
> The reason is that when the Other Side (the force of evil) sees a man or a woman committing adultery, the Other Side also becomes brazen and dares to approach that which is holy and forbidden,

snatching away the abundance which does not belong to it. As a result, livelihood decreases.

Therefore, when a lack of abundance becomes evident in a generation, the first thing that must be examined is this sin; for this sin, more than all others, lessens prosperity.

As we have just seen, the Talmud connects sexual immorality with economic difficulties, showing how an act of adultery brought about a rise in the price of grain; and *Ben Ish Chai* explains the meaning of this connection. It is also highlighted by the similarity between three Hebrew words, all of which were spelled with the same basic letters. Wickedness (רשע) among the Jewish people damages the price (שער) of goods, thus decreasing the people's wealth (עשר).

In the same light, *Ben Ish Chai* (*loc. cit.*) explains a story told in the Jerusalem Talmud (*Taanit* 1:4). This story shows how the prevention of sexual immorality among the Jewish people opens the treasure-houses of the heavens for them.

The Jerusalem Talmud tells about a time when the Jewish people were suffering from a severe drought. Rabbi Abbahu, the leader of the generation, was told from the heavens in a dream that a certain man named Fantkakah should pray, and rain would come.

Rabbi Abbahu sent for the man and asked him about his profession. Fantkakah replied that he supplied gentile prostitutes to gentiles. Rabbi Abbahu asked him what good deed he had performed in the course of this evil work. The man answered that a Jewish woman once came to him, concealed herself behind a column, and wept. She said that her husband had been put in prison (by the Romans) and that, in order to raise the necessary ransom to free him, she had decided she would have to hire herself out as a prostitute. When Fantkakah heard this, he went and sold his bed with its bedding. He gave the proceeds to this woman, telling her: "Go ransom your husband, but do not commit the sin of *znut*."

Rabbi Abbahu told him: "You are worthy of praying for rain. This thing which you have done shows that you act for the sake of heaven; for you exerted yourself so that the women of Jerusalem would not commit the sin of *znut*."

Ben Ish Chai comments:

At first glance this story is very difficult to understand. It is true that the man himself committed no misconduct, and his business dealings were purely between the gentiles. Moreover, he had a good heart which prompted him to keep Jewish women from committing *znut*. Still, what was it that gave him such great power of prayer? What weight could he have in comparison with the light of Israel, the holy Rabbi Abbahu, to whom the heavens revealed that only this man, Fantkakah, could pray successfully for rain? Surely there were many great *tzadikim* at that time. Why wasn't Rabbi Abbahu, or one of the other learned and righteous leaders, chosen to pray?

But according to what we explained above, the story is clearly understandable. It is the sin of *znut* which damages abundant livelihood and causes drought. Therefore, with perfect intent and precision, Providence chose this man to bring rain and to cause abundant livelihood through his prayers; for he had exerted himself to prevent Jewish women from committing *znut*. Through him, the entire Jewish people could not help but take notice how severe are the results of this sin, and how much damage it does in the economic field. . . .

This would cause the masses to stay far from *znut*. Likewise, the Sages of the generation would be inspired to pay attention to this matter and to separate the people from this sin.

In his Talmud commentary *Ben Yehoyada* (*Gittin*, 84), Rabbi Yosef Chaim explains how the price of grain in the first story, and the degree of price increase, have deep meaning on both the theoretical and the practical level. He writes:

It seems to me that the original price of grain was forty measures per dinar, because people are fed and nourished through the merit of the Torah, which was given in forty days. Moreover, the amount of grain which could be purchased for a dinar was reduced by one measure, and no more, to hint to the *beit din* that the economic problem had been caused by only one sinful incident. Once they had found it out, they need look no further.

The increase of one measure contained a further hint. It indicated that the sin was committed on Yom Kippur, which is one unique day out of the whole year, and which comes at the end of forty days of repentance, i.e., the month of Elul and the ten days of repentance (the first ten days of Tishrei, from Rosh Hashana until Yom Kippur). This is why the forty measures were reduced by one measure.

In the light of Rabbi Yosef Chaim's explanation, which connects the percentage of inflation with the number of sins of forbidden relations, what shall we say about our own period, when the rate of price increase has skyrocketed?

Our Sages, of blessed memory, long ago foresaw that the time just before the coming of the Messiah would be characterized by rising prices. This is mentioned in various places in the Midrash and Talmud.

A *braissa* in *Sotah* 49b states:

> In the "heel of *Mashiach*" (the end of the Exile, just before the coming of "Mashiach Rashi), impudence will grow; prices will rise; the grape-vine will give its fruit, but wine will be expensive. [Rashi explains this last phenomenon as a result of the fact that "everyone will be occupied with drinking parties," and Tiferet Israel adds that all this drinking is "to forget the bitterness of life."] The government will become nonbe-lievers; there will be no moral reproof; the meeting place of the sages will be for *znut*.

This passage, too, shows that *znut* and rising prices go hand-in-hand.

This *braissa* is also quoted, with slight variations, in *Sanhedrin* 97a, where the Talmud discusses the identifying signs of the era known as the "heel of *Mashiach*."

> Rabbi Nechemiah says: "In the generation when the son of David will come, arrogance will increase." (Brazenness is a sign of the sin of *znut*, as the verse says in Jeremiah 3:3: "You had the brazenness of a promis-cuous woman.") "Prices will be perversely high. The grapevine will give its fruit, but wine will be expensive . . . until the penny will disap-pear from the purse."

The Maharsha, in his Talmud commentary at the end of Tractate *Sotah*, explains that the two versions of the *braissa* "Prices will rise" and "Prices will be perversely high" complement each other. They teach us that the high prices will not be due to scarcity of produce, as the Tal-mud in *Sotah* points out; rather, prices will be high on account of per-sons who act "perversely"—i.e., who raise prices for no apparent reason.

On the verse "The fruits of the fig have begun to form" (Song of Songs 2:13), Midrash Shir HaShirim comments: "Rabbi Nechemiah says: 'Just before the days of *Mashiach*, poverty will increase, and high prices will break (people).'"

The word for "break," *hoveh* (הוה), is similar to the word for "Alas!"—*Hoi* (הוי). Thus, this Midrash alludes to the Gemara in *Sotah* that says:

The number will increase of those who call bad good and good bad, and "Hoi, hoi" will multiply in the world.

The double expression, "Hoi, hoi," according to Ben Yehoyada (*Sotah* 40), refers to two kinds of trouble: disease and poverty. "Who call bad good" means, "They praise the wicked" (Rashi).

The honor paid to the wicked is another sign of the "heel of *Mashiach*." According to Rashi, this is the meaning of the *braissa* in *Sanhedrin*, "Prices will be perversely high." The word for "high prices" (יוקר) also means "honor." Thus, Rashi interprets: "The most honored among them will be a perverter and deceiver."

Here we see a mixture and equalization of bad and good. Bad men are honored as if they were good; people of twisted values are treated as if they were on an exalted level of morality. This has its parallel in the prices of goods. Rather than finding some goods inexpensive and others expensive, we find that all are equalized and all expensive. This situation is reflected in a statement of Shmuel (*Sanhedrin* 98a) regarding the end of the Exile. The Messiah will only come, he states, "When all prices are equal." Rashi explains: "Because all are high."

3

Immodesty and
Its Consequences

THE HOLY *Zohar* notes, in many places, the connection between immodesty and *znut* on the one hand, and poverty and economic difficulties on the other. In Parshat Naso (77:125b), the *Zohar* states:

> Rabbi Chelkiah said: "Torment will come upon a man who allows his wife to let the hair of her head show; for this (keeping the hair covered) is one of the aspects of modesty in the home. A woman who lets her hair show in order to appear beautiful causes poverty to the home. . . .
>
> "And if this is true in the home, all the more so in the street; and all the more so if she exhibits some other type of brazenness. Therefore it is written, 'Your wife will be like a fruitful grapevine, and I shall bless your home' (Psalms 128:3)."

Great poverty is the lot of a man who has relations with a prostitute, as Rava states in *Sotah* 4b: "Whoever has relations with a prostitute, in the end will seek for a loaf of bread." This is in accordance with the verse, "For the sake of a promiscuous woman until a loaf of bread" (Proverbs 6:26).

The Maharal, in his commentary on the *Aggadot* of the Talmud (*Sotah*), explains Rava's statement.

> Abundance of livelihood (*parnassah*) is the opposite of *znut*; for *parnassah* is a very high level of holiness . . . it is on a very exalted rung. Thus, [Rava] stated that whoever has relations with a prostitute in the

end will seek for a loaf of bread and will not find it. For *znut* is a completely physical appetite, the opposite of *parnassah*.

As we have explained elsewhere, the word *znut* means "deviation," swerving away from honesty and blessing. That is why this term (זנה, which means to swerve aside, and is the root of the word *znut*) is always the one used to refer to sexual impropriety. . . . The word means to turn aside from the true order; therefore in the end one who indulges in it will lack *parnassah*. For a man's *parnassah* is something which is arranged and ordered by *Hashem*, blessed be he. For all created things, and their sustenance, are from him. That is why [a person who departs from *Hashem*'s order of Creation] will in the end seek bread and not find it.

This matter can be understood according to the secret wisdom; for the heart [is the organ of the body that] sustains a person, and it is located in the center of the body, neither to the right nor to the left. Therefore, one who has relations with a prostitute, which constitutes a swerving and a deviation away from the straight way, in the end will seek for a loaf of bread and not find it.

The heart, the Maharal explains, in order to serve as the source of abundance and blessing, must not be displaced to the right or the left. Therefore, *znut*, prostitution, which deviates from the way of truth, lessens the source of vitality.

In *Nishmat Chaim*, his commentary on *Pirkei Avot*, the Maharal again uses the analogy of the heart to explain the damage done by *znut*. The Mishnah (*Avot* 5:9) states, "Exile comes . . . because of illicit relations." The Maharal explains:

All the other lands are under the rulership of specific angels ("supernal ministers"), but *Eretz Yisrael* is under the direct supervision of *Hashem*, blessed be he. "The eyes of *Hashem* are on it always, from the beginning of the year until the end of the year" (Deuteronomy 11:12). Moreover, it is called the land of life (*eretz chaim*), as it is said, "I shall bestow beauty on the land of life" (Ezekiel 26:20), for *Eretz Yisrael* is the center of the world.

The heart distributes vitality to the entire body by means of the circulation of the blood, which is the life force (*nefesh*), as is indicated by the verse, "Above all protection, guard your heart, for from it are all the outpourings of life" (Proverbs 4:23). In the same way, the source of life for all the other lands is within *Yisrael*; all receive their abundance from it. Therefore the nation which inhabits this land must of necessity be holy. . . . If they become polluted with illicit relations, they no longer have the trait of holiness. . . . If so, they are not fit for *Eretz Yisrael* [and must go into exile].

It is explained in kabbalistic works that the nation of Israel is meant to be the source of abundance for the whole world. The sin of illicit relations causes the source of abundance to depart from Israel and be located instead among the other nations. In that case, Israel must receive its abundance from the leftovers of the abundance of the nations.

In this light, we can understand the situation in our own day. We can see why the state of Israel steadily becomes more economically dependent upon the United States. Likewise, we can understand the constant flow of *yordim*, emigrants, who in ever-increasing numbers are leaving Israel to seek the source of their abundance and livelihood in Exile.

Rabbi Elchanan Wasserman, in his work *Kovetz Maamarim* ("Maaseh Avot Siman Lebanim," 86) discusses the difficult economic situation of the Jewish people in Exile.

> The livelihood of Israel in Exile comes through defective channels. That is, the sustenance comes down by way of the gentile nations; Israel is supported by these nations' leftovers. This is literally the situation with regard to support of Torah institutions. . . . We see this especially in our days, the era of the "heel of *Mashiach*"; for by far the greater part of the contributions collected from the Jewish people fall into the hands of the wicked of Israel, and only a tiny minority of the funds remains for the support of the Torah.
>
> And so it is regarding slander. Just as the nations constantly seek ways to slander the Jewish people, so, too, the wicked among our people seek ways to slander the Torah scholars. If it should happen that someone who studies Torah commits some improper act, they do not ridicule him alone, but the criticism falls upon Torah scholars as a whole.

This parallel, in which the relationship of the other nations to Israel is mirrored by the relationship of the secular to the religious within Israel, is explained by the holy Ari in his work *Likutei Torah* (the beginning of Parshat Shoftim).

In the time of the "heel of *Mashiach*," the economic situation of Torah scholars is especially difficult. This is revealed in *Raaya Mehemna* (*Zohar*, Bamidbar 125b):

> God-fearing men of holy deeds wander from city to city unregarded. They are given only a limited allowance, so that they should have no possibility to recover from their downfall, even for their immediate

needs. All the Sages, the men of holy acts, and those who fear sin, live lives of suffering, in poverty and sorrow, and are looked upon like dogs.

We have already quoted the statement of Rava that one who has relations with a prostitute will in the end seek for a loaf of bread (and not find it). Rabbi Yosef Chaim, in his work *Ben Yehoyada* (on *Sotah 2*, 15b), explains this punishment as an example of "measure for measure" (מידה כנגד מידה).

On the verse which states that Potiphar gave Joseph control over everything in his estate "except the bread he ate" (Genesis 39:6), the Sages comment that this refers to Potiphar's wife. Hence we see that one's wife is called "bread." Apparently the reason is that, as the Sages state elsewhere, "Abundance comes to a man's house only for the sake of his wife, as it is written, 'He benefited Abram for her sake' (Genesis 12:15)." Therefore, one who abandons his lawful wife, for whose sake his bread is blessed, and who cleaves instead to a prostitute, in the end seeks a loaf of bread and does not find it.

Although *znut* leads to a situation of starvation, the righteous man (*tzadik*) merits *parnassah*, and also causes others to merit it. *Iyun Yaakov* (*Sotah, loc. cit.*) uses the example of Joseph *Hazadik* to illustrate this point. Joseph sustained and supported others in Egypt to demonstrate that the charges against him—that he had committed *znut* with the wife of Potiphar—were false.

In Hebrew, the root זנה, in its positive aspect, refers to food and nourishment (מזון, *mazon*); in its negative aspect, it indicates sexual impropriety (זנות, *znut*) and immodesty. This shows the cause-and-effect relationship between these two factors. The sin of *znut* injures and ruins the abundance of nourishment.

For a deeper understanding of this matter, we must turn to the kabbalistic explanation of the basic source of nourishment.

According to Kabbalah, the source of nourishment is connected with the great trait of *Chesed* (kindness), as is stated by *Kehillat Yaakov* (*mazon*) and as is hinted at in the verse, "You open Your hand and satisfy the wish of every living thing" (Psalms 145:15).

The connection between nourishment (*mazon*) and kindness (*chesed*) is revealed in the numerical value of these words: *mazon* (מזון): 40 + 7 + 6 + 50 = 103; *El chesed* (God of kindness, חסד א-ל): 1 + 30 + 8 + 60 + 4 = 103. This number, 103, is also the numerical value of the word *mincha* (מנחה), which means the special sacrifices by whose merit abundance comes down to the world: *mincha* (מנחה):

40 + 50 + 8 + 5 = 103. *Chesed* is a force that, on the side of holiness, brings abundance and goodness to the world. The *chesed* of impurity (*tuma*), however, is the source of unbridled appetites and destructive illicit relations. Thus, the Torah says, regarding one who marries his sister: "This is chesed" (Leviticus 20:17).

Mazon (whose linguistic root is זנה) comes from *chesed*. *Chesed* itself, however, has both a holy and an unholy aspect. Thus, we can understand the positive and negative aspects of words formed from the root זנה.

The Hebrew words for "kindness" (*chesed*, חסד) and "nourishes" (*zanah*, זנה) reveal the close relationship between these two concepts. Each three-letter root in Hebrew has a basis of two letters. Thus, the basis of זנה is זן, and the basis of חסד is חס. The letters of זן immediately precede those of חס in the alphabet; ז precedes ח, and נ precedes ס.

The force of *chesed*, which is sanctified appetite, is creative and constructive. *Chesed* on the side of *tuma*, i.e., uncontrolled appetite, destroys and ruins.

Once we understand this connection between the holy aspect of *chesed*, which is *mazon*, and the unholy aspect, which is *znut*, we can understand why the verb "to eat" refers not only to nourishment but also to promiscuity, as in the verse describing the actions of an adulteress: "She ate, and wiped her mouth, and said, 'I have not done anything wrong'" (Proverbs 30:20).

The fine line between the forces of holiness and unholiness is revealed in the Hebrew words *kedusha* (קדושה, holiness) and *kedaisha* (קדשה, prostitute). Removing the ו from the word *kedusha* changes its positive forces to negative ones of *znut* and immodesty.

Kabbalah describes how the creative power of God descends through three upper and seven lower *sefirot*, or levels of emanation, the last of which is our material universe. The letter ו refers to the sixth of the seven lower *sefirot*; it is called *yesod* (foundation, יסוד), and its characteristic is righteousness (*tzidkut*), which is related to Joseph.

Joseph was the foundation of the livelihood of Egypt because he sanctified himself in sexual purity; he kept himself far from *znut* and immodesty. This trait opened for him the storehouses of abundance and nourishment.

The relationship between Joseph and the holiness of *Yesod* is revealed by the numerical value of his name:

Joseph (יוסף): 10 + 6 + 60 + 80 = 156

This equals six times the name of *Hashem*.

Hashem (יהוה): 10 + 5 + 6 + 5 = 26; 6 × 26 = 156

Six times the name of *Hashem* hints at the perfection of the six *sefirot* that go into the makeup of *yesod*, the *sefirah* of righteousness.

The same number, 156, is the numerical value of the word *yakum* (יקום).

yakum (יקום): 10 + 100 + 6 + 40 = 156

The Sages tell us that the word *yakum* (from the root קום, stand) refers to a person's property. A verse in Deuteronomy (11:6) states: "and all the *yakum* which was with them" (lit., "which was at their feet"). The Talmud (*Pesachim* 119a) comments: "Rabbi Eliezer said, *Yakum* means a man's property, which stands him on his feet.'"

Slightly rearranged, the letters of *yakum* spell *kiyum* (קיום), which means "permanent existence." A man's property (*yakum*) and the permanent existence (*kiyum*) of his holdings depend upon his guarding the characteristic of *yesod*, the holiness and purity symbolized by the letter ו.

The fact that holiness, symbolized by the letter ו, is the basis of the permanent existence of one's property is underscored by a word for "fortune" or "wealth": *hon* (הון). The central letter of this word is ו.

Hon refers especially to the wealth of the *tzadik*, as indicated by the verse, "Fortune (*hon*) and wealth are in his house, and his righteousness endures forever" (Psalms 112:3).

When the ו is removed from the word *hon* (הון), it becomes *hein* (הן), an expression which refers to death. *Ben Ish Chai* (Drashot al Haorah, Parshat Naso, 161) states:

> The word "holy" in its masculine form is *kadosh* (קדוש) and in the feminine, *kadosha* (קדושה). If the man or woman wins, the letter ו is removed, and they are called *kadaish* (קדש) and *kadaisha* (קדשה), meaning "promiscuous man" and "promiscuous woman," as in the verse, "There shall not be any *kadaish* among the children of Israel" (Deuteronomy 23:18), and "There shall be no *kadaisha*" (*ibid.*).
>
> Thus, *znut* causes poverty, measure for measure. They removed the letter ו from the words that refer to them, and hence the letter ו is removed from the word *hon*, and what remains is *hein*. The Sages say (*Moed Katan* 8a), "*Hein* refers to death, as it is written, '*Hein*, your days are approaching death' (Deuteronomy 31:14)." And a man in poverty is considered as if he were dead.

Therefore, in referring to the Jewish people, who guarded themselves against sexual misconduct in Egypt, it is written, "I shall gird you
with fine linen" (Ezekiel 16:10). The word for "linen" (*shesh*, שש) can
also mean "six." Thus it refers to the letter ו, whose numerical value is
6. For, among these Jews, the men were *kadosh*, and the women *kadosha*.
They preserved the letter ו in the words that describe them.

God told Moses, "Go, return to Egypt, for all the men who
sought your life have died" (Exodus 4:19). The Sages explain in
Nedarim 64b that the men who sought Moses's life were Datan and
Abiram. They had not actually died, but had lost their wealth. From
this the Sages learn that poverty is considered the equivalent of death.

This concept is discussed by the Chafetz Chaim (quoted in
Rabbi Elchanan Wasserman's *Kovetz Maamarim*, 117). The Chafetz
Chaim cites the verse, "All the sinful of My people will die by the
sword" (Amos 9:10). According to the *Zohar*, this verse alludes to the
fact that the decree of the sword will be changed to a decree of
poverty. Hence, before the final redemption, poverty will increase
among Israel, as the verse says, "I shall leave in your midst a poor and
impoverished people, and they will trust in the name of *Hashem*"
(Zephaniah 3:12). The Chafetz Chaim adds:

> Those whose wealth still remains at their disposal should not rely on
> the vain fantasy that their money will stay in their hands forever.

Rabbi Nachman of Breslav (*Sefer HaMidot*, Inyan Mamon) finds
this concept of changing the death penalty into one of poverty reflected in Isaiah 48:9–10: "So that you shall not be cut off . . . I have
chosen for you the furnace of poverty." Instead of the punishment of
karas (death at the hands of heaven) that was destined (God forbid) to
destroy the Jewish people, the Holy one, blessed be he, chose to give
them poverty.

The same idea is hinted at in the verse, "I shall exalt You,
Hashem, because you rescued me (דליתני) and did not cause my enemy
to rejoice over me" (Psalms 30:2). The root of "rescue" (דלה) can also
mean "poor" (דל). Thus, the verse can be read: "because You made me
poor, and did not cause my enemy to rejoice over me [as he would
have rejoiced if I had died]."

4

Mockery Versus
Knowledge of God

So far we have learned how *znut* (sexual conduct and impropriety), causes a lessening of livelihood to both the individual and society as a whole. Another trait that has the same effect is *leitzanut,* which means cynical mockery.

In *Avodah Zarah* 18b we find, "Rabbi Katina said: Whoever indulges in *leitzanut,* his income lessens.'"

Mockery and light-headedness are closely related to *znut,* as the Sages tell us in *Pirkei Avot* (3:16): "Joking and light-headedness accustom a person to sexual misconduct."

While light-headedness and foolishness are bad traits which bring about economic collapse, the opposite traits—seriousness and a clear, receptive mind—bring in their wake blessings and economic abundance. The Sages say (*Sanhedrin* 92a):

> Whoever has a clear mind (*daat*) eventually becomes wealthy, as it is said (Proverbs 24:4) "With a clear mind, rooms will fill with all wealth, honor, and pleasantness."

In this verse, the words for "wealth" and "honor" are *hon* (הון) and *yakar* (יקר). As the verse indicates, these two words refer to the blessings of wealth. Their letters hint at the spiritual roots of these blessings, which are connected with holiness and purity.

As we have seen, ו, a letter of holiness and righteousness, occupies the center of the word *hon.*

If the initial letter of the word *yakar* (יקר), י is moved to the end, the word becomes *keri* (קרי), which means an emission of sperm and suggests the spiritual impurity of sexual misconduct. The י stands for wisdom (*chochma*), which, in kabbalistic terms, is the supernal source of knowledge of God (*daat*). Without the י, what remains is קר, which represents the forces of evil and impurity. In the word *yakar* (יקר), the holy spark of the letter י comes first, dominating the letters קר. In *keri* (קרי), the situation is reversed. The י comes last, under the domination of the negative forces.

When the holy force of wisdom dominates the forces of impurity, the result is *yakar*, honor and great wealth.

Kabbalah relates the letter ו in the name of God (יהוה) to the quality of *daat*, knowledge of God. The י in this name symbolizes *chochma*, the divine spirit of wisdom from which *daat* emanates. The relationship between *chochma* and *daat* is symbolized by the form of the letters י and ו. *Chochma*, the infinitesimal point of inspiration that begins the process of knowledge, is represented by the tiny י, which remains suspended in the air and does not reach the ground. The ו, on the other hand, does reach the ground; it symbolizes the quality of *daat*, which brings the spiritual concepts of supernal wisdom (*chochma*) down to earth, basing them in the concrete realities of this world.

The perfection of the quality of *daat* is embodied in the Jewish people, and for this reason the letter ו is especially connected with them. As the *Zohar* (Leviticus 29a) states: "Israel has knowledge of God (*deah*, a form of *daat*), and this is the letter ו." That is why the number six (the numerical value of ו) is so often associated with the Jewish people. The number of men of fighting age who received the Torah at Mount Sinai was 600,000; the Mishnah has six orders; and so on.

Thus, according to the *Zohar*, the letter ו is the basis of righteousness and purity, truth and peace. The source of these qualities is *daat*, and these qualities give a firm foundation to the economic life of the Jewish people.

The Maharal explains the destructive effect of *leitzanut* on one's sustenance (*Netivot Olam*, Netiv Haleitzanut, Ch. 2).

> One's sustenance is one's vitality and existence. *Leitzanut* involves trickery, vanity, and emptiness, acts of no substance, mere vanity and chaos. When a person is drawn to matters of *leitzanut* which are of no substance, it is fitting that his sustenance should be reduced to the point that it has no substance; it is fitting that his sustenance should be reduced to the point that it has no reality.

The Maharal makes a connection between one's sustenance and the basis of one's vitality. This connection is also revealed by the meaning of ו, the letter of holiness, which is the basis of sustenance and also the basis of life. Of the verse "And the tree of life was in the midst of the garden" (Genesis 2:9), the *Zohar* (Genesis 241) comments: "This is the letter ו."

The quality of the letter ו as the root of nourishment and life is also shown by the order of the Hebrew alphabet. After ו comes ז (זין), whose name is related to the root זנה, hinting at the concept of nourishment. Then comes ח, which is the initial of the word "life" (*chayim*, חיים). The perfection of nourishment and life are the foundation for goodness, which is hinted at by the next letter in the alphabet, ט, the initial of "good" (*tov*, טוב). These positive foundations are all brought to ruin by *leitzanut*.

The connection between *leitzanut* and loss of income is explained differently by Iyun Yaakov (Tractate *Avodah Zarah* 18b). *Leitzanut*, he points out, causes neglect of Torah study, and Torah study is the foundation of a person's success in life. As the Sages say (*Avodah Zarah* 19b):

> One who neglects the Torah because of his wealth, in the end will neglect it because of poverty. And whoever occupies himself with Torah, his holdings prosper.

Torah is the source of a person's spiritual and material life, as we learn from Proverbs 3:16, which personifies Torah as a woman: "Length of life is in her right hand; in her left, wealth and honor."

Leitzanut is the force that negates Torah. Where Torah is lacking, *leitzanut* will be found, as we read in *Pirkei Avot* (3:3):

> If two sit down and do not exchange words of Torah, this is a place of scoffers (*leitzim*), as it is said (Psalms 1:1): "Blessed is the man . . . who has not sat in a place of scoffers."

Neglect of Torah is considered *leitzanut* and light-headedness, because it shows that a person does not take the Torah seriously. As the Maharal explains in *Nishmat Adam*, his commentary on *Pirkei Avot*:

> [Neglect of Torah study] is considered *leitzanut* . . . [because it shows] that they regard the Torah as no more than the national wisdom and religion of the Jewish people, equivalent to the customs, wisdom, and religions [of other nations].

Failure to appreciate the holiness of the Torah led to the destruction of the Holy Temple (Beit Hamikdash). This, according to the Sages, is the meaning of God's statement, cited by an Aggadic passage in the Talmud (*Nedarim* 81a) that the land of Israel was made desolate because the scholars did not recite the benediction over Torah study.

Unfortunately, the attitude that Torah is just another form of wisdom, with the consequent lack of respect for Torah study, is found in various circles in Israel today. This undoubtedly injures the economic stability of the country. This cause-and-effect relationship, as we have seen, was long ago revealed by the Sages.

The destructive force of *leitzanut*, which causes economic collapse and damages creativity and existence, is revealed by the letters of the word "scoffer": *leitz* (לץ). In the alphabet, these letters precede the letters מק: ל precedes מ, and צ precedes ק.

The root מק indicates disintegration and rot. The prophet Zachariah describes how the military hordes led by Gog and Magog will descend upon Jerusalem. Before they can carry out their evil plans, they will be struck by a great plague. The linguistic root מק plays a central role in the verse describing this plague: "Their flesh will rot (המק) while they stand on their legs; their eyes will rot (תמקנה) in their sockets; their tongue will rot (תמק) in their mouth" (Zachariah 14:12).

The scoffer (*leitz*) causes disintegration and rot (מק) to the possessions (*yakum*, יקום) and to the permanent existence (*kiyum*, קיום), of a man or a society. (*Yakum* and *kiyum* are spelled with the same Hebrew letters. Their basic two-letter root is קם, the reverse of מק.)

The letters of the word *leitz* (לץ) are the same as those of the word "shadow" (*tzel*, צל). This suggests that the spiritual root of the scoffer is emptiness and shadow, without substance or foundation, mere vain fantasy. *Leitzanut* causes a person to be cut off from the source of existence and true reality; his life becomes superficial, cut off from its roots.

This rotten foundation will cause the scoffers' complete collapse in the Messianic Age, when the light of truth of God's divine presence (*Shechinah*) will be revealed. Thus, in *Sotah* 42a, the Sages say that the scoffers will not merit to welcome the *Shechinah*.

The holiness of the *Shechinah* is what gives sustenance (*parnassah*) to the Jewish people. This is revealed by the numerical value of "the *shechinah*" and the linguistic root of the word *parnassah* (פרנס).

HaShechinah (השכינה): 5 + 300 + 20 + 10 + 50 + 5 = 390
Root of *parnassah* (פרנס): 80 + 200 + 50 + 60 = 390

For this reason, the main blessing of vitality and sustenance of the Jewish people is in the land of Israel, for this is where the *Shechinah* dwells. If the Jewish people detract from the holiness of the *Shechinah* through sins based on *leitzanut* and light-headedness, the *Shechinah* departs from Israel, taking with it the source of their vitality and sustenance.

The connection between sustenance and the spiritual wholeness of a person is revealed by the numerical value of the words "sustenance" (*parnassah*, פרנסה) and "soul" (*neshama*, נשמה).

Parnassah (פרנסה): 80 + 200 + 50 + 60 + 5 = 395
Neshamah (נשמה): 50 + 300 + 40 + 5 = 395

According to Kabbalah, the connection between the foundation of life, on the one hand, and holiness, on the other, is revealed by analysis of the letter ק. The name of this letter, *kof*, is spelled קף. The Sages say that in its positive aspect the ק stands for holiness (*kedusha*, קדושה). On the negative side, this letter symbolizes frivolity and *leitzanut*, for the word *kof* also means "monkey," an animal that plays at being a man (*Zohar*, Parshat Trumah). The letters of the word *kof* (קף) have the numerical value of 180, which equals ten times the numerical value of the word "alive" (*chai*, חי).

kof (קף): 100 + 80 = 180
chai (חי): 8 + 10 = 18, 18 × 10 = 180

Ten is the number of completion and perfection. Hence, ten times eighteen symbolizes the perfection of the force of life. On the negative side, 180 is ten times the numerical value of "sin" (*chet*, חטא).

chet (חטא): 8 + 9 + 1 = 18; 10 × 18 = 180

Through holiness, a person builds for himself and for the world the foundations of life. Through sin and frivolity, a person destroys these foundations.

The number 180 is also the numerical value of "scoffer" (*leitzan* ליצן).

leitzan (ליצן): 30 + 10 + 90 + 50 = 180

This shows the destructive power of *leitzanut*. It can undermine all the positive forces symbolized by the number 180.

"Blessed is the man who has not walked in the counsel of the wicked, nor stood in the way of sinners, nor sat in the place of scoffers" (Psalms 1:1). The Sages tell us (*Avodah Zarah* 18b) that "the place of scoffers" refers to theaters and circuses.

If people involve themselves in and habituate themselves to a life of vanity and chaos, this brings upon the world the quality of *din*, strict judgment, with its attendant punishments. The Maharal explains in *Netivot Olam* (Netiv Haleitzanut, Ch. 2):

> Through the quality of *leitzanut*, it is fitting that the quality of strict judgment should strike the world . . . for *leitzanut* is the opposite of judgment. *Leitzanut* means mere pretense and mockery, while judgment is completely necessary, the inevitable conclusion of a logical process. This is the essence of judgment. Thus judgment is the opposite of *leitzanut*, which is chaotic and completely insubstantial.
>
> Therefore (as a result of *leitzanut*) strict judgment comes upon a person or upon the whole world.

5

Wisdom, the Source of Wealth

ON A DEEPER LEVEL, the connection between *leitzanut* and economic destruction is explained in kabbalistic terms. The abundance of nourishment and sustenance depends on the force of *binah*. (*Binah*, understanding, is the second of the ten *sefirot* through which the creative power of God descends to reach this world.) Rabbi Yosef Chaim, in his work *Ben Yehoyada*, uses this concept to elucidate the following Talmud passage (*Bava Metzia* 59a):

> A man should always be careful to honor his wife, because blessing is found in a man's home only for the sake of his wife; as it is said (Genesis 12:16): "He benefited Abram for her sake." Thus Rava told the people of Mechoza: "Honor your wives, so that you will become rich."

The basis of woman is the power of *binah* (understanding or intuition). In *Niddah* 45b, the Sages derive this from the similarity between the word *binah* (בינה) and the root of "build" (בנה). On the verse "[God] built the side . . . to be a woman" (Genesis 2:22), the Sages comment, "[The use of the term] "built" teaches us that woman was given extra *binah*, more than man."

On this Talmud passage, *Ben Yehoyada* comments:

> Nourishment (*mazon*) and sustenance (*parnassah*) come from *binah*, which is the foundation of the first ה in the holy Name (יהוה). The ה is with the woman, for the word for "man" (*ish*, איש) and the word for "woman" (*ishah*, אשה) both derive from "fire" (*esh*, אש); man, by adding

the letter י; woman, by adding the letter ה; hence, if a man and wife are meritorious, together they form one of the names of God: יה.

This is why the Talmud cites the verse, "He benefited Abram for her sake." The expression "for her sake" (בעבורה) can be read as בעבורה: "for the sake of ה." That is, he benefited Abram for the sake of the ה, which is in the woman, who embodies the secret of *binah*.

On the Talmud's expression "for the sake of his wife," *Ben Yeho-yada* says:

> The expression "for the sake of" (*bishvil*, בשביל) can be broken into two parts: the prefix ב, meaning "by means of," and the word "path" (*shvil*, שביל). That is, [blessing is found in a man's house] through the "path" of his wife, who serves as a channel or path through which the abundance of goodness passes.

Ben Yehoyada goes on to point out that the woman's role as the source of a blessed plentifulness of sustenance is revealed in the numerical value of the word "woman" (*ishah*, אשה), which is equal to that of the two words "blessing" and "bread" (*berachah, lechem,* ברכה, לחם), when we add the *kollel*.

ishah (אשה): 1 + 300 + 5 = 306
brachah, lechem (ברכה, לחם): 2 + 200 + 20 + 5 + 30 + 8 + 40 = 305;
$$305 + 1 (kollel) = 306$$

Leitzanut draws a person away from seriousness and inward contemplation. It distracts his attention from truth and reality. The life of a scoffer (לץ) is in a shadow (צל): It is external and superficial, cut off from reality and truth. The understanding of the heart is beyond him. This separation from understanding (*binah*) cuts a person off from the letter ה, the letter of *binah* in the name of God, the letter of life and sustenance.

The fact that the letter ה is the source of abundance and nourishment is hinted at by a verse in Genesis (47:23): Joseph had been appointed to take charge of the economy of Egypt. When the people ran out of grain and had nothing to plant, they came to him. He gave them seed for the next year's crop, telling them: "Here is seed for you." The expression "Here is" (*hei,* הא) is also the name of the letter ה. It is as if he had said, "The letter ה is the source of seed and abundance for you."

Superficially, lack of contemplation of the truth and reality of the Holy One, blessed be he, as He is revealed in this world, borders on idol worship. This defect causes the Jewish people to suffer a heavy burden of taxes. The Midrash finds a hint of this in the first verse of Lamentations, which describes the situation of the Jewish people when the First Temple was destroyed. The verse reads: "How did she sit isolated, the city which had thronged with people. . . . The queen of the countries has become a tributary."

The Midrash notes the relationship between the word "symbol" (*semmel*, סמל) and the expression "become a tributary" (*lemas*, למס).

> Because Israel worshiped idols, they became a tributary. "Became a tributary" and "symbol" are the same thing. They are spelled with the same letters. (Midrash Rabba, Lamentations, Parshah 1:20).

The word "symbol" (*semmel*, סמל) represents externality, which is connected with the power of Satan, who is on the left side. The letters ס and שׁ are interchangeable. Thus, the word "symbol" (*semmel*, סמל) is almost identical to the word "left" (*smol*, סמאל).

The connection between *semmel* and Satan is further revealed by the two-letter base of the word סמל *semmel*: סמ. This is identical to the two-letter base of Samael (סמאל), another name for the angel of evil.

The letter ל stands for "heart" (*lev*, לב), as is stated in the Tannaitic work *Otiot D'Rabbi Akiva* (ל). In the word *semmel*, the two evil letters, סמ, come first and dominate the ל, the heart.

The letter ס is closely related to צ, since both are formed with the same parts of the mouth. Thus, the base סמ is nearly identical to צמ, which is the base of the word "limitation" (*tzimtzum*, צמצום). This fact is also shown by the shape of the letters סמ; both are completely closed on all sides. They thus represent limitation, a smallness that surrounds, confines, and closes off.

The numerical value of סמ is 100 (סמ: 60 + 40 = 100). This is also the numerical value of the letter ק (*kof*), which stands for "surrounding" (*hekef*, הקף) and limitation.

We have seen that the letter ק also stands for scoffing (*leitzanut*) and frivolity. This impure force of the ק is a source of enmity for Israel, as can be seen by the fact that the letters of "enemy" (*tzar*, צר) directly follow those of *kof* (קף) in the Hebrew alphabet: צ follows פ; ר follows ק.

We have seen that the two-letter root סמ represents a confining force of impurity (*tuma*), a force that hides the ways of God's providence from the eyes of man. For this reason, the Sages ordained that the Jewish man should recite one hundred benedictions each day, thus revealing the providence of God. These benedictions counter the power of סמ, whose numerical value is 100.

The impure force of סמ causes taxation (*mas*, מס) to come upon Israel. The punishment matches the sin. If one sins by connecting oneself with the impure *klipa* (shell) of סמ, this is tantamount to idol worship. One worships the outer appearance (*semmel*, סמל) of things. The danger of idol worship is that a person gives himself over to its oppressive domination. The result is the oppressive burden of taxation.

The skin or "hide" (*klaf*, קלף) of *tuma* is what causes a person distress (*maitzar*, מצר). This is revealed by the letters of the word *maitzar*, which directly follow those of *klaf* in the Hebrew alphabet.

מ follows ל

צ follows פ

ר follows ק

The word *klipa* (קליפה, lit., shell) is the general kabbalistic term for the forces of impurity (*tuma*) and evil. It can be analyzed as the word *klaf* (קלף) with the addition of the letters י and ה. That is, the *klipa* is like a "hide" (קלף) that covers up the name of God, יה.

The numerical value of *klipa* (קליפה) is equal to that of "pig" (*chazir*, חזיר).

klipa (קליפה): 100 + 30 + 10 + 80 + 5 = 225

chazir (חזיר):   8 + 7 + 10 + 200 = 225

The numerical equivalence of these two words teaches us that their inner content is similar: Both are based on constricted and polluted materiality.

The pig (*chazir*), according to Midrash Rabba (Vayikra, Parshat Shmini), symbolizes the sovereignty of materialism, the rule of Edom (Rome), which to this day oppresses Israel with its heavy yoke. All this only comes about through the *tuma* that Israel contracts because of its sins. It is these sins that give strength to the *klipot*.

6

The Eye:
Entry Point of Desires

THE NUMERICAL VALUE of the word "symbol" (*semmel*, סמל) is 130. This equals the numerical value of "eye" (*ayin*, עין).

semmel (סמל): 60 + 40 + 30 = 130
ayin (עין):   70 + 10 + 50 = 130

This teaches us that the basis of the impure force of the external symbol flows from the visual action of the eye. The eye is quickly impressed by external appearance, and thus serves as an entranceway for the forces of superficiality and *tuma*. These, as we have seen, are the forces of *tuma* of סמ, whose main effect is through the superficial activity of "magic," or sleight-of-hand (*kessem*, קסם). We have seen how ק and סמ both represent forces of impurity. The word *kessem* combines both of these elements.

The power of the eye awakens strong appetites and "yearnings" (*kisufim*, כיסופים). The three-letter root of *kisufim* is כסף. These letters follow directly after the letters of *ayin* in the alphabet.

כ follows י

ס follows נ

פ follows ע

This illustrates the Sages' saying: "The eye sees, and then the heart desires" (Bamidbar Rabba 10:2).

The main human appetites are rooted in sexuality, money, and possessions. With regard to possessions (*mamon*, ממון), a person is never satisfied; the more he has, the more he wants. The Sages say: "If he has a hundred, he wants two hundred" (Kohelet Rabba 1:34). The Chida (חיד'א) points out that the insatiable appetite for possessions is reflected in the word itself. If we write out in full the names of this word's letters, we find that each letter is spelled by doubling the letter itself. ממון is spelled מם, מם, וו, נן. In other words, the second letter of each letter-name is identical to the first. This teaches us that no matter how much *mamon* a person has, his feeling of lack remains.

The numerical value of *mamon* (ממן) is equal to that of "for taxation" (למס) and "symbol" (סמל).

mamon (ממן): 40 + 40 + 50 = 130
lemas (למס):   30 + 40 + 60 = 130
semmel (סמל): 60 + 40 + 30 = 130

The numerical value of "eye" (*ayin*, עין), 130, equals that of "poverty" (*oni*, עני).

ayin (עין): 70 + 10 + 50 = 130
oni (עני):   70 + 50 + 10 = 130

This teaches us that the basis of poverty is the eye. The eye causes a person to "collapse" (התמוטטות). Stupidity and impurity (טם) lead to a downfall and collapse (מט).

Another word whose numerical value is 130 is *kal* (קל, "light, easy"). It is also the two-letter root of the word "ruin" (*kilkul*, קלקל). This shows the connection between light-mindedness (קלות הדעת) and ruination (קלקל), both of which are rooted in the superficiality of the eye.

If a person is light-minded, he is close to being a scoffer (*leitz*, לץ). This is reflected in the closeness of the letters of "light" (*kal*, קל) and "scoffer" (*leitz*, לץ) in the alphabet. The letter ל is common to both words; the other letter of *kal* is ק, and the other letter of *leitz* is צ. These two letters are adjacent in the alphabet.

The letters of "light" (*kal*, קל) immediately precede those of "bitter" (*mar*, מר) in the alphabet.

ק precedes ר

ל precedes מ

This teaches us that bitterness in life results from light-mindedness.

The word *kilkul* (קלקל) means "ruin," "spoilage," or "sin." If one spoils one's soul through sin, one becomes greatly embittered. Thus, the letters of the root of "embitterment" (*hitmarmerut*, התמרמרות), מרמר, directly follow the letters of *kilkul* in the alphabet.

מ follows ל

ר follows ק

מ follows ל

ר follows ק

The foundation of "ruination, sin" (*kilkul*, קלקל) is in the two eyes. Thus, the numerical value of *kilkul* is twice that of "eye" (*ayin*, עין).

kilkul (קלקל):   100 + 30 + 100 + 30 = 260
ayin (עין): 70 + 10 + 50 = 130; 2 × 130 = 260

This quality of *kilkul* limits and closes off a person's heart, bringing him to collapse (God forbid). The two-letter root of the words for "stupidity" (*timtum*, טמטם) and "impurity" (*tuma*, טומאה) is טם. By simply reversing these two letters, we have מט, the two-letter root of "collapse" (התמוטטות). Stupidity and impurity (טם) lead to a downfall and collapse (מט).

When a person lacks the power of *bina* (understanding), which "builds" (*boneh*) and creates, he is beset with troubles and problems. These, in turn, arouse him to begin thinking at last about his way of life, which brought him to this undesirable state. This type of thought, which a person undertakes in time of trouble, is discussed by Rabbi Eliahu Dessler in his work *Michtav MiEliahu* (Part 3, 339). In this passage, Rabbi Dessler discusses the trend toward materialism and the tendency to place faith in secular learning that preceded the Holocaust.

When *Hashem*, blessed be he, saw that this form of idol worship was gaining the upper hand, he gave the command that all these preparations (for success, i.e., secular training) should cease to be effective. And it came to pass that he created mass unemployment, so that the "trained professionals" were left with nothing. And when he perceived that the blind still did not have their eyes opened, because they had no desire to see, he went further and showed them a whole country (Germany) where previously there had been practically no poverty among our brothers the Jews, and where all, Orthodox and non-religious alike, had "prepared themselves for life," as they thought, from early youth. All of them had taken the most full and painstaking care to prepare themselves for the needs of this world. And it came to pass that he sent the implacable enemy, to convey the message: "Where now are all your preparations? Did the professor teach you how to be skillful at window-washing?"

The examples could be multiplied. It was not for nothing that *Hashem* sent suffering to his people. He only did it as a means to reveal to them the right way of life.

Troubles and sufferings are like a window through which one can perceive God's providence, which metes out punishment for the sins of individuals or societies. The kabbalistic works point out that this is reflected in the similarity between the words *tzohar* (צהר), meaning "window" or "glowing" and *tzura* (צרה), meaning "catastrophe." The *tzura* serves as a *tzohar* by which our eyes can perceive the revelation of divine Providence.

If the Jewish people are meritorious, they are able to perceive God's providence in times of abundant blessing and security, as the verse says: "You shall eat your bread to satiety, and you shall dwell in security in your land" (Leviticus 26:5). Economic comfort and national security are the blessings that result from fulfilling the *mitzvot* of the Torah.

If the Jewish people are not meritorious, they must be shown the ways of God's providence through their troubles, as we read in Midrash Rabba (Lamentations, Petichata Rabbati), which expounds on the verse, "Judea was exiled through poverty" (Lamentations 1:3):

> The Holy One, blessed be he, said to Israel: "If you had been meritorious, you would have read in the Torah, 'and you shall dwell in security.' Now that you are not meritorious, you must read, 'Judea was exiled through poverty.'"

The connection between "secure" (*betach*, בטח) and "holy" (*kadosh*, קדוש) is revealed by spelling out the names of the letters of *betach*.

The letters of *betach* (בטח) are spelled בית, חית, טית. As *Ben Ish Chai* points out (Drashot Al haTorah, Vayyikra, Parshat Bechukotai), these are the only three letters in the Hebrew alphabet whose names are completed by the letters ית. The numerical value of ית is 410, which equals the numerical value of "holy" (*kadosh*, קדוש).

ית: $10 + 400 = 410$
kadosh (קדוש): $100 + 4 + 6 + 300 = 410$

Furthermore, the letters of *betach* are the initials of the words house (*bayit*, בית), goodness (*tovah*, טובה), and life (*chayim*, חיים). The basis of these three things is holiness. Thus, we learn that security in the home, and goodness and life in the world, depend upon holiness (*kedusha*). The sins of sexual misconduct, light-headedness, and *leitzanut* (scoffing) damage the foundation of *kedusha* and rob Israel of security.

Without a foundation of faith and *kedusha*, the constructions of man have no enduring existence.

> If *Hashem* does not build the house, those who build it work in vain; if *Hashem* does not guard a city, the watchman watches in vain (Psalms 127:1).

Evil—i.e., "deviation" (*sareh*, סרה) from the straight path—arouses and causes "destruction" (*heres*, הרס), as can be seen from the fact that these two words are spelled with the same letters. This teaches us that the root of destruction and ruin is in sin (*chet*, חטא).

The concealing force of "wickedness" (*roa*, רוע) in the world produces a "skin" (*or*, עור) or "blindness" (*ivur*, עור) that covers the light of *kedusha*. Thus, the letters of these three words are the same.

The source of these negative powers is sin (*chet*, חטא). This word is composed of two parts. The final א, *alef*, stands for God, who is the *aluf*, "chief," of the world. The first two letters, reversed, spell טח, which means "plasters." Thus, *chet* is something that plasters over and conceals the influence of God in the world.

In other words, the powers of evil set up a smokescreen that conceals the light of God. This "smoke" (*ashan*, עשן) is the source of the "punishment" (*onesh*, ענש) that is visited upon an individual or a society. The concealment (*seter*, סתר) of the light causes destruction (*seter*, סתר) of the holy Temple.

Leitzanut is one of the greatest factors that conceals the face of the divine Presence (*shechinah*) and God's providence in the world. *Leitzanut* casts a shadow over the eye of providence, as it were. This is shown by the fact that "scoffer" (*leitz*, לץ) and "shadow" (*tzel*, צל) have the same letters. The identity of the letters points to a cause-and-effect relationship.

The great destruction brought about by the quality of *leitzanut* can be seen by the fact that the numerical value of this word is equal to that of "force" (*tokef*, תוקף).

leitzanut (ליצנות): 30 + 10 + 90 + 50 + 6 + 400 = 586
tokef (תוקף):   400 + 6 + 100 + 80 = 586

Tokef alludes to the forceful quality of strict judgment (*din*), which is aroused in the world as a result of the sin of *leitzanut*. *Ben Yehoyada* (*Avodah Zarah* 73b), citing the Arizal, states:

> Leitzanut causes dominance of the forces of strict judgment (*dinim*). These judgments are the 120 permutations of the name *Elokim* (אלקים, the name of God which represents his quality of strict judgment; this name consists of five letters, and produces a total of 120 words through all the possible combinations of letters). This same number (120) is the numerical value of the word "scoffer" (*leitz*, לץ). The *leitz* increases these forces of strict judgment and raises them up opposite the quality of *keter*. (This kabbalistic term, meaning "crown," refers to the highest level of emanation of the divine creative force.) Then the illumination of *keter* ceases to illumine below.

The world of *keter* is the ultimate source of all abundance. The foundation of sustenance (*kalkalah*) depends upon the maintenance of a connection between the supernal world of *keter* and this lower world of ours. This is revealed by the two-letter root of the word "sustenance" (*kalkalah*, כלכלה): כל. The Talmud (Tractate *Shabbat*, Haboneh) states that the first of these two letters, כ, stands for the world of *keter* (כתר). The second letter, ל, refers to the heart (*lev*, לב) of the person or the world (*Otiot d'Rabbi Akiva*, s.v., ל). Together, the letters כל refer to the qualities of *yesod*, "foundation," and holiness (*Kehillat Yaakov*, כל). When a person is pure and holy, the world of *keter* (כ) is unified with the person's heart (ל), and this unity is reflected in the world.

7

Amalek and Related Forces

THE "SPOILAGE" (*kilkul*, קלקל) of one's actions through sin causes destruction of sustenance. The root of *kilkul* is קל. Here the letter ק, representing the evil force of frivolity and scoffing (*leitzanut*), dominates the letter ל, representing the heart.

The letter ק can be analyzed into two elements. Above is כ, which stands for the supernal world of *keter*, which should be the head and should be placed above. The long line that descends from the כ indicates that the *yetzer hara*, the evil inclination, drags the supernal force of כ down into matters of gross materiality.

The *tuma*, impurity, of the letter ק has its source in the wicked nation of Amalek, whose whole goal is to cover and hide the eye of Providence, as is written (Exodus 17:16): "The hand is on the throne of God; *Hashem* has a war against Amalek throughout the generations."

The negative force of Amalek (עמלק) is hinted at by the letters of the word. It can be divided into ע (*ayin*, eye) and מלק (*malak*, sever). The desire of Amalek is to sever the eye of Providence.

According to the *Zohar*, this name can also be divided into עמל (*amal*, labor) and ק. This hints that the main will and labor of Amalek is the impure force represented by ק, which is the foundation of *tuma* of קר.

Through these evil forces, Amalek robs Israel of abundant livelihood, as is stated by *Kehillat Yaakov* (Amalek). Amalek draws its strength from the sins of Israel. These sins cause a covering (*kisui*,

כסוי) and a shadow (*tzel*, צל) over the light of God's providence. This is shown by the letters that precede those of "Amalek" in the alphabet. They spell כס (covering) and צל (shadow).

כ precedes ל

ס precedes ע

צ precedes ק

ל precedes מ

The letters that follow those of "Amalek" in the alphabet are פנמר.

פ follows ע

נ follows מ

מ follows ל

ר follows ק

Here, the letters for "bull" (*par*, פר), symbolizing strictness and judgment, surround and restrict the letters for "manna" (*man*, מן), symbolizing abundant sustenance.

The connection between "covering" (כסה) and "judgment" (*din*, דין) is revealed by the fact that the former follow the latter in the alphabet:

כ follows י

ס follows נ

ה follows ד

The strength of Amalek grows from the falsity that is in the world. Falsity is prevalent wherever the light of truth is concealed by the shadow of materiality. Thus, Amalek succeeds in robbing Israel of sustenance. That is why the Torah puts the laws of honesty in weights and measures (Deuteronomy 25:13–16) immediately adjacent to the commandment of wiping out the memory of Amalek (*ibid.*, 17–19).

Falsity (*sheker*, שקר) is the root of the *tuma* represented by the letters קר. Falsity brings into the world the power of קר, which is that of Amalek. *Kehillat Yaakov* (Amalek) states:

> Through the quality of falsity, people arouse the *klipa* (impure force) of Amalek, as is stated by the Sages. This is why [just before the commandment to wipe out the memory of Amalek] the Torah says, "You shall not have in your pocket a weighing-stone and a weighing-stone, one large and one small" (for the purpose of cheating in weights) (Deuteronomy 25:13); for the *klipa* of Amalek robs Israel of sustenance.

The foundation of evil in *sheker* (falsity), according to the *Zohar*, are the letters קר. These letters are associated with the *tuma* of Amalek, as we read in Deuteronomy 25:13: "Remember what Amalek did to you on the way, when you went out of Egypt; for he fell upon you (קרך) on the way."

The essence of Amalek (עמלק) is to make crooked (לעקם) the honesty (יושר) and truth of Israel (ישראל) and Jeshurun (ישורון).

It is Amalek (עמלק) who blocks (מעקל) the channels of abundance, preventing them from pouring out blessing upon Israel.

The force of Amalek also causes a person the *tuma* of seminal emission (*keri*, קרי), which is based on the letters קר. The letters of *keri* also spell *rik* (ריק), emptiness. Because of *keri*, *rik* comes to a person. It causes him impoverishment, as is seen by the fact that the letters of "impoverished," *rash* (רש), immediately follow קר in the alphabet.

ר follows ק

ש follows ר

Reversed, the letters of *rash* spell "prince" (*sar*, שר), which indicates governance and control. When a person governs and controls his urges, he cancels the evil decree of poverty.

The force that prevents livelihood from reaching Israel, Amalek, is also the main enemy of Israel, falling upon the Jewish people and attacking them at their moment of weakness. This happens when the children of Israel sin, becoming attached to the bad deeds and *tuma* of Amalek. If the children of Israel cheat in their business dealings, they are handed over to Amalek. Thus, Rashi explains why the Torah places the commandment against false weights and measures just before the recounting of Amalek's attack on Israel (Deuteronomy 25:13–19): Rashi states:

> If you have cheated with measures and weights, you should worry about harassment from the enemy, as it is said (Proverbs 11:3–4): "Deceptive scales are an abomination to *Hashem*. . . . When willful disobedience comes, humiliation will come."

The Maharal explains why the use of false weights and measures brings Amalek to prey against Israel. He writes (*Gur Aryeh*, Deuteronomy 25:17):

> You must know that when the Holy One, blessed be he, created and established the world, He measured, weighed, and balanced every created thing, providing each thing with its own existence, with nothing encroaching upon anything else at all, not even by a hairsbreadth. This is

how it was with all that exists, and this is the divine measure which he measured out to all. Therefore, when a person cheats with the measurements and quantities by which people conduct business, the enemy attacks. Before this, the enemy had a measured territory with which the Holy One, blessed be he, had provided him, and to which he was not to add; he should not have expanded his border to encroach upon the border of another nation beyond what had been measured out to him and established for him by the Holy One, blessed be he. But when one cheats in measures, this means that, with regard to him, there is no longer any accurate measurement; either he adds to the measure, or he detracts from it. Then, in the same way, the enemy attacks and overpowers him, going beyond the measured borders, i.e., exceeding the established measure.

Amalek, whose power of *tuma* robs Israel of abundance, also detracts from her security and peace (*shalom*). These two negative functions are interdependent, for peace and abundance of sustenance are nourished from the same root. Ben Ish Chai explains this in his *Drashot Al Hatorah* (Parshat Pinchas, 194):

> It is known that abundance and sustenance are referred to as "peace" (*shalom*); for abundance comes about through the combination of the name יהוה (indicating *chesed*, kindness) with the name of judgment (אדנ-י) in such a way that they strike against each other. This produces the number of "peace" (*shalom*, שלום).
>
> Therefore it is written: "He puts your border at peace; he satisfies you with the richness of wheat" (Psalms 147:14). And this is why the gift of *shalom* was given to Pinchas (see Numbers 26:12). By his act of zeal he separated Israel from the sin of *znut* (sexual misconduct). Through this they received abundance of sustenance, which is referred to as *shalom*. Otherwise, they would have been deprived of abundance because of that sin.

The dependence of sustenance (*parnassah*, פרנסה) upon the holiness of the name of God (יהוה) that indicates *chesed* can be derived from the numerical values of these two words. The "reduced" of *parnassah* is equal to the numerical value of *Hashem*.

parnassah (פרנסה): 80 + 200 + 50 + 60 + 5; small gematria:
        8 + 2 + 5 + 6 + 5 = 26
Hashem (יהוה): 10 + 5 + 6 + 5 = 26

When the numerical value of *parnassah* is compressed still further by adding together the two digits of the number 26, it equals 8. This number symbolizes the upper world, which is beyond nature.

Thus, the source of *parnassah* depends upon the upper world.

The method of *gematria* that adds together the digits of large numbers to arrive at a one-digit number reveals the equivalence of *parnassah* and goodness (*tov*, טוב).

parnassah (פרנסה): 80 + 200 + 50 + 60 + 5; 8 + 2 + 5 + 6 + 5 = 26;

$$2 + 6 = 8$$

tov (טוב):   9 + 6 + 2 = 17; 1 + 7 = 8

This equivalence teaches us that *parnassah* depends upon the perfection of the quality of *yesod* (foundation), which is referred to by the word "goodness" (*Kehillat Yaakov*, טוב).

Eight is also the numerical value of the word *Torah*.

Torah (תורה): 400 + 6 + 200 + 5; 4 + 6 + 2 + 5 = 17; 1 + 7 = 8

Torah is the source of *tov* (goodness) and *parnassah*.

By combining the numerical values of *Torah* (תורה), *tov* (טוב), *Hashem* (יהוה), and *neshamah* (נשמה, soul), we arrive at the number 36. We have already seen that *tov*, *Torah*, and *Hashem* all contract to the number 8. The same is true with the word *neshama*.

neshama (נשמה): 50 + 300 + 40 + 5 = 395; 3 + 9 + 5 = 17; 1 + 7 = 8

Thus, these four words, each of which has the numerical value of 8, total 32. When we add 4 for the number of words, we have 36. Six, as we have seen, represents the *tzadik*. When this number is multiplied by itself (6 × 6 = 36), it represents the perfection of the quality of *tzadik*, by whose merit the world exists. That is why there are thirty-six *tzadikim* in each generation, by whose merit the world endures.

A breach of the peace (*shalom*) because of disagreement (*machloket*) and fighting robs Israel of *parnassah*. Thus, the Shlah (*Shnei Luchot Haberit*, p. 242) states: "One *machloket* pushes away one hundred *parnassot*."

The letters of *machloket* (מחלוקת), when rearranged, spell "portion" or "death" (מות, חלק). This teaches us that *machloket* kills every good portion for Israel.

Why did the Shlah choose the number 100? Apparently, he wished to suggest that the root of *machloket* is the power of Satan, symbolized by the letters סמ, whose numerical value is 100. This is also the numerical value of the letter ק, which stands for the root of the power of *tuma*, spiritual impurity.

The three-letter linguistic root of *machloket*, as well as other words having to do with dispute and divisiveness, is חלק. These letters can be analyzed as חל (*chal*, take effect) and ק. That is, by means of חלק, the evil power of ק takes effect, pushing away one hundred *parnassot*.

The numerical value of חלק is 138, which equals the numerical value of "leavened bread" (*chametz*, חמץ).

חלק: $8 + 30 + 100 = 138$
chametz (חמץ): $8 + 40 + 90 = 138$

Chametz symbolizes the *yetzer hara*, the evil inclination. This equivalence of numerical values shows that the evil inclination to pride and sexual misconduct, as symbolized by *chametz*, is the source of divisiveness and causeless hatred.

We may further observe that the Shlah's statement that one *machloket* pushes away one hundred *parnassot* is intended to allude to a similar dictum: "One scoffing remark (*leitzanut*) pushes away one hundred moral admonishments (*tochachot*)." *Leitzanut*, like *machloket*, adversely affects a person's *parnassah*. In fact, disputes among people lead to the development of *leitzanut*, as each person attempts to belittle his antagonist. This connection between *machloket* and *leitzanut* is reflected in the numerical value of these words.

"in *machloket*" (במחלוקת): $2 + 40 + 8 + 30 + 6 + 100 + 400 = 586$
leitzanut (ליצנות): $30 + 10 + 90 + 50 + 6 + 400 = 586$

Through disagreement and fighting, the evil of *leitzanut* takes root, and with these developments the economic foundations of a home or a society are shaken.

We previously discussed the Maharal's explanation of the connection between unfair weights and measures and military attack by the enemy. The blurring of boundaries caused by inaccurate measurement in business transactions leads to the breakdown of national borders through military invasion. Similarly, a severe danger is caused by *machloket* within a society. As each side of the dispute attempts to invade the domain of the opposing party, the channels of abundance are set askew, and the society suffers loss of *parnassah*.

The process is similar regarding the sin of *znut*, sexual misconduct. Here, too, creative forces are diverted in the wrong direction, as is indicated by the linguistic root of *znut*, זנה, which means to deviate from the straight path. As a result, the supernal channels that should bring down *parnassah* to this world are likewise diverted.

Machloket results from lack of faith in the fact that the Creator of the world exercises providence, giving every single person and nation the right place and the right tools for development and growth. A person imbued with this faith would not attempt to encroach upon his neighbor's boundary or to injure him. Thus, we see that faith (*emunah*) is the foundation of existence and sustenance. As we read in Proverbs 28:20: "A man of faith has many blessings, and he who rushes to become rich will not be acquitted."

Truth (*emet*, אמת) is the foundation upon which the world stands. If one fails to acknowledge the א (*alef*), symbolizing God, who is the Chief, (*aluf*) of the world, one removes the א from *emet*. What remains is "dead" (*met*, מת), complete depletion and destruction.

The Sages tell us that the "man of faith" referred to in Proverbs was our teacher Moses, through whom we received the holy Torah. The Midrash states:

> We find that whenever a person is trustworthy, the Holy One, blessed he be, grants blessings through him. . . . The "man of faith" is Moses. Whatever he was given charge of was blessed, because he was trustworthy. (Midrash Rabba, Shemot, 51:1).

In Kabbalah, Moses is considered to represent the inner meaning of the prime trait of Jacob: truth. This is revealed by spelling out the names of the letters that form "Moses." Their total numerical value is equal to that of the term "the truth" (*haemet*).

Moses (משה), spelled מם שין הא: 40 + 40 + 300 + 10 + 50 + 5 + 1
$$= 446$$
haemet (האמת):   5 + 1 + 40 + 400 = 446

The equivalence of numerical values teaches us that Moses is the foundation of truth, and through him the Torah of truth was given to Israel.

The same Midrash goes on to say that the verse "He who rushes to become rich will not be acquitted" refers to Korach, who challenged the truthfulness of Moses. Korach wanted to take more than his due. The Midrash states:

> He was a Levite, and he tried to take the position of High Priest. And what was his end? "The earth opened its mouth [and swallowed him]" (Numbers 16:32).

The name Korach (קרח) is made up of the letters קר and ח. According to Kabbalah, this indicates the evil forces symbolized by קר and ח, the initial of "sin" (*chet*, חטא). These forces took control of Korach and brought him to his downfall. It was Korach who left a "bald spot" (קרחה) in the Jewish people because of his bad deeds.

Korach tried to encroach upon a sphere that did not belong to him. He became the symbol of *machloket* based on ulterior motives. In the end, he and all that belonged to him were destroyed. Moses, by contrast, remained faithfully attached to his life's goal, his task and place in the world. He merited a multitude of blessings for himself, for all the Jewish people, and for the entire world.

The *Zohar* (Bereishith, Miketz, 199), discussing the economic success of Joseph in Egypt, also mentions our verse from Proverbs.

> "The man of faith has many blessings. . . ." This refers to a person who has within him faith in the Holy One, blessed be he."

The fact that faith (*emunah*, אמונה) is the foundation of nourishment (*mazon*, מזון) is revealed in the numerical value of these words. *Emunah*, with the addition of the *kollel*, totals 103, as does *mazon*.

emunah (אמונה): 1 + 40 + 6 + 50 + 5 = 102
adding the *kollel*:   102 + 1 = 103
mazon (מזון):   40 + 7 + 6 + 50 = 103

The addition of the *kollel* to the numerical value of a word indicates that the word is a cause. *Emunah* is the cause of the blessing of *mazon*.

Injury to the traits of truth and faith, and the prevalence of economic and moral problems, are signs of the period just before the coming of the Messiah, the time known as the "heel of *Mashiach*." The *braissa* in *Sotah* 49b states:

> In the "heel of *Mashiach*," prices will rise; truth will disappear; youths will publicly embarrass elders; the great will stand up before the small.

In this era, the explanations of the Sages regarding the relationship between sin and punishment will be realized. The blurring of boundaries (as exemplified by the failure to distinguish between the great and the small), and the lack of honesty and truth, will bring in their wake a situation of high prices and runaway inflation ("prices will rise"). All sectors of the economy will be equally affected ("all the prices will be equal"). The main causes of economic collapse will be lack of *binah* (understanding)—i.e., failure to distinguish between different categories of values and people; *znut* (sexual misconduct); *leitzanut* (scoffing); and *machloket* (divisiveness). These factors will appear in full force in the time just before the coming of the Messiah. The Sages refer to his coming as the "sprouting" (*tzemach*) of the son of David. Before this sprouting there must be a period that resembles rot and disintegration, just as a seed in the earth seems to split open and disintegrate before it sprouts.

The public embarrassment of elders and the lack of respect for Torah scholars and God-fearing men deprive these scholars of aid and economic support. This lack of support for Torah institutions is another sign of the period called the "heel of *Mashiach*." The Torah alludes to this situation in the story of Jacob's struggle with the angel Samael (Genesis 32:24–32). The struggle continued throughout the night—which symbolizes the long night of exile—and only ended at dawn, which symbolizes the dawn of redemption. The Torah says:

> A man wrestled with him until dawn; and he saw that he could not overcome him; and he touched the hollow of his thigh (*ibid.*, 25–26).

This blow to Jacob's thigh at the blow that Satan will strike against later generations, the descendants of Jacob's loins. According to the *Zohar*, this indicates primarily an attack of Satan against the supporters and upholders of Torah institutions. The *Zohar* (Bereishith, 171a) states:

> When he [Samael] saw that he could not touch [Jacob's] Torah, he sapped the strength of those who support Torah scholars.

Rabbi Elchanan Wasserman relates this *Zohar* passage to our present era. In *Kovetz Maamarim* (Ikvata Demashichah, 111) he writes:

> Everywhere, even in countries where at the moment people can still afford to give monetary contributions, they give to all kinds of causes. But for the Torah, only a few pennies are left over. . . . And what is the response of Heaven? "For the sin of neglecting Torah study, war and pillage come, as it is said, 'I shall bring upon you an avenging sword, avenging the covenant,' and 'covenant' means Torah" (*Shabbat* 33a).

The decree of an "avenging sword," as we explained earlier, will be changed to a decree of poverty, which is considered the equivalent of death.

The aid given to Torah scholars parallels the tithes (*maasros*) of produce given to the Levites. The Rambam (*Hilchos Shmitah Veyovlos*, 13:13) writes:

> It is not only the tribe of Levi [who are separated from worldly occupations to devote themselves to the service of *Hashem*]. Anyone in the world whose spirit moves him and whose knowledge makes him understand, may separate himself to stand before *Hashem*, to serve

him and to work for him, in order to know *Hashem* . . . and [*Hashem*] will grant him in this world enough to take care of his needs, just as he granted (the *maasros* and other gifts) to the Kohanim and the Levites.

Just as the blessing of wealth depends upon the faithful giving of *trumos* and *maasros* to the Kohanim and Levites, so, too, the blessing of a fruitful and peaceful land depends upon aiding Torah scholars. That is why Satan attacked this particular point; he introduces disruption in order to rob the Jewish people of blessings.

Failure to give *trumos* and *maasros* results in rising prices and erosion of wages. The Sages state (*Shabbat* 32b):

> Through the sin of neglecting *trumos* and *maasros*, the heavens are prevented from giving dew and rain; high prices break [people]; wages disappear; people run after their livelihood but do not attain it.

"High prices break [people]" and "wages disappear" are signs of the "heel of *Mashiach*." The prophet Zachariah writes regarding this period: "Before those days, a person's wages will not exist" (Zachariah 8:10). The Maharsha, in his commentary on *Sanhedrin* 98b, explains the prophet's statement.

> Before those days, after all the sufferings [of exile], it will come about that a person's wages will not exist. . . . Even if a person wants to hire himself out, no one will want to hire him.

This refers to the phenomenon of unemployment.

Midrash Shir Hashirim also describes the time of the "heel of *Mashiach*" as one during which "poverty will increase, and high prices will break [people]" (Shir Hashirim Rabba 2:29).

These descriptions provided by the prophets and Sages closely match the reality of our time. Ben Yehoyada (on Tractate *Shabbat* 13b) remarks:

> "High prices break [people], and wages disappear." Normally, in a time of high prices, a small number of people, those who own the sources of fruit and grain, make high profits (wages). But in this era, the profits that these people make will not last, but will disappear. The Holy One, blessed be he, will arrange it that their profits will afterward be lost.

Against the background of our times, when money rapidly loses its value and wages and profits alike are eroded, the words of Ben Yehoyada shine a clear light.

The Maharal explains why neglect of *trumot* and *maasrot* causes poverty. In his commentary on the Aggadot of the Talmud (*Shabbat* 32b) he writes:

> Because of the sin of not giving *trumot* and *maasrot*, blessing disappears from the world, and wages and livelihood are not to be found at all. Wages and livelihood come from *Hashem*, blessed be he, and [if people sin] *Hashem*, blessed be he, takes away everything that he gave; for it is *Hashem*, blessed be he, who gives dew and rain. Thus it is he who gives wages and livelihood. And he takes everything away.

This passage is characteristic of the Maharal's way of explaining the Jewish people's problems in the areas of economics and security. At the root of the problem lies a lack of faith: People fail to recognize the purpose of their lives and the purpose for which the Creator, blessed be he, gave them property. A person fails to recognize the place and task in the world that Providence has assigned to him. This lack of awareness typifies our time, in which everyone tries to damage his fellow man.

In Tractate *Berachos* (63a), the Sages discuss how poverty and decreasing income result from the failure to give the required gifts and tithes to the Kohanim and the Levites, the servants of God. The Talmud points out that a verse about the tithes—"The holy things [tithes] of each man shall be his own" (Numbers 5:10)—immediately precedes the passage about an unfaithful wife (*sotah*): "If a man's wife goes astray . . ." (*ibid.*, 12). If a man fails to give the proper tithes, and instead diverts them for his own use, the Talmud explains, this causes his wife to be unfaithful, so that in the end he must resort to the services of the *kohen* to perform the Temple ritual of the *sotah*, which reveals her sin and brings about her punishment. Not only this, but the man will remain with a decreasing return of produce from his fields until finally it dwindles to the amount that originally should have been given to the Kohanim and Levites. This is hinted at by the verse, "The holy things of a man shall be his own." If he does not give the "holy things," the tithes, in the end they will be "his own"; that is, his field will provide only the amount of the tithe itself.

From this talmudic passage we see clearly that failure to help those worthy of receiving contributions causes an increase in *znut* and poverty among the Jewish people.

The connections between the *znut* of a husband and that of the sinner's wife is ingeniously explained by Rabbi Yehonatan Eubeshitz, as cited in *Chidushei HaGeonim* (Ein Yaakov, *Berachot* 63b).

> When a man lacks money, his wife suspects that he is occupying himself

with prostitutes, as it is written: "He who occupies himself with prostitutes will lose a fortune" (Proverbs 29:3). As a result, the wife will not
fear the *mayim hameorarim*, "the water of the curse" [which is adminis-
tered in the Holy Temple to determine whether a woman has committed adultery]. For the *halacha* is that if the husband is not free of sin,
this water has no effect on his wife. The wife thinks, "He goes among
the pumpkins, and she among the squashes." (This folk saying means
that if a husband engages in sexual misconduct, his wife will do likewise, as the Sages say in *Sotah* 10a: "Whoever betrays his wife, his wife
betrays him.")

The reason that a person's *parnassah* (livelihood) depends upon
his spiritual level is because *parnassah* is connected with the quality of
strict judgment (*din*). According to *Kehillat Yaakov* (פרנסה), this is
shown by the fact that *parnassah* begins with the letters פר, which indicate *gevurot*, the severity of strict justice.

It is true that *parnassah* depends on *chesed* (kindness), which is the
opposite of *din*, strict judgment. In fact the numerical value of "nourishment" (*mazon*, מזון) is equal to that of "God of kindness" (אל חסד):
103. This, however, is not a contradiction. As *Kehillat Yaakov* explains,
the source of nourishment and livelihood is kindness and mercy
(*chesed* and *rachamim*); but the vessel that receives these blessings can
only hold firm by the strength of *din*, strict judgment. *Din* is the quality that says, "Enough!" and thus forms firm boundaries within which
the blessing can be contained. When the "vessels" of the Jewish people—that is, the Jewish people themselves, who make themselves into
fit vessels—are unblemished, then "the vessel contains the blessing."
This is suggested by the letters of the word "vessel" (*kli*, כלי), which
are the initials of Kohanim (כהנים), Leviim (לויים), and Israel (ישראל),
the three groups that together constitute the entirety of the Jewish
people. When this *kli* is perfect, the people merit abundance and
blessing.

The numerical value of *kli* is 60.

kli (כלי): 20 + 30 + 10 = 60

This hints at the perfection of the quality of *yesod* (foundation), which
is the sixth of the seven lower qualities (*midot*) discussed by Kabbalah.
Multiplying a number by ten symbolizes the perfection of its quality.

The perfection of the number six, which represents holiness,
peace, and truth, is the foundation of the vessel that can receive and
contain blessing.

The linguistic root of "vessel" (*kli*, כלי) is כל. This is also the root of "sustenance" (*kalkalah*, כלכלה). As we have seen, the letters כל symbolize the quality of *yesod*, wherein the crown (*keter*), which is the supernal source of all abundance, is united with the heart (*lev*)—in this case, the heart of the Jewish people as a whole.

The fact that *parnassah* depends upon strict judgment (*din*) makes it very hard to attain. The Sages say in Tractate *Pesachim* (118a): "Providing a man's livelihood is more difficult than redemption." The Talmud goes on to explain that, regarding redemption, Jacob says, "The angel who redeemed me" (Genesis 48:15). Thus, we see that redemption can come about through an angel. *Parnassah*, on the other hand, comes about only through the Holy One, blessed be he. We have already seen a similar concept expressed by the Maharal, who states that those things given directly by the Holy One, blessed be he, are taken away by him when the people sin.

In the same talmudic passage, the Sages compare the difficulty of attaining *parnassah* to that of splitting the Red Sea. When the children of Israel stood at the edge of the sea, many accusations were leveled against them in the heavenly court. Likewise, many accusations are leveled against a man when he seeks *parnassah*.

8

The Relationship Between Respect for Justice and Economic Well-being

THE RELATIONSHIP BETWEEN *parnassah*, on the one hand, and judgment and law, on the other, is highlighted by the fact that Scripture in various places uses the word "law" (*chok*, חוק) to mean income or sustenance. Thus, "Help me attain my daily bread" means, literally, "the bread of my law," לחם חקי (Proverbs 30:8). The Gemara (*Beitzah* 16a) comments on this verse: "This word, *chok*, is an expression for income (*mezonot*)."

The Hebrew language contains several words for "law." *Chok* refers especially to those statutes whose rationale is not readily apparent. The faithful observance of such statutes has a special power to draw down abundance of sustenance from the upper world. Thus, we read in Leviticus 26:3–4: "If you go in My statutes (bechukotai), and keep My *mitzvot*, and do them, I shall give your rains in their fit season, and the land will give its produce." Observance of *chukim*, statutes that are beyond our understanding, brings in its wake the fulfillment of the *mitzvot*, which is a trustworthy guarantee of economic blessing and supernal abundance.

According to *Kehillat Yaakov* (חק), the word *chok* is also a name for the sixth of the kabbalistic qualities (*midot*), *yesod* (foundation), which stands for holiness.

The numerical value of *chok* is 108.

chok (חק): 8 + 100 = 108

The number 108 is equal to the number 6 multiplied by the number 18. Eighteen is the value of "alive" (*chai*, חי).

chai (חי): 8 + 10 = 18

This teaches us that a life (18) of holiness (6) causes a man to merit *chok* (18 × 6 = 108)—i.e., income and sustenance.

The connection between *chok* and a life of holiness is also shown by the significance of the letters that make up this word: חק. Previously, we have dwelled on the negative significance of these two letters; however, like all the fundamental forces, these letters have a positive meaning as well. The letter ח is the initial of the word "life" (*chayim*, חיים), and ק is the initial of "holiness" (*kedusha*, קדושה). Thus, the letters of חק indicate "a life of holiness." A complete life of holiness is the foundation of a stable economic situation.

The linguistic root of "sustenance" (*kalkalah*, כלכלה) is כלכל. The connection between this root and the concept of holiness is revealed by their numerical equivalence. The root כלכל and the letter ק both have the numerical value of 100.

כלכל: 20 + 30 + 20 + 30 = 100; ק = 100

We have seen that the numerical value of *chok* (חק) is 108. This equals the value of "the nourishment" (*hamazon*, המזון).

hamazon (המזון): 5 + 40 + 7 + 6 + 50 = 108

Chok is the foundation of *mazon*. By perfecting the observance of the Torah's statutes, one arrives at perfect nourishment and sustenance.

The connection between "statute" (*chok*, חק) and "purity" (*tohar*, טהר) is emphasized by their closeness in the Hebrew alphabet. The feminine form of *chok* is *chukah*. Chukah (חקה, statute) and *tohar* (טהר, purity) share the letter ה; the remaining two letters of *tohar* immediately follow those of *chukah* in the alphabet.

ט follows ח

ר follows ק

The word "statute" (*chok*, חק) is based on a root that means "to carve out." The Torah's statutes "carve out" gross materiality and produce from it *tohar*, purity.

Purity and cleanliness are the source of sustenance (*kalkalah*). On the other hand, filth and pollution are the opposite of sustenance, and undermine it. This can be seen in the letters of "filth" (לכלק), which are the reverse of the root of "sustenance," כלכל.

According to the commentary *Siftei Kohen* on the Torah, the concept of spiritual filth as a force that negates sustenance is expressed in the beginning of Lech Lecha (Genesis 12:1). God tells Abram, "Get thee gone from your land and from your birthplace, and from your father's home, to the land which I will show you." Why, asks *Siftei Kohen*, does the Torah use the lengthier expression "Get thee gone" (לך לך), when it could simply have said, "Go" (צא)? (Rabbenu Bechaya asks the same question about this verse.) *Siftei Kohen* answers that the Holy One, blessed be he, wished Abram to realize that the place where he was contained filth and pollution, and that in order to sanctify himself he would have to separate himself from this place. (Rabbenu Bechaya offers a similar explanation.) *Siftei Kohen* states:

> This is why He told him, "Get thee gone" (*lech lecha*, לך לך). He meant: "Remove the filth (*lichluch*, לכלך) from the land. You must cleanse it . . . and you shall also cleanse and purify those who dwell in the land, removing their pollution and taking them out of the category 'cursed' into the category 'blessed.' This you shall do by means of nourishment and sustenance (*kalkalah*, כלכלה)." That is why He said *lech lecha* (לך לך); these are the same letters as "sustain" (כלכל).

Of the righteous Joseph the Torah says, "Joseph sustained his father and his brothers and the whole house of his father" (Genesis 47:12). He merited to do so because he was clean and pure, unsullied by the filth and pollution of Egypt. Joseph (יוסף, 156) equals six times the name of God (יהוה, 26 × 6 = 156). He thus represents the perfection of the six qualities (*midot*) that culminate in *yesod* (foundation).

The special power of the name Joseph is also revealed by the fact that it comes from a linguistic root that means "gathering" (אסיפה). This hints at Joseph's ability to gather and unify all the tribes of Israel.

As we have seen, the letters כל, which relate to unification, are related to Joseph, who represents *yesod*. This quality of כל is also the foundation of sustenance (*kalkalah*, כלכלה); the letters כל spell "all" (*kol*, כל), indicating that Joseph sustained and unified all the tribes. Likewise, peace (*shalom*, שלום) is the foundation of *parnassah*, livelihood.

Joseph is the one who brought, and will bring, "conciliation" (*piyus*, פיוס) to Israel. In fact, the letters of his name, rearranged, spell this word (Joseph, יוסף; *piyus*, פיוס). The *piyus* will come about through the Messiah of Joseph, who will bring unity to the Jewish people in preparation for the complete redemption that will be accomplished by the Messiah of David. This will lead to the situation when "he makes your border peace; he shall satisfy you with the fat of the wheat" (Psalms 147:14).

Through this special power, Joseph counteracts the wicked Esau and his offspring Amalek. Only upon the birth of Joseph, the antagonist of Esau, did Jacob feel ready to return to his land, as it is written: "And it came to pass, when Rachel gave birth to Joseph, Jacob said to Laban, 'Send me away, and I shall go to my place and my land'" (Genesis 30:25).

Nourishment (*mazon*) is derived from the quality of kindness (*chesed*). Thus, as we saw, the numerical value of *mazon* (מזון) is equal to that of "God of kindness" (אל חסד). Likewise, the word "nourish" (*zan*, זן) equals the name of God (יהוה) that indicates mercy (*rachamim*) plus the name (אל) that indicates kindness (*chesed*).

zan (זן): $7 + 50 = 57$
Hashem (יהוה): $10 + 5 + 6 + 5 = 26$
Kel (אל): $1 + 30 = 31$; $31 + 26 = 57$

Livelihood (*parnassah*), on the other hand, depends not only on kindness and mercy, but also on the quality of strict judgment, which is the vessel that may contain blessing and abundance. This combination of kindness (*chesed*) and strict judgment (*din*) is revealed in the word "peace" (*shalom*, שלום), which is both the source and the precondition of abundance. The first letter of *shalom*, ש, is connected, according to *Sefer Yetzira*, with the element of fire (*esh*, אש). Fire is the source of strict judgment (*din*) and discipline (*gevura*). The final letter, ם, is connected with the element of water (מים), which symbolizes kindness and mercy. The two central letters, לו, have the numerical value of 36. We have already learned that 6 is the number of the *tzadik*. The number 36, which equals 6×6, thus represents the perfection of the quality of the *tzadik*. It is this quality that brings about harmonious coordination of the two opposites, fire and water (strict judgment and kindness).

Likewise, if we take the letters of the name of God (אדני) that indicates strict judgment (*din*) and multiply them by the numerical value of the letters of the name of God (יהוה) that indicates mercy (*rachamim*), the result is the numerical equivalent of "peace" (*shalom*).

אדני:	1	4	50	10
יהוה:	× 10	× 5	× 6	× 5
	10	+ 20	+ 300	+ 50 = 380

shalom (שלום):   300 + 30 + 6 + 40 = 376

Add 4 for the four letters of *shalom*: 376 + 4 = 380

Joseph embodies the perfection of all these forces of *shalom* by means of the *tzadik*. He was the ruler (*moshel*, מושל) of the land of Egypt. The letters of *moshel* are the same as those of *shalom* (שלום). Thus, Joseph was the man of sustenance who succeeded in drawing down the channels of abundance to the world.

A close relationship exists between Joseph, who embodied the perfection of the quality of peace, and Pinchas. According to *Megaleh Amukot* (beginning of Pinchas), this relationship is reflected in the fact that the letters of Pinchas's name can be rearranged to spell the "grace of Joseph" (*chen Yosef*, חן יסף).

Pinchas merited that God gave him a covenant of *shalom* because, through his righteousness, he saved Israel from immorality (*znut*) and annihilation. *Shalom* is the vessel that can contain an abundance of livelihood (*parnassah*) for Israel. We have already had occasion, in that context, to quote the explanation of *Ben Ish Chai* (Drashot Al Hatorah, Pinchas 194):

> *Shalom* was given to Pinchas because, through his zeal, he separated Israel from this sin of *znut*. Because of this, they were given abundance of sustenance, which is called *shalom*.

According to Midrash Rabba (beginning of Pinchas), Pinchas returned to the world as Elijah the Prophet. Through Elijah, *shalom* will return to the children of Israel after they have completely repented of their sins; then abundance of food and sustenance will return to the Jewish people.

The special power of Elijah to bring abundance of nourishment to Israel is revealed by the letters of his name. They allude to *Kel* (אל), the name of God that indicates kindness (*chesed*), and *Hashem* (יהוה), the name that indicates mercy (*rachamim*). We have already seen that these two names together have the numerical value of "nourishes" (*zan*, זן), 57. This is also the numerical value of "food" (*ochel*, אוכל).

ochel (אוכל): 1 + 6 + 20 + 30 = 57

Chesed and *rachamim* are the source of food, which nourishes. They are, likewise, the source of "nourishment" (*mazon*, מזון), whose numerical value equals that of "God of kindness" (אל חסד). When the children of

Israel repent of their sins, and the Father is united with his children through the work of Elijah the Prophet, the storehouses of abundance will be opened for the Jewish people from the upper world, whose root is *chesed* and *rachamim*.

The announcement with which Elijah will proclaim the coming of the Messiah is closely related to the blessing recited in the Shemona Esrei prayer, Birkat Hashanim, which requests a year of fruitful crops. In Tractate *Megilla* (17a), we learn that fruitful crops in the land of Israel are a sign that the redemption is approaching. The Talmud discusses the order of the blessings of the Shemona Esrei.

> Why did [the Sages institute that we] recite the blessing concerning the in-gathering of the exiles immediately after the blessing for a fruitful year? Because it is written (Ezekiel 36:8): "And you, o mountains of Israel, give your branches and bear your fruit for My people Israel, for they are drawing close to come."

The blessing for a fruitful year is the ninth blessing of the Shemona Esrei prayer. The Talmud explains that it corresponds to the ninth chapter of Psalms. (It is actually numbered Chapter 10; the Maharsha explains that the Talmud counts the first two chapters as one.) The connection with the ninth chapter of Psalms alludes to price-fixers, whose activities produce the opposite of the abundance we request in the ninth blessing. Their punishment is mentioned in the ninth chapter of Psalms (15): "Break the strength of the wicked"—i.e., the price-fixers, whose main victims are the poor. As we find earlier in the same chapter of Psalms, "He lies in ambush to snatch the poor; he snatches the poor, drawing him into his net." Those who suffer most from high prices and a bad economic situation are the poor and weak, the lower economic stratum, as is painfully evident in our own time. With the complete redemption, the price-fixers will receive severe punishment. Hence, the Sages connected the ninth blessing, with its portent of redemption, to the ninth chapter of Psalms.

According to Ben Yehoyada (*Megilla* 15b), the wicked person who fixes high prices is hinted at in the letters of the word for "wicked one" (*rasha*, רשע). Rearranged, these letters spell "price" (*shaar*, שער). The order of the letters of *shaar* indicates honesty and truth; the word *rasha* indicates the perversion of this order.

The word *rasha* (רשע) can be analyzed as *rash* (רש, impoverished) and *ayin* (ע, eye). The eye of the *rasha* is always impoverished and lacking, never satisfied with what it has; therefore, the *rasha* cheats the poor and pursues profit. The word "crime" (*pesha*, פשע) can be analyzed in a similar way. It consists of *pash* (פש), which means to expand or increase, and *ayin* (ע, eye). If one's eye constantly seeks increase and expansion, this leads to crime.

"Wicked one" (*rasha*, רשע), "commotion" (*raash*, רעש), and "wealth" (*osher*, עשר), are all spelled with the same letters. The wicked one is thrown into commotion and confusion by his thirst for profit. His urges lead him to do acts of wickedness, and in the end these acts cause him to lose the wealth of his home and all his possessions.

We have seen that *chesed* (kindness), in its negative aspect, is sexual misconduct (*znut*). If a person uses the powers of discipline and strict judgment (*gevurat din*) to gain control over his urges, refraining from feelings of impure *chesed* so that those feelings do not govern him, he is a man of *shalom* (peace). This is the quality that unites strict judgment (*din*) with kindness (*chesed*). In this way, he merits an abundance of food (*ochel*) and nourishment (*mazon*). This process, according to *Beer Moshe* (Shoftim, 231), is revealed by the numerical value of another word for "food," *maachal* (מאכל), which equals the combined value of the name of God (יהוה) that indicates *chesed* and the name (אדני) that indicates *din*.

maachal (מאכל): $40 + 1 + 20 + 30 = 91$
יהוה: $10 + 5 + 6 + 5 = 26$
אדני: $1 + 4 + 50 + 10 = 65$; $26 \times 65 = 91$

Another word whose numerical value equals 91 is *amen* (אמן).

amen (אמן): $1 + 40 + 50 = 91$

When a person says *Amen* after a prayer or blessing, he indicates belief and acceptance of the words he has just heard. *Amen* (אמן) has the same linguistic root as "faith" (*emunah*, אמונה). This numerical equivalence (*amen* = *maachal*) teaches us that in order to merit the blessing of food (*maachal*), one must have faith (*emunah*).

As we have seen, "A man of faith has many blessings" (Proverbs 28:20). Through the merit of *emunah* (faith), one receives the blessing of food. It follows that lack of food stems from a lack of faith among the Jewish people. On the spiritual level, the evil force that casts doubt upon faith is the power of Amalek. Thus, when the children of Israel were in the wilderness, they lacked water because, through the evil spiritual force of Amalek, they began to have doubts about their faith. Afterward, Amalek attacked them in its material form, as an enemy nation (see *Exodus* 17:7–16). The Sages teach (*Zohar*, Vilna ed., 255): "The evil urge, Satan, and the angel of death are the same thing." This thing manifests itself on the spiritual level as the evil urge (*yetzer hara*) and on the material level as the angel of death (*malach hamavet*). In the same way, Amalek manifests itself on the spiritual level as doubt or lack of faith, and on the material level as the archetypal anti-Semitic nation.

Amalek (עמלק) has the same numerical value as "doubt" (*safek*, ספק).

Amalek (עמלק): 70 + 40 + 30 + 100 = 240
safek (ספק):   60 + 80 + 100 = 240

Amalek, on the spiritual level, stirs up doubts in a person's heart; with the doubts comes trouble. Thus, when the children of Israel asked, "Is *Hashem* in our midst, or not?" (Exodus 17:7) immediately they faced a war.

The misleading provocations of Amalek has an ancient precedent: the provocation of the snake against Eve, which led to a curse upon the fruitfulness of the land and decreased the abundance of man's food. Eve said, "The snake misled me, and I ate" (Genesis 3:14). The expression "misled me" (אשי אני) can be broken into two parts: היש, and אין, meaning, "Is there or isn't there?" This hints at the power of Satan, who plants doubts in a person's heart as to whether or not there is a Creator who exercises providence over his world.

Adam's sin brought about a curse that reduced the abundance of food. In the same way, the sin of lack of faith, throughout the generations, has caused the same curse.

"Misled me" (השי אני) can also be broken into יש (*yaish*, there is), and אני (*ani*, I). This, pointed out in kabbalistic works, indicates that wickedness and the curse of lack of abundance stem from the power of pride in a person's heart, the power that convinces him of the importance of his existence ("there is") as an independent self ("I").

The power of pride is also derived from the evil force of Amalek. This can be seen in the numerical value of the word *ram* (רם), which means "high" or "exalted."

Ram (רם): 200 + 40 = 240
Amalek (עמלק): 70 + 40 + 30 + 100 = 240

When a person considers himself high and exalted, he is under the influence of Amalek.

Now we can understand why Amalek robs Israel of abundant livelihood. *Ohev Israel* (Zachor) explains the matter, quoting the verse in which God declares war against Amalek:

> "The hand is on the throne of God; a war against Amalek generation after generation" (Exodus 17:16). The word for "throne" (*kes,* כס) comes from a linguistic root which means "covering" (*kisui,* כסוי). This means that the "hand," which is related to the concept of *kaf* (כף meaning both the letter כ and the palm of the hand), covers (God forbid) the light of the divine face, as represented by the name of God, *Kah* (יה). Then the children of Israel receive only a bare minimum of nourishment, as is known, but they do not receive from the light of the divine face (see *Zohar,* part 2, 152b). But when, speedily in our days, the verse [about Amalek] is fulfilled, and "he is destined to be destroyed forever" (Numbers 24:20), he and his descendants will be eradicated from the world. Then the *kaf* will not cover the divine face, and beneficial outpourings, salvation, and consolation will be drawn down upon [the Jewish people].

From this, it follows that the way to remedy the Jewish people's lack of abundance is through *emunah,* faith. Thus, after Amalek attacked Israel at Refidim, Moses waged war against them with his hands, as it is written (Exodus 17:12): "His hands were faith."

We have seen many times that the abundance of sustenance depends upon the holiness of the relationship between husband and wife. The letters of the name of God (יה) that Amalek attempts to cover are the source of abundance, and are especially connected with the marital relationship. Thus, the word for man (husband) (*ish,* איש) contains the letter י, and the word for wife (*ishah,* אשה) contains the letter ה. If the יה are removed from husband and wife, what remain are two fires (*esh,* אש), which (God forbid) destroy the household. Similarly, when Amalek removes the יה, the result is a destructive force that ruins the world and cuts off abundance.

The power of pride of Amalek causes suffering and pain to the world. This is revealed in the numerical value of the word "pride" (*gaava,* גאוה), which equals that of the word *dava* (דוה), meaning to have sickness or pain.

gaava (גאוה): 3 + 1 + 6 + 5 = 15
dava (דוה):   4 + 6 + 5 = 15

We have seen that the numerical value of Amalek (עמלק) equals that of "high" or "exalted" (*ram*, רם). The letters of *ram*, reversed, spell *mar* (מר, bitter). The pride of Amalek causes a bitter life.

We learn from Midrash Rabba (Bamidbar, 13) that the essence of Amalek is pride. On the verse "The pride of a man humiliates him, but the lowly in spirit bears honor" (Proverbs 29:23), the Midrash comments: "The pride of a man refers to Amalek, who acts arrogantly toward the Holy One, blessed be he."

This quality of pride, which causes bitterness in life, is the root of sins involving sexual misconduct. As we have seen, such sins are a prime cause of economic difficulties.

The Talmud (*Sotah* 4b) states: "Anyone who has an arrogant spirit is as if he had committed every form of forbidden relations." One who is gross-spirited and given to pride will come to be physically gross as well, and thus will fall prey to the grossly materialistic appetite of forbidden relations.

The connection between pride and physical appetite is explained by the Maharal in his commentary on the Aggadot of the Talmud (*Sotah* 4b):

> A person who is gross-spirited (proud) has a soul with a tendency toward abominable and disgusting materiality. . . . Therefore he is considered as if he had committed every form of forbidden relations.

Forbidden relations (*erva*, ערוה) is the basis of badness (*roa*, רועה) in the world. Thus, these two words are spelled with the same letters.

The numerical value of *erva* is 281, which is also the numerical value of *pere* (פרא), meaning "lawless, uncontrolled."

erva (ערוה): 70 + 200 + 6 + 5 = 281
pere (פרא):   80 + 200 + 1 = 281

Pere (פרא) stands for permissiveness and uncontrolled urges; it results from a person's glorifying (פאר) himself.

The quality of pride has a particularly ruinous and disruptive effect on the abundance that should be revealed in the land of Israel. The eyes of God are continually watching this land (see Deuteronomy 11:12), and here his providence is apparent for all to see. According to the Chida, the especially close relationship between the land of Israel and the qualities of humility and submissiveness is revealed in the name by which this land is known in the Five Books of Moses: ארץ כנען (the land of Canaan). The Chida writes, in *Nitzutzei Orot* (*Zohar*, Part 3, 159b):

The spies were commanded to "spy out the land of Canaan (ארץ כנען)"
(Numbers 13:2), i.e., the land which is given to those who "submit"
(nichna, נכנע) to the Holy One, blessed be he, and do his will. (The letters of Canaan can be rearranged to spell nichna.)

The Shlah (Torah Shebichtav, Lech Lecha) likewise writes:

A person who lives in the land of Israel must always remember the
name Canaan, which indicates servitude and submission (hachnaah,
הכנעה).

The force that is the exact opposite of the land of Israel is that of
uncontrolled appetite, which is kindness (chesed) and submissiveness
(hachnaah) in their aspect of impurity (tuma). This force was embodied, in all of its evil facets, by the Canaanite nation.

The evil power of appetite, as opposed to the holiness of Israel, is
revealed in the numerical value of the expression ארץ כנען, 481. This
equals the numerical value of Lillit (לילית), a name mentioned in Kabbalah as representing the forces of sexual impurity.

ארץ כנען: 1 + 200 + 90 + 20 + 50 + 70 + 50 = 481
Lillit (לילית):   30 + 10 + 30 + 10 + 400 = 480
plus the kollel: 480 + 1 = 481

If the Jewish people are involved in illicit relations and gross appetites, they lose the privilege of dwelling in the land, as happened
with the destruction of the First and Second Temples. The seven
fruits with which Eretz Israel is especially blessed (see Deuteronomy
8:8) are connected, according to Kabbalah, to the seven nations who
were dwelling in the land before Joshua's conquest. Moreover, each of
the seven fruits corresponds to one of the seven kabbalistic qualities
(midot), which also indicate seven basic character traits. In order to
merit the land of Israel, a Jew must refine and purify all seven midot;
then he merits the blessings of the seven fruits of the land.

Amalek, the power of evil, prevents the children of Israel from
purifying themselves of evil. As a result, Amalek delays the Jewish
people from entering their land. This, the Sages tell us (Midrash
Rabba, Devarim, beginning of Ki Tavo), is why the Torah passage that
discusses the commandment of the first fruits (bikurim) comes just
after the commandment to destroy Amalek (Deuteronomy 25:17,
26:11). The bikurim are brought from the seven fruits. The juxtaposi-
tion of the two passages teaches us that only when we have purged

ourselves of the evil represented by Amalek will we merit to enter the land of Israel and benefit from the blessings of its fruits and nourishment, for it is Amalek that prevents Israel from achieving this bounty.

The evil force of Amalek is what holds and prevents the children of Israel from settling in peace and tranquility in their holy land.

9

Holiness: The Source of Abundance

HOLINESS AND PURITY in the land of Israel affects not only the quantity, but also the quality, of the produce of the land. The Talmud (*Sotah* 49b) discusses the changes that took place in the fruits of the land of Israel when the Temple was destroyed. "Purity," says the Talmud, "eliminated taste and fragrance." This means that when the laws of ritual purity (*tahara*) were no longer observed, the Jewish people ceased to experience the flavor and fragrance that they had previously enjoyed in the fruits of the land (see Rashi).

The Maharal, in his commentary on the Aggadot of the Talmud, explains this talmudic passage.

> Purity means the elimination of dirtiness. When dirtiness is eliminated, the strength of the fragrance increases, for fragrance is the opposite of dirtiness. . . . When there was purity in the world, the force of fragrance predominated, and this was what gave the fruits flavor; fragrance and flavor are the same thing, since both of them have strength (*koach*). Hence, when purity ceased, the flavor of fruits also ceased.

The sanctity of God is the source of all blessing and wealth. Thus, disrespect (חרי) toward the sanctity of God and his name causes poverty. The Talmud (*Nedarim* 7b) states:

> Wherever mention of *Hashem*'s name is common (i.e., wherever it is mentioned needlessly, *ran*), poverty is common; and poverty is equivalent to death.

The Maharal (*op cit.*) explains this passage as follows.

> Created things cannot maintain their existence in the presence of His name, blessed be He. Thus, Moses split the sea with His name. . . . ("Kabbalah tells us that Moses split the sea with the name of God that contains 72 letters; for the three consecutive verses in Exodus, 14: 91-22, each contain 72 letters; and this is a proof that Moses uttered His name, blessed be He, at the sea, and split the sea with His name" [the Maharal, *Gevurot Hashem*, Ch. 40]). And since created things cannot maintain their existence, hence, when the name of Heaven is common, poverty is common. And as for the verse (Exodus 20:21), "Wherever I shall cause My name to be mentioned, I shall come to you and bless you," this refers only to situations when it is proper that His name be mentioned.

Disrespect and frivolity toward sacred values and the related phenomenon of desecration of God's name are connected with *leitzanut* (mocking) and *schok* (clowning). As we have seen, these qualities lead to the collapse of a person's economic structure.

As one commentator explains it, the name of God is the source of blessing. Hence, when one mentions the name of God needlessly, this counteracts the force of blessing; the result is poverty (*Likutei Batar Likutei*, citing *Lashon Limudim*, Tractate *Sotah*).

Disrespectful and wasteful treatment of food is another thing that causes poverty. The Talmud in *Pesachim* 113b says that the angelic minister in charge of food is not pleased when crumbs are thrown down to be trampled underfoot.

According to Kabbalah, crumbs of bread that are treated carelessly symbolize wasted sperm, which is a desecration of the covenant of circumcision. The potentially holy sparks wasted by seminal emission give birth to harmful spiritual forces (*mezikim*) that work to ruin a person, especially his economic life. Similarly, the sin of *znut*, sexual misconduct, causes poverty and economic insufficiency.

Seminal emission (*keri*, קרי) causes emptiness (*rik*, ריק) and expensiveness (*yoker*, יקר) of prices. All three of these words are spelled with the same letters.

The two basic letters of *keri*, קר, refer to the impurity of Amalek, about whom the Torah says, "He fell upon you" (Deuteronomy 25:18). The word used for "fell upon you") is קרך, whose basic letters are קר. If we write out the names of these letters in full, we have *kof*

raish (קוף ריש), whose combined numerical value is 696. This equals
the numerical value of "troubles" (*tzarot*, צרות).

> *kof, raish* (קוף, ריש): 100 + 6 + 80 + 200 + 10 + 300 = 696
> *tzarot* (צרות):   90 + 200 + 6 + 400 = 696

The connection between poverty and the impurity of *keri* is
hinted at in Psalms 34:11: "Young lions became poor and went hun-
gry." The word for "young lion" (*kefir*, כפיר) has the numerical value of
310, which is also the value of *keri*.

> *kefir* (כפיר): 20 + 80 + 10 + 200 = 310
> *keri* (קרי):   100 + 200 + 10 = 310

According to Rabbi Nachman of Breslav (*Sefer Hamidot*, Mamon),
the verse just quoted suggests that non-belief (*kefira*, כפירה) leads to
poverty and hunger. The word for young lion (*kefir*, כפיר) is spelled with
the same main letters as non-belief.

The *kefir* symbolizes one who is brave and strong and puts his
trust in his own strength. A man who behaves like a *kefir* thereby denies (*kofer*, כופר) the providence of God, trusting instead in his own
strength and the might of his own arm. Such a man will eventually arrive at a state of impoverishment and hunger, to learn the lesson that
it is not through his might and accomplishments that a man overcomes difficulties, but through faith and by the spirit of God.

In this light, we can understand the talmudic passage (*Sotah* 11a,
Yevamot 64a): "Whoever engages in construction becomes poor."
Rashi explains that this profession "brings a man to poverty." This
passage refers to a man whose constant occupation is construction. He
sees the product of his efforts, and he lacks awareness of and faith in
the fact that, as we read in Psalms 127:1, "If *Hashem* does not build a
house, its builders work on it in vain." The man whose occupation
leads him to forget this fact will, in the end, come to poverty.

A man of faith sees in every small detail of his life the hand of
God. And when he finds himself or his fellow man in trouble, he joins
the name of heaven to his troubles by reciting the blessing over bad
news or by praying for mercy. Such a man merits redoubled sustenance, as the Talmud (*Berachot* 63a) states: "Whoever joins the name
of heaven to his troubles, his *parnassah* is doubled." The reason is that
a man of this type sees that his task in life is to achieve spiritual goals.
He uses all his property for these goals, and, therefore, through his
prayers, he merits abundant property.

The man of faith sees it as his function to help others. He regards his property as belonging to heaven, and considers that the Holy One, blessed be he, put these possessions into his hands so that he could give to those in need. The exact opposite of the man of faith is one who lends money at interest. This man is obligated to practice the *mitzvah* of lending money to his fellow Jew in time of trouble; instead, however, he takes advantage of the other man's troubles to charge him interest. Of such a person, the Sages said (*Bava Metzia* 71a): "Whoever lends at interest, his holdings collapse." It is true, the Talmud goes on to explain, that sometimes people's holdings collapse even if they do not practice usury. However, "Those holdings collapse and then recover; these collapse and do not recover."

The reason is explained by the Maharal (*Netivot Olam*, Netiv Hatzedakah, Ch. 6):

> The mitzvah of *tzedakah* (charity) is life. Usury, on the other hand, is gouging and removal. . . . Since the transgressor cleaves to something whose essence is removal, he brings upon himself the total removal of his own possessions.

If a person makes his profits through sin and transgression, the forces of removal and lack cling to them, and the profits do not last long.

Tzedakah is the opposite of usury and is the foundation of life, especially in Israel. "Justice, justice pursue, that you may live and possess the land" (Deuteronomy 16:20). Justice (*tzedek*, צדק) has the same linguistic root as charity (*tzedakah*, צדקה). *Tzedek* is the foundation of *tzedakah* because, in truth, an act of charity is an act of justice. A person's money is not his own; it is given to him so that he can use it to fulfill the commandments of the Holy One, blessed be he, distributing to those who deserve it.

The letter ק, as we have learned, in its impure aspect represents the power of the *klipa*, the external illusory shell that causes lack of income and livelihood. The word *tzedek* (צדק) can be analyzed as *tzad* and ק (צד–ק), meaning, "hunt down the ק." One who hunts down the forces of impurity brings justice, *tzedek*, to the world.

The same breakdown of the word *tzedek* into *tzad* and ק can also be read as "the side (*tzad*, צד) of the ק." According to *Ben Ish Chai* (Drashot, 224), this suggests that we should look at the letters that are "beside" the letter ק in the alphabet. These letters are צ and ר. Together, they spell *tzar* (צר), meaning "enemy" or "difficulty."

Troubles and difficulties arise through the power of impurity of the letter ק. Hunting down and subduing this power of impurity annuls the enemies and difficulties of Israel, and brings life and abundance.

When a man fulfills his purpose in life with justice and truth, as divine providence intended, he is supplied all his needs from heaven, so that he can carry out his assigned goals. Sin, transgression, and unworthy deeds, however, lead to the reduction of his sustenance. As the Talmud records in *Kiddushin* 82b:

> Rabbi Shimon ben Elazar says: "In my whole life I have never seen a deer working as a farmhand, nor a lion as a porter, nor a fox as a storekeeper; and yet they receive their livelihood without suffering. And they were created only to serve me, while I was created in order to serve my Creator. If those were created only to serve me, and they receive their livelihood without suffering, how much more that I, who was created to serve my Creator, should receive my livelihood without suffering. But I have done unworthy deeds and have deprived myself of my livelihood.

The Maharal, in his commentary on the Aggadot of the Talmud, explains the above passage:

> A man's livelihood (*parnassah*) is his existence. If a man lacks *parnassah*, he is lacking existence. Existence cannot be derived from actions which themselves are not of enduring existence. It can only be derived from perfect actions, whose effect is through wholeness.

Ben Yehoyada (*Kiddushin* 57b) also interprets our talmudic passage. He says that a person's innate powers are symbolized by the animals mentioned. If a person utilizes these powers in holiness, they are the source of abundance. If one is swift as a deer in the service of his Creator; if he is as brave as a lion, and uses this bravery for the sake of heaven; and, likewise, if he utilizes his intelligence and cleverness to go in the way of God, he merits abundant *parnassah*.

One of the main reasons for the economic difficulties and the downfall of companies and employers is the injury perpetrated against wage-earners by the delay or nonpayment of salaries. The Talmud states in *Sukkah* 29b:

> Because of four transgressions, the property of the well-to-do is lost: Because they delay the wages of workers; because they deprive the

workers of wages; because they shirk the yoke from their own shoulders and put it on the shoulders of their friends; and because of arrogance.

Pride is the basis of these offenses against the wage-earner, as the Maharsha explains in his commentary on this passage: "Because of their pride, they tell the workers, 'Come back another time.' "

When the Jewish people find themselves dependent upon loans and aid from other nations, it reduces their world prestige. This is part of the curse that the children of Israel were told they would receive as a rebuke if they transgressed the *mitzvot* of God.

He [the non-Jew] will lend to you, and you will not lend to him. He will be the head, and you will be the tail (Deuteronomy 28:44).

Similarly, the Talmud states in *Sotah* 47b:

Ever since the increase in those [Jews] who receive charity from the non-Jews, Israel has been on top, and [the non-Jews] on the bottom; Israel ahead, and they behind.

This passage is an example of the rhetorical device known as *sagi-nahor* (euphemism). The Talmud, therefore, tactfully reverses the terms "top" and "bottom," and "ahead" and "behind."

The opportunity for the gentile countries to give charity and to do kindness (*chesed*) for the Jewish people adds to those countries' merit, thus allowing them to continue to hold the upper hand over Israel, keeping the Jews under firm subjugation. This may be compared to the Talmud's statement in *Bava Batra* (10b) that, because of Daniel's advice to King Nebuchadnezzar to give charity to impoverished Jews, Nebuchadnezzar's reign was extended for a whole year.

This situation, according to the Sages, is reflected in Proverbs 14:34: "Charity exalts a nation, but the *chesed* (kindness) of the states is a sin." On this, the Sages comment:

"Charity exalts a nation": This refers to Israel, who is called a nation, as in the verse, "Who is like Your people Israel, one nation on the earth." "But the *chesed* of the states is a sin": For the gentile states of the world, it is counted as a sin.

The Talmud goes on to explain that the charity of gentile states is considered a sin because their intent is only to further their own benefit.

10

"Turn Aside from Evil and Do Good"

IN ORDER TO ESTABLISH the basis for a firm and stable economic life, the Jewish people must remedy the spiritual failings that injure the economy. The basic failings are looseness (*pritzut*) in sexual morality; frivolity and *leitzanut*; and lack of support for Torah scholars. The remedying of these problems constitutes the step of "Turn(ing) aside from evil" (Psalms 34:15), and will prevent economic collapse. After remedying the evil comes the next step: the spiritual self-strengthening indicated by the second half of the above verse: "and do good." This will increase and magnify economic abundance.

On the side of "and do good," one of the bases for economic blessing is the *mitzvah* of *Shabbat*, in which is contained a special power to bring wealth. In Proverbs 10:22 we read, "The blessing of *Hashem* is what makes a person wealthy, and will not add any sadness with it." The Midrash explains that "the blessing of *Hashem*" refers to the *mitzvah* of *Shabbat*, concerning which it is written (Genesis 2:3): "*Hashem* blessed the seventh day."

Honoring the Sabbath also brings wealth to those Jews who live outside Israel. In Tractate *Shabbat* (119a), the Talmud asks, "In other countries, how do the Jews merit wealth?" It answers: "By honoring *Shabbat*."

The special power of *Shabbat* (שבת) is revealed by its numerical value: 702. This equals three times the numerical value of the word "blessing" (*berachah*, ברכה) plus the numerical value of God's name, אהיה.

Shabbat (שבת): $300 + 2 + 400 = 702$
berachah (ברכה): $2 + 200 + 20 + 5 = 227; 3 \times 227 = 681$
אהיה: $1 + 5 + 10 + 5 = 21; 21 + 681 = 702$

This teaches us that the blessing (*berachah*) of each of the three upper worlds—*bria* (Creation), *yetzira* (formation), and *asiya* (action)—is united with its supernal root, the world of *keter* (crown), which is represented by the name of God, אהיה, the source of existence and of abundant *parnassah*. This unification depends upon the observance of *Shabbat*.

Torah study, *Shabbat*, and *tzedakah* have the special power to bring wealth to Israel after the people have remedied the sins that have been wreaking havoc on their economic life. *Shabbat*, Torah study, and *maaser* (tithes), as the source of abundance and wealth, embody the basis of complete faith in the Holy One, blessed be he, who created the world and exercises providence over it, and in his goodness renews the Creation every day.

Faith (*emunah*) is the root of blessings, as it is written (Proverbs 28:20): "A man of faith has many blessings." This *emunah* is strengthened, first of all, by the observance of *Shabbat*, which testifies to God's Creation of the world and constant providence over his world.

Torah study strengthens faith in reward and punishment for the observance or non-observance of the *mitzvot*.

The *mitzvah* of *maaser* teaches a person that he is not the owner of his property. Everything he has is the property of the Holy One, blessed be he, who gives it to a person so that the person can use it to accomplish spiritual goals and serve those who serve God. If one does not use his property in the right way, in the end he will lose it.

The Sabbath's special power to increase a person's livelihood is also due to the principle of *daat* (knowledge of God) that is connected with *Shabbat*. We have seen that the quality of *daat* has the power to bring wealth. This is the deeper meaning of the interpretation of the Sages quoted earlier:

> The blessing of *Hashem* is what makes a person wealthy (Proverbs 10:22). This refers to the blessing of *Shabbat* (Jerusalem Talmud, *Berachot*, Ch. 2).

Maaser is the portion of the Levites. According to Kabbalah, the Levites are connected with the quality of strict judgment, *din*. The connection between *din* and wealth is revealed by our forefather Isaac, who is the root of the quality of *din*, and who merited enormous wealth, as we read in Genesis 26:12: "In that year he found one hundred measures." (Rashi: His fields produced one hundred times the normal yield.) Isaac used his power of *gevura*—meaning heroism, might, and discipline—to wage war against the forces of evil. Therefore, he merited very great wealth.

The source of wealth is what Kabbalah refers to as the left side, the side of *gevura* (might, strict judgment). The holy Ari (*Likutei Torah*, Vaeshev, ויהי אחר הדברים האלה) discusses Joseph, who was the source of sustenance for the land of Egypt. He states, "all wealth (*mezonot*) comes from the side of *gevura*, the left side."

In *Likutei Shas* (*Berachot*), the Ari states:

> Nourishment (wealth) is drawn from the quality of *chesed* (kindness), but it is revealed by means of *gevurot*, as Scripture says (Proverbs 14:4), "Great crops through the strength of the ox."

The ox symbolizes Joseph, as in the blessing of Moses for the tribe of Joseph: "The firstborn of the ox, splendor is his" (Deuteronomy 33:17).

The left side, as the source of wealth, is also alluded to in the verse in Proverbs 3:16 that speaks of the good qualities of Torah: "In her left hand are wealth and honor."

By giving *maaser*, a person connects himself to the Levites, who embody *gevura* and *din*. Likewise, by aiding Torah scholars, a person connects himself with them and merits the blessing of wealth.

Moreover, by giving *maaser*, a person shows that he has the spiritual might (*gevura*) to overcome his urges, including the desire for property. This connection with the source of the holiness of *gevura* causes a person to merit wealth.

An especially great power of *gevura*, self-discipline, is required in matters of *ariot*, forbidden relations. The person who overcomes temptation in this area is referred to as a "mighty one" (*gibor*). Thus, the *Zohar* (Part 1, 189b) cites the verse (Psalms 103:20), "Bless *Hashem*, you angels of his, you mighty ones of strength who do his command." The *Zohar* comments: "The angel of *Hashem*, the mighty one of strength, is Joseph the righteous." Because Joseph overcame the temptation of illicit relations, the *Zohar* connects this verse to him.

Because he guarded himself against forbidden relations, Joseph merited to be a shepherd of the people, the minister in charge of Egypt's economic life. Ben Yehoyada (*Sotah* 34) points out that the same letters spell both "forbidden relations" (*erva*, ערוה) and "shepherd" (*roeh*, רועה). In the blessing Jacob gave to Joseph (Genesis 49:24), we read: "From there the shepherd, the stone of Israel." Ben Yehoyada explains:

> From there [from his power to overcome the temptation of forbidden relations] Joseph had merit, and became the shepherd of Israel, as it is said (Psalms 80:2): "O shepherd of Israel, listen! He who leads (them) like the flock of Joseph."

Joseph, through his power of *gevura*, brought economic success. Similarly, Isaac, the archetype of *din* and *gevura*, symbolizes the economic success that the children of Israel achieve when they overcome their evil inclinations. This is seen in the story of Isaac's struggle against Abimelech, king of the Philistines, and his followers. The Philistines challenged Isaac's ownership of water wells, which symbolize the sources of abundance.

These struggles are an example of the principle. "The deeds of the fathers are an omen for the sons." They teach us a lesson concerning Israel's struggles, throughout the generations, against the forces of spiritual impurity (*tuma*), as symbolized by the Philistines, who always rose up to block Israel's efforts to settle the holy land. Throughout Judges we clearly see how, whenever Israel found disfavor in the eyes of God, the Philistines wreaked havoc on their agricultural produce and economic life. Thus, in Judges 10:7, we find: "The wrath of *Hashem* burned against Israel, and he gave them over to the hand of the Philistines." And again: "*Hashem* gave them over to the hand of the Philistines for forty years" (*ibid.*, 13:1).

Every force in holiness has a corresponding force in *tuma*. The Philistines, on the side of *tuma*, correspond to the holiness of Israel with regard to *din* and *gevura*. This is revealed in the numerical value of the word "Philistines" (*plishtim*, פלשתים): 860. This equals ten times the name of God (אלהים) that represents the quality of *din*.

plishtim (פלשתים): $80 + 30 + 300 + 400 + 10 + 40 = 860$
Elohim (אלהים): $1 + 30 + 5 + 10 + 40 = 86; 10 \times 86 = 860$

The number ten represents totality or completion. Thus, *plishtim* represents the totality of the strength of *din*. Isaac, who personified the quality of *din* on the side of holiness, opposed the *plishtim*, who embodied this same quality on the side of *tuma*. Thus, when the children of Israel sinned, the execution of strict judgment against them took place by means of the *plishtim*.

In Kabbalah, the negative forces are called *klipot* (shells). The *klipa* of the *plishtim* is that of *leitzanut*, mockery. The Sages say, in *Avodah Zarah* 19a:

> "Blessed is the man who has not sat in the place of mockers" (Psalms 1:1). This refers to Abraham, who did not sit in the place of the Philistine men because they were mockers.

And in Midrash Shmuel we find: "'Strike a mocker' (Proverbs 19:25). This refers to the *plishtim*."

Moreover, *Tikunei Zohar* (23b) tells us that the verse quoted above, "in the place of mockers," refers to Lillit, a negative force personifying sexual impurity. Thus, the root of the *klipa* of the *plishtim* is illicit relations and *leitzanut*.

In this light, it is understandable why the *plishtim* (Palestinians), throughout history, even down to the present generation, have always tried to undermine the economy of the Jewish people. We have seen that the main transgressions that destroy prosperity are *znut* and *leitzanut*, sexual misconduct and mockery, and the *plishtim* embody precisely these two forces.

Our Patriarch Isaac, the personification of *din* and *gevura* on the side of holiness, so completely overcame this *klipa* that, in the end, the Philistines admitted to him that his success was from heaven. Like all the anti-Semites of history, they had claimed that the success of the Jews was achieved parasitically at the expense of the gentiles: "Go away from us, for you have become very wealthy from us" (Genesis 26:16). In the end, however, they acknowledged: "We have seen that *Hashem* is with you" (*ibid.*, 28). Likewise, the nations of the world will one day realize that their success depends upon the spiritual level of the Jewish people, upon whom rests the prosperity of the world.

The world being what it is, this realization currently escapes the gentiles, and therefore they hate the Jewish people. Midrash Shochar Tov, on the verse, "Instead of my love, they hate me, and I am (in) prayer" (Psalms 109:4), comments:

> The foundation of wealth (*osher*, עשר) is joy (*simcha*, שמחה). As the Sages said: "Who is wealthy? He who rejoices in his portion." The word joyful (*sameach*, שמח) expresses the concept of a fully aware brain (*moach*). The letter ש, when properly written as in a Torah scroll, consists of a baseline to which are connected the letters ז-י-ו. Thus, "joyful" (*sameach*, שמח) can be analyzed into זיו (*ziv*, shining) and מח (*moach*, brain). When the shining light of awareness illuminates the

brain, this brings a person a feeling of wealth (*osher*, עשר). On the other hand, perfection of the traits of the heart brings a person to a feeling of satiety (*sova*, שבע).

> Israel said to the nations of the world: "All these benefits, the Holy One, blessed be he, gives you for our sake, and yet you hate us."

In the Messianic Age, when the nations of the world come to realize that it is the high spiritual level of Israel that brings abundance to the world, the nations will aid and support the Jews, as Isaiah prophesied: "Foreigners will rise up and herd your flocks; strangers will be your farmers and your vintners" (Isaiah 6:5). When this takes place, the Jewish people will be able to devote themselves to Torah study, and this will bring great abundance to the world. As the Rambam writes (*Hilchot Melachim* 12:5): "At that time . . . great benefit will be granted, and all the delicacies will be as common as dust."

The abundance that will be granted to the world in the Messianic Age will come through the merit of the *daat* (knowledge of God) that will then fill the world, as it is written in Isaiah 11:9: "Knowledge of *Hashem* will fill the earth, as water covers the sea." We have seen that *daat* is the source of abundant livelihood. When the world becomes filled with *daat*, it will be filled with abundance and blessing.

Until the Messianic Age, mockery, frivolity, and cynical ridicule will be the predominant forces in the world, deriving from the root of *tuma* of the Philistines and Amalek. In opposition to them stands Isaac, who symbolizes laughter in its aspect of holiness (*yitzchak* means "he will laugh"), a laughter that ridicules the emptiness of idol worship.

At the end of days, this struggle between ridicule on the side of *tuma* and ridicule on the side of holiness (*kedusha*) will be revealed in the war of Gog and Magog. The numerical value of "Gog and Magog" is 70, representing the seventy nations of the world.

Gog and Magog (גוג ומגוג): 3 + 6 + 3 + 6 + 40 + 3 + 6 + 3 = 70

Gog and Magog will stir up laughter and ridicule against the holy values of Israel, as it is written in Psalms 2:1: "Why do the nations agitate. . . ." According to the Sages (Tractate *Berachot* 7b), this verse refers to the time just before the coming of the Messiah. Then the nations, under the aegis of Gog and Magog, will say, "Let us untie our reins, let us cast our ropes from off us" (*ibid.*, 3). This refers to ridicule of the *mitzvah* of *tefillin*. As against the laughter and ridicule of the nations, who will mock at the Torah of Israel, the heavens will laugh at the deeds of the gentiles.

> He who resides in the heavens will laugh, *Hashem* will ridicule them. Then he will speak of them in his fury, and in his anger he will panic them (*ibid.*, 4–5).

In the wake of the ridicule and laughter the nations level at the holy values of Israel, the quality of fierce justice will be revealed.

This attitude of ridicule and laughter directed against the sacred values of Israel is being revealed more and more, in all its strength, in our age. On the other hand, we are witness to the laughter of heaven toward a Jewish society based on such skepticism, for success somehow eludes all its plans and initiatives in the areas of politics, economics, and security.

The number seven represents the natural world. For example, the seven days of the week include the full cycle of time in the natural world. Eight, which goes beyond seven, stands for that which is above nature. The numerical value of the name of Isaac, who symbolizes perfection in holiness and *gevura*, is 208, eight times the numerical value of the name of God (יהוה).

יהוה: $10 + 5 + 6 + 5 = 26$
Isaac (יצחק): $10 + 90 + 8 + 100 = 208$; $8 \times 26 = 208$

Through the merit of *gevura*, which is above nature, one overcomes the power of the seventy nations that represent 10×7, the perfection of materiality within nature.

This power of *kedusha* (holiness) above and beyond nature was also revealed in Pinchas. He halted the plague that had begun to destroy Israel because of the sin of *znut* with the women of Moab and Midian. According to the *Zohar* (beginning of Pinchas), through his righteous act, Pinchas merited to receive the letter י from the name of God. When we spell Pinchas with a י, its numerical value equals that of Isaac, 208.

Pinchas (פינחס): $80 + 10 + 50 + 8 + 60 = 208$

This teaches us that the strength of Pinchas came from the quality of *din* and *gevura* of Isaac, who was the source of life, peace, and abundance.

Wealth (*osher*, עשר) represents the perfection of livelihood and nourishment, for its numerical value equals ten times that of the words "nourishes" (*zan*, זן) and "food" (*ochel*, אוכל). When one word is ten times the value of another, this indicates that the first word represents the perfection of the root of the second.

osher (עשר): 70 + 300 + 200 = 570
zan (זן): 7 + 50 = 57
ochel (אוכל): 1 + 6 + 20 + 30 = 57; 10 × 57 = 570

Another word whose numerical value equals 57 is "altar" (*mizbeach*, מזבח). This teaches us that by the merit of the *kedusha* of the *mizbeach* the world receives an abundance of nourishment and food.

Wealth (*osher*, עשר) is spelled with the same letters as "ten" (*esser*, עשר). This teaches us that the root of perfection depends upon the perfection of the ten *sefirot*, the ten worlds through which the emanation of Creation reaches us. These are paralleled by the ten *midot*, traits of thought and feeling, which are located in the brain and the heart, and which a person must work to perfect in himself.

The person who has perfected himself in brain and heart, with the *kedusha* of Torah, merits *osher*, wealth.

The word *osher* also indicates *gevura*, self-discipline. This is shown by analyzing its letters into ע (*ayin*, eye) and שר (*sar*, rule). This suggests that the eye is in control, and rules so that it cannot be affected by the forces of emptiness and vanity that attempt to attract it. When the same letters are arranged in a different order, we have רשע (*rasha*, wicked one). Here, the letters רש (*rash*, impoverished) precede and rule over the ע (*ayin*, eye), so that a person sees only the poverty and emptiness of the world. The *rasha* is produced by the forces of emptiness of Satan. Thus, the letters that precede rasha in the alphabet are ק, ר, ס.

ק precedes ר

ר precedes ש

ס precedes ע

These letters symbolize the forces of spiritual impurity (*tuma*), קר, followed by the letter ס, which, according to Midrash Rabba, Bereishith, is the letter of Satan.

When the poverty and emptiness of the world rule over the eye, the result is summed up in the Sages' dictum, "The eye sees, and the heart craves." This is reflected in the fact that the letters of *kisuf* (כסף, craving) immediately follow the letters of *ayin* (עין, eye) in the alphabet.

פ follows ע

כ follows י

ס follows נ

Excessive multiplication of pleasures (*taanugot*, תענוגות) is the cause of economic losses (*hefsedim*, הפסדים) to the individual and the world. This can be seen in the letters of the linguistic root of "loss," פסד. These letters immediately follow those of pleasure (*oneg*, ענג) in the alphabet.

פ follows ע

ס follows נ

ד follows ג

The letter ר, according to the Sages (Tractate *Shabbat*, Haboneh), symbolizes the "wicked one" (*rasha*, רשע). This letter also stands for "head" (*rosh*, ראש), of which it is the initial. This teaches us that the basis of the *rasha* is his pride, his desire always to be the "head." It is this negative trait that causes a person to become impoverished (*rash*, רש).

In contrast to the trait of pride, which blocks abundance, the trait of humility draws down abundance to the world. This can be seen in the letters of "abundance" (*shefa*, שפע), which are composed of two elements: שפ and ע. The first element, שפ, is the two-letter root of *shiflut* (שפלות), meaning "lowliness" or "humility." The second element, ע, means "eye." When one looks at the world with a lowly and humble eye, being satisfied with even a little, this draws down abundance from above.

Similarly, another word for humility, *anavah* (ענוה), can be analyzed into ע, eye, and נוה (*nava*, pleasant). One who is humble sees something pleasant wherever his eye turns.

When a person does complete repentance (*teshuvah*) for his acts of crime (*pesha*, gap) and wickedness (*resha*, רשע), even deliberate sins are transformed into merits. The letters are rearranged, and wickedness (*resha*, רשע) becomes wealth (*osher*, עשר), while "crime" (*pesha*, פשע) turns into "abundance" (*shefa*, שפע). Thus, on the verse, "[He] forgives (lit., passes over) crime" (Exodus 22:8), the *Zohar* comments:

"He 'transfers over' the שׁ in the word 'crime' (pesha) so that it becomes 'abundance' (shefa)."

The perfection of wealth and abundance depends upon a person's spiritual perfection. As we have seen, "wealth" (osher, עשר) can be analyzed into עשר, indicating that the ayin (eye) rules. But ayin (עין) also means iyun (עיון, thought). When a person's power of thought and reflection is in control, he merits osher, wealth. Similarly, a person merits wealth when he is filled with wisdom (chochma). Thus, when we write out in full the letters of osher, their numerical value totals 1,000.

osher (עשר) is spelled: ayin (עין), shin (שין), raish (ריש): 70 + 10 + 50 + 300 + 10 + 50 + 200 + 10 + 300 = 1000

The word for "one thousand" is elef (אלף). It comes from a root that means to learn or teach. Thus, ulpan (אולפן) means a place where one learns wisdom, and in Job 33:33 we find, "I shall teach you (ואאלפך, vaa'alefcha) wisdom." As we learned earlier, knowledge of God (daat) and wisdom (chochma) are the source of wealth and abundance for the world.

In addition, the number 1,000 stands for the highest of the worlds mentioned in Kabbalah, the world of atzilut, which is the source of abundance for all the worlds below it.

While the word "wealth" (osher, עשר) is connected with "ten" (esser, עשר), the word "satiety" (sova, שבע) is connected with "seven" (sheva, שבע). In Hebrew, the labial letters ב, ו, מ, בומפ, are interchangeable, so that the word, sheva (שבע) can be analyzed into the word שב–ע, which is שב, the two-letter root of "break" (shever, שבר) plus ע (ayin, eye). Breaking the appetites of the eye is what gives one a feeling of satisfaction and satiety (שבע).

The ten sefirot, or stages of divine creative emanation mentioned in Kabbalah, are paralleled by ten midot, or traits of character. The first three of these are related to the brain, and the remaining seven to the heart. Thus, the number seven alludes to the seven midot that depend upon the heart. Perfecting these traits of the heart brings a person to satiety (sova, שבע) and abundance (shefa, שפע).

The connection between joyousness and economic perfection is also revealed when we write out in full the letters of the word kilkul (כלכל), which means to give sustenance. Spelling out the letters of a word expresses the perfection of the concept represented. In this case, the numerical value of kilkul equals that of "joyful" (sameach, שמח).

kilkul (כלכל) is spelled: *kof* (כף), *lamed* (למד), *kof* (כף), *lamed* (למד)
20 + 80 = 30 + 40 + 4 + 20 + 80 + 30 + 40 + 4 = 348
sameach (שמח):   300 + 40 + 8 = 348

The letters of "joyful" (*sameach*, שמח) can also spell *chimush* (חמש), which means supplies or equipment, and alludes to being economically equipped or supplied. The Torah says of Joseph that "He supplied (*chimesh*, חמש) the land of Egypt" (Genesis 41:34). Being economically supplied makes a person joyful.

Another term that means economic supplies is *tzayid* (ציד), or, in the feminine form, *tzeidah* (צידה). Rearranged, the letters of *tzeidah* spell *ditza* (דיצה), "rejoicing."

The letters of *tzayid* (ציד, supplies) can be rearranged to spell *tzadi*, the name of the letter צ. This is yet another hint that the righteous person, the *tzadik* (צדיק), is the source of "supplies" and sustenance.

Moreover, the numerical value of *tzadi* and *tzayid* is 104. When we add the *kollel*, it equals 105. This is the numerical value of "sustenance" (*kalkalah*, כלכלה).

tzadi (צדי):   90 + 4 + 10 = 104
Plus the *kollel:*   104 + 1 = 105
kalkalah (כלכלה): 20 + 30 + 20 + 30 + 5 = 105

Righteousness and purity are the foundation of *kalkalah*, sustenance.

The two dental letters, ש and צ, are interchangeable. Thus, *tzadi* (צדי), the name of the letter צ, which represents *tzidkut* (צדקות, righteousness) is equivalent to one of the names of God, *Shaddai* (שדי). According to the *Zohar* (Part 2, 253a), this name alludes to the source of abundance of nourishment and livelihood. It is also connected to the quality of *yesod* (foundation), which is the *midah* of righteousness. This quality causes a person to feel that he has "enough" (*dai*, די), and gives him satisfaction with his life. The rewards of righteousness (*tzidkut*) will be revealed in the Messianic Age, when the Jewish people will have completed their process of purification, and "their lips will be worn out from declaring, 'Enough!'" because of all the abundance they will receive.

When the evil of the world has been remedied, the name *Shaddai* will be revealed on the earth, as we say in the prayer, Aleinu Leshabeach:

Therefore we hope . . . to see speedily the glory of your might, to remove the idols from the earth, and completely cut off the false gods, to perfect the world through the sovereignty of *Shaddai*.

When all the evil and perverted philosophies have been eliminated from the world and annulled, the source of abundance and mercy for the world will be revealed. Then all will see true abundance of goodness and blessing.

11

Ways of Increasing
One's Livelihood

A NUMBER OF SPECIAL METHODS (*segulot*) exist for improving one's livelihood (*parnassah*). This chapter includes some of the main *segulot*.

Above all others, the primary segulah for *parnassah* is prayer (*tefillah*).

The following *tefillah* is to be recited in the Shemona Esrei prayer, in the blessing called Shomea Tefillah, ("Who hears prayer," just before the words: "for You hear prayer" (כי אתה שומע תפילה) at the end of the blessing.

> You are the One, *Hashem*, o God, who nourishes, supports, and sustains all creatures, from the mighty antelopes to the eggs of lice. Cause me to attain my allotted bread, and provide me and my whole household with our income before we need it, in ease and not through suffering, in permitted ways and not in forbidden ways, with honor and not with humiliation, for life and peace, with an abundance of blessing and success, with an abundance of supernal blessing, so that I can do your will and be engaged in your Torah and fulfill your mitzvot. Do not cause me to need the gifts of flesh and blood. In me may the verse be fulfilled, "You open your hand and satisfy every living being."

The kabbalists teach that one *segulah* for *parnassah* is to recite with great concentration the verse, "You open Your hand and satisfy every living being" (Psalms 145:16). This verse contains seven words, which hint at the seven days of Creation, as well as the seven (*sheva*, שבע) qualities (*midot*) upon which the satiety (*sova*, שבע) of the world depends. One should concentrate especially on the initials of the three words פותח את ידך ("You open your hand"), which form the word, פאי (*Pai*), one of the seventy-two names of God that are connected with *parnassah*.

The numerical value of this name is 91, equal to the combined numerical value of two names of God—the one that stands for kindness (*chesed*, יהוה), and that stands for strict judgment (*din*, אדני).

יהוה: $10 + 5 + 6 + 5 = 26$
אדני: $1 + 4 + 50 + 10 = 65; 26 + 65 = 91$
Pai (פאי): $80 + 1 + 10 = 91$

As we have learned, the combination of these two qualities serves as the basis for abundant *parnassah*.

The final letters of these same three words ("You open your hand") spell *chatach* (חתך, cut), a word that alludes to the Holy One, blessed be he, who "cuts off," a fixed allotment for each living being.

By the *Atbash* (א״ת-ב״ש) transformation, *chatach* (חתך) becomes *Sal* (סאל), which, according to Kabbalah, is the name of the angel in charge of *parnassah*. *Sal* (סאל), like *Pai* (פא-י), has the numerical value of 91.

Sal (סאל): $60 + 1 + 30 = 91$

One of the things the *halacha* tells us to do on Friday in order to honor the Sabbath is to sharpen the knives. According to Kabbalah, the reason is that *chatach* (חתך, cut) is a name that has special power to increase *parnassah*. Therefore, one sharpens the instrument of "cutting" to prepare for the Sabbath, which is the source of blessing.

Another *segulah* for *parnassah* is the daily recitation, with concentration, of Parshat Hamon (Exodus 16:11–36), the Torah passage that describes how God gave the Jewish people manna in the wilderness. It is also desirable to recite the Targum, the Aramaic translation of the passage, if feasible. Likewise, the concentrated recitation of the Song of the Sea ("Then Moses and the children of Israel sang . . .") in the daily morning prayer service is considered effective in improving *parnassah*.

It is said that the recitation of Psalm 23 ("A song of David . . .") before meals has special importance for the blessing of *parnassah*. This psalm contains fifty-seven words, corresponding to the numerical value of the word "nourishes" (*zan*, זן). Fifty-seven is also the combined numerical value of two names of God, אהיה and יהוה.

אהיה: 1 + 5 + 10 + 5 = 21
יהוה: 10 + 5 + 6 + 5 = 26
plus the number of words: 2
plus the number of letters: 8
           21 + 26 + 2 + 8 = 57

This alludes to the unification of *keter* (crown), represented by אהיה, with *tiferet* (beauty), represented by יהוה. Through this unification, abundance of *parnassah* descends to our world.

Sefer Zechirah mentions that a *segulah* for economic success is to be truthful and trustworthy in one's business dealings, and also to give interest-free loans and to do other acts of kindness.

When a person sets out on a business venture, he should express his confidence that the Holy One, blessed be he, will grant blessing and success to his efforts. And, after success has been achieved, a person should give thanks to God.

Sefer Devek Mehaach (340) mentions the following *segulah* for *parnassah:*

1. To recite the verse "From [the land of] Asher, the bread is rich with oil: and [the land] produces royal delicacies" (Genesis 49:20) ten times in the morning and ten times in the evening.
2. To recite Psalms 145 three times.
3. To recite Psalms 29.
4. To recite the Thirteen Attributes (Exodus 35:6–7) nine times, finishing each time at the word ונקה ("and forgives").
5. To recite the verse beginning, "Their father, Israel, said to them . . ." (Genesis 43:11) seven times.
6. To recite the verse "And Saul sent a message to Jesse, saying, 'Let David please stand before me, because he has found favor in my eyes' (Samuel 16:22).
7. To recite the verse beginning, "Nard and saffron . . ." (Song of Songs 4:14).

Sefer Heach Nafsheinu (224, Parnassah) mentions a *segulah* for gaining one's income without pain and suffering: Each week, on the departure of *Shabbat* (*Motzei Shabbat*) one recites the name, Elijah, exactly seventy times, concentrating each time on a name of God, אגלא. (The author adds that one should not tell people that one is doing this.)

PART IV

REPENTANCE IN WORDS AND LETTERS

THE LETTERS AND WORDS of the Hebrew alphabet are the building blocks of the human soul. To understand how a person can achieve perfect repentance and thereby correct his God-given soul, we must first delve into and understand the secrets of the letters of the holy tongue from which the Jewish soul is built.

Ours is a generation in which the prophet Amos said there would be: לא רעב ללחם ולא צמא למים כי אם לשמע את דברי ה', "Neither a hunger for bread nor a thirst for water, but to hear the words of God" (8:11). It is due to this spiritual thirst that the phenomenon of people returning to their roots—doing תשובה (*teshuva*, return and repentance)—is prevalent in our age. Thus, elucidating the different angles and dimensions of repentance can be an invaluable asset to those yearning and searching for the truth found in Judaism.

The importance of repentance regarding the coming of the משיח (Messiah) is seen from the numerical values of the prophetic verses calling upon the Jewish people to repent. For instance, it is written in Malachi 3:7: שובו אלי ואשובה אליכם, "Come back to Me, and I will come back to you." The numerical value of this verse equals 776 (314 + 41 + 378 + 101 = 776)—the same numerical value as the words המשיח ביאת ("the coming of Messiah"; 413 + 363 = 776). The same applies to the words of the prophet Jeremiah (3:22): שובו בנים שובבים, "Return, you faithless children of Israel," which also equals 776 (314 + 102 + 360 = 776). The number 776 is also the numerical value of the word שלמות (*shlaimut*, perfection; 300 + 30 + 40 + 6 + 400), teaching us that the

children of Israel will come to שלמות by doing תשובה. That is, the fulfillment of the directive שובו בנים שובבים (= 776) will cause ביאת המשיח
(= 776). Our Sages tell us that the final future redemption is dependent on the merit of repentance: אין ישראל נגאלים אלא בתשובה, "The
children of Israel will be redeemed only with repentance" (*Sanhedrin*
97b).

Introduction to the
Interpretive Methods Used

THROUGHOUT THIS BOOK, we utilize various methods of analyzing Hebrew words. Since an understanding of these methods will greatly enhance appreciation of this work, each method is briefly explained below.

1. Gematria

(a) Primary Gematria (Numerical Value of Each Letter)
    The thirty-two principles of exegesis used by the Sages to interpret the Torah are set forth in a *baraita* (a teaching of the Oral Tradition not codified in the *Mishna*) in the name of R. Eliezer, the son of R. Yossi HaGalili. The twenty-ninth principle is the primary gematria. The commentary *Midrash Tannaim* states that the numerical values of the Hebrew letters were given to Israel at Mt. Sinai. The Hebrew letters and their values are as follows:

100 - ק (*koof*)	10 - י (*yood*)	1 - א (*alef*)
200 - ר (*raish*)	20 - כ (*kaf*)	2 - ב (*bet*)
300 - ש (*shin*)	30 - ל (*lamed*)	3 - ג (*gimel*)
400 - ת (*taf*)	40 - מ (*mem*)	4 - ד (*dalet*)
500 - ך (*final kaf*)	50 - נ (*noon*)	5 - ה (*hai*)
600 - ם (*final mem*)	60 - ס (*samech*)	6 - ו (*vav*)
700 - ן (*final noon*)	70 - ע (*ayin*)	7 - ז (*zayin*)
800 - ף (*final peh*)	80 - פ (*peh*)	8 - ח (*chet*)
900 - ץ (*final tzadeh*)	90 - צ (*tzadeh*)	9 - ט (*tet*)

For example, the primary gematria of פרנסה (*parnasah*, livelihood) is 395 (80 + 200 + 50 + 60 + 5).

Note: In this work the word *gematria* refers to the primary gematria.

The last five letters listed above (corresponding to the numbers 500–900) are the "final" forms of the letters כ מ נ פ צ and are used when the letter occurs at the end of a word. At times these letters are assigned the same value as the regular form; for example, ך is counted as 20, just as is כ. At other times, the final forms as shown above are used to represent the multiples 500 through 900. For example: the gematria of the word מלך can be either 90 or 570: by reckoning the letter ך as an ordinary כ equal to 20 (מלך = 40 + 30 + 20) or by its true final form (ך) equal to 500 (מלך = 40 + 30 + 500).

(b) Reduced Gematria (*Gematria K'tanah*) or Small Numerical Value
   (*Mispar Katan*)

The *Mispar Katan* is the primary gematria (see previous section), except with the removal of the final zeroes. For example, 10 and 100 are both counted as 1.

This type of gematria is basic to the teaching of the *Tikunei Zohar,* one of the central works of Kabbalah. It is connected to what the kabbalistic writings refer to as *Olam HaAsiyah,* the World of Action. This, the lowest of the worlds, is symbolized by the units (the "ones"), while the tens and hundreds symbolize the higher worlds (Ramchal, *Adir BaMarom*). Thus, when we reduce a word to its *mispar katan,* we discover how the concept represented by that word relates to *Olam HaAsiyah.*

Sometimes the primary gematria or *mispar katan* is reduced even further by adding together all the digits of the number until a single digit is presented. For example, the gematria of פרנסה (*parnassah*) is, as noted above, equal to 395. Using this technique we could ultimately reduce 395 to 8, as shown:

$$3 + 9 + 5 = 17$$
$$1 + 7 \quad\;\; = 8$$

(c) Full and Inner Full Gematria (Spelling out the Name of
   Each Letter)

In these forms of gematrias, each letter of a word is written out in full, and the numerical values of all the resulting letters are counted.

For example, the full gematria of the word קר (*kar*, cold) is 696—the numerical total of the letters that spell out the name of the letters of this word. Therefore, קר is spelled out thus: קוף ריש (the letters *koof* and *raish*): ק (100) + ו (6) + ף (80: its regular-form, not its final-form, value) + ר (200) + י (10) + ש (300).

Similarly, an Inner Full Gematria considers letters spelled out in full, but counts only the numerical values of the inner (that is, those following the initial) letters. For example, the Inner Full Gematria of קר is 396 (its Full Gematria minus the initial letters ק (100) and ר (200).

(d) The Addition of the *Kollel*

Sometimes, in finding the numerical equivalent of a word, we increase the total by one. Rav Y. A. Chaver in *Pitchei Sh'arim* explains that in such cases the root of a word is still attached to the upper worlds, and therefore dependent upon them. When we add the *kollel* (= 1), we thereby note the word's unique connection and dependence Above.

A striking example of this is the word ברית (*brit*, covenant). Its numerical equivalent, including the *kollel*, is 613.

ברית = 2 + 200 + 10 + 400 = 612
plus the *kollel:*   1 + 612 = 613.

Since there are a total number of 613 Scriptural mitzvot (commandments), the gematria therefore teaches us that the concept of covenant (ברית) is attached and cleaves to the 613 mitzvot.

A related practice in gematria is to find the total numerical value of a word and then add the number of letters of the word to the numerical value. By this method, the word דגל (*degel*, flag) has the numerical value of 40:

דגל: 4 + 3 + 30 = 37
plus the number of letters in דגל: 3 = 40.

The Baal HaTurim finds a Scriptural basis for the practice of adding the *kollel* to a gematria. In the Scriptural phrase (Genesis 48:5): אפרים ומנשה כראובן ושמעון יהיו לי—"Efra'eem and Menashe will be to me the same as Reuven and Shimon," the words "Efra'eem" and "Menashe" have the numerical value of 726, while "Reuven" and "Shimon" have the numerical value of 725. Thus, when we add the *kollel* to the second pair of words, the values are equal. The Torah itself testifies that they are "the same." This is a hint that sometimes it is necessary to add the *kollel*.

Efra'eem, Menashe (אפרים ומנשה)

$1 + 80 + 200 + 10 + 40 + 40 + 50 + 300 + 5 = 726$

Reuven, Shimon (ראובן שמעון)

$200 + 1 + 6 + 2 + 50, + 300 + 40 + 70 + 6 + 50 = 725$

plus the kollel: $1 + 725 = 726$.

(e) The Sequential Developing or Progressive Gematria

This gematria totals the gematrias of the first letter of a word or phrase, plus that of the first two letters of the word or phrase, plus that of the first three letters, and so on. An example found in this book is the progressive gematria of the words כסא הכבוד (*Kisai HaKavod*, Throne of Glory), which equals the gematria of the word תשובה.

כסא הכבוד + כסא הכבו + כסא הכב + כסא הכ + כסא ה + כסא + כס + כ

$20 + 80 + 81 + 86 + 106 + 108 + 114 + 118 = 713$

$713 = $ תשובה $= 300 + 400 + 300 + 6 + 2 + 5$

2. Transformation Codes

(a) Interchangeability of Letters Formed with the Same Part of the Mouth

The ancient kabbalistic work known as *Sefer HaYetzira* (*The Book of Formation*), written by our forefather Abraham, states that the letters of the Hebrew alphabet may be divided into five groups according to the part of the mouth where the letter is produced:

(1) אחה"ע—These are the guttural letters, formed in the throat, using the back of the tongue and/or the pharynx.

(2) בומ"פ—These are the labial letters, formed primarily by closing the lips.

(3) גיכ"ק—These are the palatal letters, formed mainly by contact between the palate and the back third of the tongue.

(4) דטלנ"ת—These letters are produced with the tip of the tongue against the front of the palate, just behind the teeth.

(5) זסשר"ץ—These are the sibilants-produced by expelling air between the teeth, with the tongue held flat.*

Thus, for example, the word שבע (*sheva*, seven) and שפע (*shefa*, abundance) are closely related since the letters ב and פ are interchangeable.

(b) The At-Bash Transformation (א"ת ב"ש)

According to *Midrash Tannaim*, this transformation code was also given with the Torah at Mt. Sinai. Examples of it are therefore found in the Talmud and Midrash. In the At-Bash transformation, the first letter of the alphabet is interchangeable with the last letter of the alphabet, the second with the next-to-last, and so on. This results in the following table of equivalences:

ט – נ	ה – צ	א – ת
י – מ	ו – פ	ב – ש
כ – ל	ז – ע	ג – ר
	ח – ס	ד – ק

(c) The Al-Bam Transformation (א״ל–ב״מ)

The Al-Bam transformation code was also given with the Torah at Mt. Sinai (*Midrash Tannaim*). Here the letters of the alphabet are divided into two groups. The first letter of the first group is interchangeable with the first letter of the second group, and so on.

ג–נ	ב–מ	א–ל
פ–ו	ע–ה	ד–ס
ר–ט	ק–ח	צ–ו
	ת–כ	ש–י

(d) The Ik-Bechar Transformation (אי״ק בכ״ר)

According to the *Midrash Tannaim*, the twenty-seven letters of the Hebrew alphabet are divided into three groups whereby each of the letters in the same group have the same small gematria (the final letters are included in this transformation).

זען = 7	דמת = 4	איק = 1
חפף = 8	הנך = 5	בכר = 2
טצץ = 9	וסם = 6	גלש = 3

Rav Yaakov Emden, in his commentary on *Pirkei Avot* entitled *Lechem Shamayim*, sets forth the following basic principles for the use of gematria:

> "*One cannot use gematria . . . to introduce into the Torah innovations which are not confirmed by our forefathers, who had direct and trustworthy traditions. One may, however, use gematria to uphold the teachings of our Sages and the traditions of our forefathers, and whoever originates such gematrias more power to him, and his reward will be great. For this purpose, the scholar is allowed to search tirelessly for a gematria with which to support the words of truth.*"

---

*Although grammarians include the letter י in group 1, the Kabbalah classifies it in group 5.

It is in this spirit that the author has not only cited many gematrias and related exegeses from other authorities, but has also included some which do not appear elsewhere.

The Holy Attributes (*Sefirot*)

Now and at every moment, God brings forth the Creation יש מאין—that is, *ex nihilo*, "something from nothing." His purpose? To make for himself a דירה בתחתונים—"a dwelling place in the lower worlds"—and thereby to reveal himself as the Supreme King. To this end, God irradiates his creative life force from above by means of his holy attributes, known in Kabbalah as *sefirot*.

These ten spiritual powers, or potencies, are at once the spiritual conduits through which God creates all, and the means by which he portrays himself to man. More important, because man was made in God's image—that is, an earthly creature created to be like his Creator—man has only to strive to know and emulate these ten holy attributes in order to perfect himself and complete his task here on earth.

crown	*keter*	כתר
wisdom	*chochma*	חכמה
understanding	*binah*	בינה
knowledge	*daat*	דעת
lovingkindness	*chesed*	חסד
severity	*gevura*	גבורה
beauty	*tiferet*	תפארת
victory	*netzach*	נצח
glory	*hod*	הוד
foundation	*yesod*	יסוד
kingdom	*malchut*	מלכות

The four worlds:

Emanation	אצילות
Creation	בריאה
Formation	יצירה
Action	עשיה

1

The Negative Effect of Sin

Sin: The "Plastering Over" of the Spiritual Aspect of Man

SIN HAS A NEGATIVE influence on the godly soul of a person, surrounding the soul with a coarse, materialistic covering that impedes its spiritual powers. The result is that the soul's various parts—the רוח (*ruach*, spirit) and the נפש (*nefesh*, soul)—are unable to receive and facilitate spiritual energy. This idea can be seen by the structure of the word for sin: חטא (*chet*), which is composed of טח–א (the word *tach*, "it plasters," and the letter א, *alef*). Thus, sin is the plastering over of the א in a person. The א represents the spiritual aspect of a person that is derived from God, the אלוף (*aluf*, master), Master of the world. The letter א represents God, as can be seen by its very shape: א is a composition of ו (its diagonal; the *gematria* of 6); a י above (*gematria* of 10); and a י below (10). These letters equal 26, as do the letters of God's four-lettered name (the tetragrammaton): יהוה (10 + 5 + 6 + 5 = 26).

God is hidden not only from man, but also from the world at large. The verse כי אם עוונתיכם היו מבדילים ביניכם לבין אלקיכם, "For only your sins separate you from your God" (Isaiah 59:2) explains why the Divine Light is hidden. חטא (sin) causes a חיץ (*chetz*, barrier or screen); both of these words are numerically equivalent, according to the *Ik-Bechar* transformation: חטא = (8 + 9 + 1; חיץ = 8 + 10 + 90).

This teaches us that sin has two negative implications. Primarily, it creates a distance between a person and his Creator; it also prevents the godly light from reaching the person's soul. The Rabbi of Varky explains that these two disadvantages are found in the psalm: שתה עוונותינו לנגדיך עלומינו למאור פניך, "You have set our iniquities before you, our secret sins before the light of your countenance" (Psalms 90:8).

The idea that sin covers the spiritual eyes of a person can be seen by the spelling of the letter חית (*chet*). This letter symbolizes sin by its vocalization (חת, *chet*), which is similar to the word for sin (חטא, *chet*). Even its shape (ח) is open at the bottom, indicating downfall. The connection between חט and the letter ח appears in the small numerical value of the word חט, which equals 8 (8 + 9 = 17; 1 + 7 = 8)—the value of the letter ח. According to the *Atbash* transformation, this word can be exchanged for סמא (*sama*, blinding: ח-ס, ט-מ, א-ת). The power that the angel Samael (סמאל; *samokel*, "obscuring God") utilizes to blind a person is sin (חטא is טח-א, "plastering of the א"), for it blinds the ל (*lamed*), which represents the heart and, thus, God, as we will see.

The numerical value of the "negative" letters of the word חטא—that is, חט (8 + 9 = 17)—is the same as the numerical value of the word אגוז (*egoz*, nut; 1 + 3 + 6 + 7 = 17), symbolizing the materialistic shells of the physical world (קליפות, *klipot*). Sin, therefore, encircles and covers the soul just as a shell encircles and covers the fruit of a nut.

According to the *Albam* transformation, these negative letters (חט) are the same as those of the letters קר (*kar*, cold; ק-ח, ר-ט). This teaches us that sin causes coldness—that is, laziness—in a person. חט (*chet*) is also related to חטט (*chatat*, digging), which teaches that חטא (sin) is חטט-א: the "digging away of the א." The coldness of sin is a consequence of the evil power of the nation of Amalek (עמלק). The nation of Amalek lay in wait for the nation of Israel when it left Egypt, as it says: אשר קרך בדרך, "when they encountered you on the way" (Deuteronomy 25:18).

The word קר (*kar*, cold) of the word קרך (*korchicha*) is also the root of the word מקרה (*mikre*, occurrence). Note the similarity of the English word "occur" and קרה (*kara*, happens). This is also the root of the word קרי (*keri*, nocturnal emission), showing that the nation of Amalek is indeed the source of impurity. The word חטא, in the *Albam* transformation, is ח-ק, ט-ר, א-ל (קרל); according to *Letters of Rabbi Akiva*, the ל symbolizes לב (*lev*, heart), teaching us that חטא (sin) is a result of קר (*kar*, coldness) in the heart (ל). Moreover, the letters חטא, in *Atbash*, are סתן (Satan, adversary), indicating the evil force that causes man to sin.

The letters of the word פגם (*pigam*, blemish) alphabetically follow those of בלע (*bela*, corruption), teaching us that a person's spiritual sensitivity is blemished by evil or corrupt deeds. A פגם in the soul creates a מגף (*magaf*, cover). Both of these words have the same letters in a different order, a concealment that prevents the spiritual light from entering the soul of man.

ע precedes פ

ב precedes ג

ל precedes ם

According to our Sages, the letter ס (*samech*) refers to Satan (Midrash Rabba on Genesis 17:6). The letters סמך (*samech*) are the same as those of מסך (*masach*, screen), which, alphabetically, precede those of נעל (*naal*, lock). This teaches us that the destructive power of סתן (Satan) creates a screen (מסך) that separates and "locks out" (נעל) the divine light.

מ precedes נ

ס precedes ע

ך precedes ל

The numerical value of the words פגם and מגף is 123 (80 + 3 + 4), which is the same as נגע (*nega*, plague; 50 + 3 + 70), and teaches us about the common source of these words, which is בלע (*bela*, corruption; 2 + 30 + 70).

מגף (*magaf*) is related to מגפה (*magaifa*, plague), the letters ג and פ combining to form the word גוף (*guf*, body) and showing that מגפה comes as a result of overindulgence in the material world.

The word אלף (*alef*, instruction or learning; also the name of the letter א) refers to אולפן תורה (*ulpan Torah*, study of Torah), the acquisition of divine wisdom, as is written in the book of Job (13:33): אאלפך חכמה (*aalfecha chochma*, I will teach you wisdom). Through אולפן תורה, the study of Torah, a person merits the revelation of the divine light of א, for the light of Torah has the ability to penetrate the barriers created by sin. From this we learn that the repentant should involve himself in אולפן תורה as much as possible. Rabbenu Yona, in The Foundation of Repentance (found in *Gates of Repentance*), teaches that for one who is accustomed to learn one page of Torah, a proper repentance includes learning two pages of Torah.

The opening of the letter ח (*chet*) is directed downward, which symbolizes the sinner whose tendencies and desires are also directed downward—that is, to his materialistic and baser nature. Opposed to this is the letter ה (*hei*), of the same shape but with an opening at the top, suggesting higher spiritual aspirations. Therefore, if a person blocks his spiritual striving and closes the upper opening of the ה, it becomes a ח (*chet*, sin).

The difference between these letters can be seen in the words חמץ (*chametz*) and מצה (*matzah*). חמץ, the leavened food we are forbidden to eat or even to possess during passover, is a symbol of the evil inclination: It is filled with emptiness, like the yeast that puffs up dough to make it expand but essentially adds nothing). The word מצה (*matzah*, unleavened bread), on the other hand, is the symbol of the good inclination. The only difference in the letters of these two words is the "window of repentance"—the slight opening at the top of the ה.

Impurity: The Blockage of the Spiritual

Just as the composition of the word חטא (*chet*, sin), טח–א, hints at the negative effect that sin has on the soul and mind of man, so, too, does the word טמא (*tameh*, impure) hint at טמ–א—the טמטם (*timtum*, dulling) of the soul (the טומאה). א (*tuma*, impurity) causes a צמצום (*tzimtzum*, diminishing; ט and צ are interchangeable according to the Ik-Bechar transformation). As the Torah mentions regarding forbidden foods: ונטמתם בם, "That you should be defiled thereby" (Leviticus 11:43), referring mainly to forbidden food that defiles the soul of man. One of the most impure foods is the חזיר (*chazir*, pig), equal to 225 (8 + 7 + 10 + 200), as is the word קליפה (*klipa*, shell; 100 + 30 + 10 + 80 + 5).

טמא (*tameh*, impure) has the same letters as אטם (*otem*, obstruction). Impurity causes a general breakdown of the spiritual structure of a person. Just as an אטם in the body is a barrier that prevents the flow of blood to the heart, so, too, does impurity (טומאה, *tuma*) prevent spiritual abundance and existence from reaching the heart and brain of a person. The evil impurity caused by an עברה (*aveira*, transgression) can be clearly seen in its letters: רע בה (*ra ba*, evil in it). This is what our Sages mean when they say: עברה מטמטמת לבו של אדם, "Sin dulls the heart of man" (Yoma 39a). Rabbi Eliyahu Dessler (*Michtav MiEliyahu*) writes: "The sin itself is the dullness—the desire for and cleaving to the sin does not allow a person to find something to oppose it."

The Letters of the Word עבר

The root עבר (*avar*, transgress) provides us with a deep insight into the consequences of an עברה (*aveira*, transgression). An עברה causes an עב ריש (*av raish*), a cloud over the head; according to *Letters of Rabbi Akiva*, the letter ר (*raish*) symbolizes ראש (*rosh*, head). This causes one's mind (that is, rational thought) to become clouded.

An increase of desires also causes a clouding over and grossness in a person; the letters of תאוה (*taava*, desire) and תעבה (*toava*, abomination) are similar (the letters ע and ב are more emphatic than those of א and ו). The root עבר (*avar*) is similar to עכר (*achar*, befoul, pollute; ב and כ are interchangeable, according to the *Ik-Bechar* transformation). Transgressions thus befoul the soul and the quality of man, causing him to do תעבה, abominable deeds, and bringing about עכירות (*achirut*, pollution). The letters following עכר are ש (*shin*), פ (*peh*) and ל (*lamed*), which spell שפל (*shafel*, degraded), and teach us that pollution brings one to a state of degradation. Moreover, שפל is made up of שף (*shaf*, lowering) and ל (the letter *lamed*, an abbreviation for לב, *lev*, heart).

ש follows ר

פ follows ע

ל follows כ

The word אשם (*asham*, guilt; note the similarity to the English word "ashamed") causes man to feel ashamed (אשם, *ashem*, guilty). The word אשם can be read א-שם (*alef shem*), whereby the א, the divine within man, becomes שם (from the word שמם, *shamem*, desolate) as a result of the guilt caused by the sin. In the וידוי (*vidui*, the alphabetical confessional prayer), the word אשמנו (*ashamnu*, we have sinned) expresses the deep pain and desolation (שממה) felt by the divine soul (the א) after sin. This pain comes to man (אדם, *adam*) through the transgression of an אסור (*issur*, prohibition), which can be read א-סור (*alef soor*), the removal of the א. This teaches that sin causes an סור-א, a removal and desolation of the א (the divine). When one does *teshuva*, he revives the א within himself and thus builds himself back into an אדם (*adam*). This teaches that, however great a person's transgressions, they will never damage the innermost part of the soul, the א. Through *teshuva*, a person rebuilds and remolds himself to the depths of his soul. Nothing can stand in the way of *teshuva*.

The Book of Formation (*Sefer Yetzira*) states that the letters אמש are those with which the three central elements of the world were created: א, as in אויר (*avir*, air); מ, as in מים (*mayim*, water); and ש, as in אש (*esh*, fire).

Because the alphabetical order of a word's letters changes when a sin takes place, we can learn how sin produces and effects a change in the sinner. For example, the word אשם (*asham*, guilt; these same letters rearranged) is dominated by the letters אש (*esh*, fire). Since physical fire is connected to the supernal source of fire above, this shows that the force of judgment is so strong that it rules over the sinner in the form of אשם (guilt). As a result of the soul's desolation, the fire (אש) in a person (that is, his burning power of desire) causes the אש (fire) of judgment and guilt to rule him.

חטא (sin), טומאה (impurity), and אשם (guilt) all damage the spirituality of אדם (man) by separating the א. His situation then becomes one of דם (*dam*, blood), which refers to the דמם (*domem*, inanimate), the materialistic and nonspiritual part of him. (Note the similarity to the English word "dumb.") Once a person is disposed toward the material and is subsequently spiritually stagnant, his imagination and desires become exaggerated. His life then turns into a constant quest to satisfy his insatiable desires. The result is a lack of peace and contentment; even if he were to succeed, the fulfillment of these desires could never satisfy the Divine soul.

The word רשע (*rasha*, a wicked person) stems from רעש (*raash*, noise). The wicked have no peace, being pursued throughout life by a strong evil inclination, as is written: והרשעים כים נגרש כי השקט לא יוכל, "But the wicked are like the troubled sea, for it can never be at rest" (Isaiah 57:20). The word רשע is also related to רשה (*rasha*, permitted; the ע and ה are interchangeable). The evil person (רשע) permits (רשה) everything to himself, thus paving the way to permissive life.

The strong evil forces that affect the רשע (*rasha*) are indicated in the preceding letters: קרס (*karas*, collapse).

ק precedes ר

ר precedes ש

ס precedes ע

Mystically, the letters קרס represent the evil forces. Our Sages speak about the letters קר (*kar*, cold), which form the basis of the word קרי (*keri*, nocturnal emission). This refers to the impurity of the

Amalekite (עמלק), about whom it is written (Deuteronomy 25:17): אשר
קרך בדרך, "when they encountered you on the way." The force of קר
brings man to קרס (*karas*, collapse). The letters קרס (note the similarity
to the English word "cross") are like סרק (*srak*, emptiness), indicating
that emptiness brings wickedness. The letters of סרק (*srak*) and קרס
(*kras*) are the same as the word סקרן, meaning curious. This teaches us
that incorrect סקר (*seker*, curiosity) can turn one into a רשע (*rasha*,
wicked one).

When the numerical value of the word דם (*dam*, blood; 4 + 40 =
44) is multiplied by ten (440), we see that it has the same value as that
of the word מת (*met*, dead; 40 + 400 = 440). This provides us with a
deep insight into what our Sages mean when they say: רשעים בחייהם,
קרויים מתים "The wicked, while alive, are as if dead" (Berachot 18b)—
for true life lies in the observance of the *mitzvot*, as we say in the
evening prayer: כי הם חיינו וארך ימינו, "For they are our life and the
length of our days." For the wicked, this life has been lost (see *Michtav
MiEliyahu*). If the א, the divine aspect, is missing from אמת (*emet*,
truth), then מת (*met*, death) results. Also, regarding ארץ (*aretz*, land),
when the א (*alef*) is removed, only צר (*tzar*, trouble) remains. The letters preceding the letters צר are פ and ק (*peh* and *kof*; פ precedes צ, and
ק precedes ר). Rearranged, they form the basis of the word קוף (*kof*,
monkey), alluding to the mystical power of impurity that copies the
power of purity, like the animal that apes the human before him.

2

The Prerequisites
for Repentance

Repentance: The Return of the *Hei*

THE LETTERS OF THE WORDS תשובה (*teshuva*, return or repentance) reveal
the essence of repentance. They are the first letters of five verses in
the Tanach (Bible):

ת: תמים תהיה עם ה׳ אלקיך, "You shall be wholesome with the Lord
your God" (Deuteronomy 18:13). According to Rashi, this
means that one should follow God without questioning his
ways.

ש: שויתי ה׳ לנגדי תמיד, "I have placed God before me always"
(Psalms 16:8). A man should consider God's will to be before
his at all times, indicating that a man should strengthen his
belief in divine Providence.

ו: והלכת בדרכיו, "You should go in his ways" (Deuteronomy 28:9).
This means that a person should emulate God and his thirteen
attributes; that is, to be kind and merciful, not to anger, etc.

ב: בכל דרכיך דעהו, "In all your ways you should know him"
(Proverbs 3:6). A person should always act with the knowledge
that God is present and sees all.

ה: הצנע לכת עם אלקיך, "Go humbly with your God" (Micha 6:8).
A man should be modest and humble in his ways and deeds.

310

The word תשובה is made up of (*tashuv hei*, the letter ה will return). The letter ה is made up of two letters, ד (*dalet*) and י (*yud*); the ד
is its primary component, and the י is below it. The ה is the letter with
which the world was created (Rashi, Genesis 2:4), and with which man
re-creates himself through repentance (*teshuva*). Repentance causes
holiness, symbolized by the letter ה, the letter symbolizing God's
name—to return.

The letter י (*yud*), which, together with the letter ד (*dalet*), forms
the letter ה, symbolizes the power of חכמה (*chochma*, wisdom); the primary and fundamental element, according to Kabbalah, necessary for
repentance. According to *Sefer Yetzira*, the letter י is the reference letter for אלול (Elul), the late-summer month leading into Rosh Hashana
and designated primarily for repentance. (Each month has a reference
letter symbolizing its inner essence.) Indeed, a person gains much wisdom by contemplating the bitter consequences, heartache, and דוה
(*daveh*, grief) that will be brought about by his sins. This great suffering and דוי (*dvai*, pain) leads one to the rebuilding of the letter י (*yud*,
which is spelled out as follows: יוד, the same letters as the word דוי, but
rearranged). When the letter י is blended with the ד (*dalet*; its gematria
is 4, which is equal to the four basic elements, fire, air, water, earth), it
forms the letter ה and leads to תשובה (*teshuva* and *tashuv hei*), the return of the ה.

The letter י also symbolizes life. The word חיים (*chayim*, life),
then is מח (*moach*, brain) surrounding י. The connection between חכמה
and חיים is seen in the numerical value of חיים (8 + 10 + 10 + 40) and
חכם (*chacham*, wise; 8 + 20 + 40), both 68. Through תשובה (*teshuva*),
which comes from deep understanding, one gets life; בינה (*binah*, understanding) is one before 68 (2 + 10 + 50 + 5 = 67).

Reuben: The First Repentant

According to our Sages, the verse (Genesis 37:29) וישב ראובן
אל הבור "And Reuben returned to the pit [into which Joseph was put]"
hints at the fact that Reuben repented of his sin. Our Sages say
(Midrash Rabba 84:19): "God said to him: Never has a person sinned
before me and repented. You are the first to show the way to repentance. By your life, your grandson הושע (Hosea) will be the first to
open the path to repentance." As it is said: שובה ישראל עד ה' אליך, "Israel, return to God, your God" (Hosea 14:2).

Reuben's repentance was different from the repentance of previous generations (that of Adam, Cain, etc.) in that he reached the point of complete repentance through contemplation and awareness of the future. The very name ראובן (Reuben) reveals the word ראיה (*reiya*, "sight" or "perception," whose root is ראה) and בינה (*binah*, "understanding," from the root בנה). With his perception and understanding, Reuben realized the terrible implications and consequences of the sin involved in the sale of his brother Joseph. The basis of true repentance is the realization of the extent to which sin and evil deeds negatively influence man and the world.

Understanding and Wisdom: Enabling a Person to Elevate Himself

בינה (*binah*, understanding), which is derived from the root בנה (*bana*, building), stems from wisdom and is symbolized by the letter ה. Fundamental to repentance, בינה (2 + 10 + 50 + 5 = 67) has the same gematria as the name of the month of repentance: אלול (Elul; 1 + 30 + 6 + 30 = 67). The word Elul, in Aramaic, means "searching"; its zodiac sign is Virgo, which symbolizes renewal. During this month, therefore, a person should search with the purpose of renewal; he should consider his past actions and repent of any sins. This agrees conceptually with the letter symbolic of Elul, the י (*yud*), for the י represents חכמה (*chochma*, wisdom), which refers to the initial spark of an idea or process.

חכמה (*chochma*, wisdom) and בינה (*binah*, understanding) are the fundamental aspects of the re-establishment and reintegration of a person after he falls into the תהום (*tihom*, depths) of sin. The word תהום contains the same letters as the word המות (*hamavet*, the death), the final, physical disintegration. The sinner, who is in a deteriorated and weak (מק, *mak*) state (note the English word "meek"), is able to rise (קם, *kam;* the word מק reversed) by implementing the twin qualities of חכמה and בינה. The sum of the two gematrias (חכמה + בינה = 8 + 20 + 40 + 5 + 2 + 10 + 50 + 5 = 140) is equal to the gematria of the word קם (100 + 40 = 140). This same idea is found in Leviticus: והנשארים בכם ימקו בעונם בעונם באוצת אויביכם, "And they that remain of you shall pine away (ימקו, *yimaku*) in their iniquity in your enemies' lands; and also in the iniquities of their fathers shall they pine away with them" (Leviticus 26:39).

The digits of this *gematria* (140) may be rearranged to form other numbers, thereby revealing deep mystical significance. (The re-arrangement of *gematriot* into other number sequences alludes to the transduction of parallel spiritual energies in higher worlds.)

Here, the gematria of the word קדוש (*kadosh*, holy; 100 + 4 + 6 + 300) is 410. Therefore, the way to attain holiness is to raise oneself (קם, *kam*) spiritually by means of חכמה (*chochma*, wisdom) and בינה (*binah*, understanding; חכמה + בינה = 140), thus achieving קיום (*kiyum*, existence). This קיום is dependent on holiness and purity, as can be seen from the numerical value of the word קיום (156 = 100 + 10 + 6 + 40), as well as other especially holy concepts: יוסף (the righteous Joseph; 10 + 6 + 60 + 80) and ציון (the holy mountain Zion; 90 + 10 + 6 + 50).

Wisdom and understanding are the basis of Creation, as seen by their *gematriot*:

$$\text{חכמה ובינה} = 146 \ (73 + 6 + 67)$$

This equals the word עולם (*olam*, world; 70 + 6 + 30 + 40 = 146).

The Creation of the world with wisdom and understanding appears in the verse: ה' בחכמה יסד ארץ כונן שמים בתבונה, "The Lord has through wisdom founded the earth; he has established the heavens through understanding" (Proverbs 3:19).

The word את (*et*, the undefinable word that specifies the direct object; 1 + 400 = 401) symbolizes the entire alphabet from א to ת, as is described in *Ohr Torah:* "It is learned in kabbalistic works that, first of all, the letters of the alphabet were formed, and thereafter, using these letters, God created all the worlds. This is the secret esoteric meaning of the verse: . . . בראשית ברא אלקים את, "In the beginning God created . . ." (Genesis 1:1). That is, He first created the letters of the alphabet from א to ת. The verbal confession וידוי (*vidui*), when recited in the correct alphabetical sequence (represented by את = 1 + 400 = 401), allows the sinner to arise and exist (קיום, *kiyum*), restoring him to a level of holiness (קדוש = 410) and to the status of a צדיק (*tzadik*, righteous man), who is symbolized by the letter צ (*tzadi;* צדי = 90 + 4 + 10 = 104).

The negative forces of אף וחמה (*af vechaima;* wrath and anger: 1 + 80 + 6 + 8 + 40 + 5 = 140) destroy wisdom and understanding (חכמה + בינה = 140). These forces are created by the sins of a person, causing him to weaken (מק, rot) and to be susceptible to these negative forces (Magen Avraham on Deuteronomy, Netzavim).

את	=	401
חכמה בינה קם	=	140
קדוש	=	410
צדי	=	104

The various permutations of the numbers 401, 140, 410, and 104 are all part of a total process. The sinner, by using his wisdom and understanding (חכמה and בינה = 140), becomes aware of his sin and its consequences. By activating all the letters of the alphabet (את = 401) in the וידוי (verbal confession), he is able to arise and exist (קם = 140). He thus restores himself to holiness (קדוש = 410) and clears the path to becoming a righteous man (צדי = 104).

The Power of Humility: A Prerequisite for Overcoming One's Sins

חטא (*chet*, unintentional sin) involves a lack of thought at the time of the transgression. When one's mind—the אלף (א, *alef*)—is plastered over (טח, *tach*), the result is sin, חטא. Intentional sins (עוונות) comprise עוות-נ (*avut nun*, the distortion or corruption of the letter נ, which represents understanding). These letters also allude to the power of thought and purity (עיון, *iyun*), which is connected to the fifty (נ = 50) gates of impurity and understanding.

The Chida says that the power of humility is so great that it can mend one's sins; the letters of ענוה (*anava*, humility) are the same as those of the word העון (*haavon*, the sin). As our Sages say: כל המעביר מעבירין לו על כל על מדותיו פשעיו, "Whoever overcomes his feelings, all his sins are passed over" (Rosh Hashana 17a).

Repentance out of humility and love for God changes negative actions into positive ones. This amazing concept is unique to Torah thought: Not only is a person capable of wiping the slate clean, he also has the ability to turn the negativity he has caused in the world into a positive force.

The source of humility (ענוה) is עין נוה (a pleasant eye). The name of the letter ע (עין, *ayin*) is the same as עין (*ayin*, eye). This refers to one who observes God's world without any jealousy. If a person relates to others humbly and without jealousy, so, too, will God relate to him, and ignore and nullify his bad deeds.

The humble repentant is strengthened by the realization that, despite his sins, God shows great kindness toward him. This strengthens his belief (אמונה, *emunah*) and faith (בטחון, *beitachon*), enabling him to grow and build upon his good deeds. That good and graceful deeds strengthen man's confidence and trust in God can be seen in the word בטחון, which is built from the words טוב (*tov*, good) and חן (*chen*, grace).

Another example of how a rearrangement of letters causes a change of meaning from positive to negative and vice versa involves the words פשע (*pesha*, sin) and שפע (*shefa*, abundance). The *Zohar* questions the verse: מי אל כמוך נושא עון ועבר על פשע, "Who is a God like you, who pardons sin and passes over transgression?" (Micha 7:18). Specifically, it asks, what is the meaning of "passes over transgression (פשע)"?

Answers the *Zohar:* "Abundance (שפע)!" That is, in the combination of letters composing the word שפע (abundance), the ש (*shin*) precedes the other two letters of the word (both of which symbolize other attributes). When the פ (*peh*, which also means "mouth," which symbolizes the emotional attributes of the heart) precedes the ש (which refers to the power of understanding stemming from שינון, *shinun*, repetition), the negative situation—פשע—results. On the other hand, if the ש (*shinun*, repetition) precedes the פ, then the positive situation—שפע—is attained.

A further example, using the words ענג (*oneg*, enjoyment) and נגע (*nega*, plague), is explained by the Chatam Sofer: When the ע (for עין, *ayin*, eye, denoting spiritual awareness) begins the word, this quality predominates and man enjoys (ענג) life. When, however, the ע ends the word, spirituality is of secondary importance, thus leaving man with נגע (*nega*, plague).

The Letter Dalet: Poverty and Subservience

The letter ד (*dalet*), found in the words דוה (*daveh*, pain) and ודה (*vadeh*, confession), suggests the attribute of subservience and humility that is essential for repentance. The feeling of poverty (דלות, *dalut*)—whether spiritual, intellectual, emotional, or rational—arouses a person to confess and repent. Rabbenu Yona, in his *Gates of Repentance*, states:

The seventh principle is humility, achieved through subservience with all one's heart. . . . King David, may peace be upon him, when confessing his sin when Nathan the prophet came to him, concluded:

"The sacrifices of God are a broken spirit; a broken and contrite heart, you, God, will not despise" (Psalms 51:19). "A broken spirit" connotes a humbled spirit. We learn from this that humility is one of the principles of repentance.

Through the action of ודה (*vadeh*, confession), the דלות (*dalut*, poverty) of man, symbolized by the letter ד (*dalet*), becomes enveloped in the holy light of God's name. In the word ודה, the וה of God's name surrounds the ד—like the broken, empty man who, because of his sins, has surrendered himself to God and is rewarded by becoming enveloped in the *Shechinah* (the Divine Presence in this world). This idea is brought down in *Letters of Rabbi Akiva*: "The one whose heart is broken and whose spirit is humbled merits to become a vehicle for the *Shechinah*." Furthermore, the Torah considers such a person as if an altar has been built in his heart. הוד (*hod*, glory), which refers to the Temple, is built in each person who has felt the pain (דוה) caused by sin, and has confessed (ודה).

King David was the epitome of subservience, as is indicated by the letters of his name: דוד. The two ד (דלת, *dalet*) represent דלות, as is evident from the Book of Psalms, in which King David repeatedly emphasizes his humility before God. The importance of ענוה (*anava*, humility) in bringing man to the fulfillment of the Torah is seen by the full *gematria* of the word ענו (*anav*, humble: עין נון וו = 70 + 10 + 50 + 50 + 6 + 50 + 6 + 6), which equals 248, the number of positive commandments of the Torah. This shows us that only the humble person has the potential to fulfill the commandments of the Torah.

King David, whose essence was subservience and humility, established the offering of repentance (עולה של תשובה) by which means the children of Israel could return to God. On the verse: נאם דוד בן ישי ונאם הגבר הוקם על, "The saying of David the son of Jesse, and the saying of the man raised on high (על)" (2 Samuel 23:1). Our Sages comment as follows: The word על refers to עולה (*olah*), the offering of repentance (Moed Katan 16b), which is an instruction and a provision to return—that is, to repent.

The word על (*al*) has a *gematria* of 100 (70 + 30 = 100), which refers to the one hundred blessings incumbent upon every man to recite daily. The Levush explains (Section 46):

At a time when one hundred Jews were dying daily, King David understood by means of the divine inspiration granted him that the cause was the Jews' failure to praise and bless God appropriately for all the goodness He had showered upon them. They were, in fact, dying as a result of this sin. King David, therefore, issued a decree of rectification for the nation of Israel that all men should pronounce one hundred blessings daily to counteract the daily death of one hundred people.

This decree apparently was effective, and the deaths subsequently ceased, as hinted at in the verse in 2 Samuel (23:1): "The man who was raised up on high" (על = 70 + 30 = 100), referring to the one hundred blessings of rectification. There is a related idea in the verse: מה ה' אלקיך שאל מעמך, "What (מה, *mah*) does the Lord your God require of you" (Deuteronomy 10:12). The Levush comments: "Don't read מה, but מאה" (*maiya*, one hundred), referring to the one hundred daily blessings.

The full *gematria* of the word על (עין למד = 70 + 10 + 50 + 30 + 40 + 4 = 204) is equivalent to the letters of the word צדיק (*tzadik*, righteous person; 90 + 4 + 10 + 100 = 204)—one who is elevated. According to the *Atbash* transformation, the letters of the word על parallel those of זך (*zach*, pure), teaching us that purity of spirit is the hallmark of an elevated, righteous soul.

The letters of the word על, which is the root of the word עולה (*olah*, offering, referring to repentance), provide an indication of the word's intrinsic meaning. According to *Letters of Rabbi Akiva*, the shape of the letter ע (*ayin*), as written in the Torah scroll, resembles a bent-over person, the characteristic of humility (ענוה, *anava*) and subjugation. This letter also refers to עיון (*iyun*, in-depth study). The ל (*lamed*) denotes לימוד (*limud*, learning), which essentially refers to the לב (*lev*, heart), as is stated in *Letters of Rabbi Akiva*: "The letter ל (*lamed*) connotes the heart." This is also revealed by its shape (as written in the Torah scroll), with blood vessels going up and down. The letter ב (in לב) equals 2, and refers to the two chambers of the heart. The letter ב also represents בינה (*binah*), learning and understanding. Contemplation and humility (symbolized by the ע), together with an understanding heart (symbolized by the ל), creates the fundamental essence of the word על, the elevation of a person through repentance.

The 613 Commandments and the Daily Recital of One Hundred Blessings

100	+ 613	= 713
blessings	*mitzvot*	(תשובה)

Subservience, as a fundamental element of repentance, was the main attribute of King David, who established the daily recital of one hundred blessings and raised up the offering of repentance. The number of *mitzvot* (613) plus the number of blessings (100) equals 713, the *gematria* of the word תשובה (*teshuva*, return and repentance; 400 + 300 + 6 + 2 + 5). The number 100 (מאה, *maiya*), whose outer letters form the word מה (*mah*, what), indicates the attribute of humility, as expressed by Moses and Aaron: ונחנו מה, "What are we?" (Exodus 16:7,8), denoting their great humility. The letters preceding מאה are דלת, which can be read as דלות (*dalut*, poverty), referring to humility.

ל precedes מ

ת precedes א (the alphabet is cyclical)

ד precedes ה

According to Kabbalah, the number 100 is connected to the aspect of בינה (*binah*, understanding), and that of חכמה (*chochma*, wisdom) is related to the number 1000. The letters of the word מאה, rearranged, form the word האם (*ha'em*, the mother). The basic attribute of the mother is her בינה, her understanding—as opposed to the father (אב, *av*), who is connected to the attribute of חכמה (*chochma*, wisdom). The word אם, according to the *Albam* transformation, is לב (*lev*, heart), the seat of בינה, from whence repentance originates. It is said in Isaiah: ולבבו יבין ושב ורפא לו, "And he will understand with his heart and repent and be healed" (Isaiah 6:10).

The importance of חכמה for keeping the 613 *mitzvot* can be seen in the full numerical value of the word חכמה:

חכמה = חית כף מם הי = 418 + 100 + 80 + 15 = 613

A *baal teshuva* (a person who returns to his Torah roots) must, in addition to fulfilling the 613 *mitzvot*, strengthen his humility and understanding, both hinted at by the number 100 (מאה): 613 + 100 = 713 = תשובה. He should also strengthen his faith by saying one hundred blessings daily. The *baal teshuva* becomes humble when he understands the effect of his past wrongdoings. According to Resh Lakish, the *baal teshuva* is considered greater than a *tzadik* (צדיק, righteous person). The *tzadik* concentrates on punctilious observance of the 613 mitzvot; the *baal teshuva* excels in humility and faith. These qualities are a result of his recognition of the lovingkindness of God, who receives him in repentance—an outcome of the 100 added to the 613, resulting in 713 (תשובה).

Moreover, the letter ק (*kof*), which represents קדושה (*kedusha*, holiness), equals 100. A repentant person who recites one hundred blessings daily and who fulfills the 613 *mitzvot* in holiness is considered to be "doing תשובה" (תשובה = 713 = 613 *mitzvot* + 100, קדושה).

Sanctity in worldly matters is strengthened by uttering the one hundred blessings with great intent. The connection between these hundred blessings and repentance (תשובה) is revealed in Midrash Rabba on Genesis 21, which connects the verse ועתה מה ה' אלקיך שאל מעמך כי אם ליראה את ה', "And now, Israel, what does the Lord your God request of you but to fear him" (Deuteronomy 10:12) to the verse in Genesis 3:22: ועתה פן ישלח ידו, "And now, lest He put forth His hand." Our Sages (Midrash Rabba, Genesis 21:6) teach us that the word ועתה (*veatah*, "and now"; 5 + 400 + 70 + 6 = 481) equals תלמוד (*talmud*, study; 400 + 30 + 40 + 6 + 4 = 480 + 1 [*kollel*]). That is, proper study of Torah is the basis of ועתה תשובה (*teshuva* now!).

According to the Sefat Emet, the word אלול is made up of the words לו לא (*lo lo*, nothing to Him). This teaches us that a person who nullifies himself merits to be לו (*lo*, "to Him"—that is, to God), as is seen in the interpretation of the verse (Psalms 100:3): הוא עשנו ולו אנחנו, "He created us and we are his." Because the word ולו may also be spelled ולא (and nothing), we can interpret the verse as follows הוא עשנו ולא אנחנו, "He created us and we are nothing."

The progressive *gematria* of the word אלול (אלול = 1 + 31 + 37 + 67 = 136) is also the value of סולם (*sulam*, ladder), indicating that Elul (as well as humility) is the ladder to elevate man. The number 136 is the numerical value of the word עניו (*anav*, humble person; 70 + 50 + 10 + 6 = 136), as well as that of הענוה (*haanava*, the humility: 5 + 70 + 50 + 6 + 5 = 136). According to Rabbenu Yona in *Gates of Repentance*, humility is one of the obligations of a penitent. Interestingly, the numerals of 136, rearranged, make 613, the number of *mitzvot*. This teaches us that the 613 commandments of the Torah serve as a ladder, סולם (= 136), to raise man to the upper worlds. This power of a *mitzvah* (מצוה, commandment) to elevate is seen in the root of the word: צוות (*tzevet*), which means "joining."

Introspection and Shame: Motivating a Person to Repentance

Contemplative reflection is the basis of repentance; the letters of the word שוב (*shuv*, return) alphabetically follow those of the word ראה

(*r'ei*, look). For this reason, on the last Sabbath of the month of Menachem Av, during which the month of Elul (the month of repentance) is announced, the Torah portion "Look!" (ראה, R'ei) is read. This portion enjoins man to delve into and contemplate that which takes place in both his private life and the world-at-large, as it says (Deuteronomy 11:26, 27): ראה אנכי נתן לפניכם היום, "Look, I give to you today [a blessing and a curse: a blessing that you should listen to the commandments of God your God, which I command you to do, and a curse if you will not listen to the commandments of God]."

ש follows ר

ו follows ה

ב follows א

The fact that introspection (ראה, *r'ei*) precedes repentance (שוב) is also seen in the sequence of blessings in the Shemona Esrei (the standing prayer often called Amidah) Our Sages, commenting on the order of the Shemona Esrei prayer, note that the blessing for knowledge (אתה חונן לאדם דעת ומלמד לאנוש בינה, "You favor man with knowledge and teach mankind understanding") (Megilla 176) precedes the blessing of repentance (השיבנו אבינו לתורתך, "Restore us, our Father, to your Torah"), which is followed by the blessing of forgiveness (כי חטאנו סלח לנו אבינו, "Forgive us, our Father, for we have sinned"). Knowledge through learning and introspection must precede repentance, which leads to forgiveness.

When a person recognizes the way of God and is aware of divine providence in the world, he becomes ashamed of his deeds, thus meriting forgiveness of his sins. Our Sages comment (*Berachot* 12b): מוחלין כל העושה דבר עבירה ומתבייש בו לו על כל עונותיו, "Whoever transgresses and is ashamed by it is forgiven for all his iniquities."

The word בראשית (*bereishith*, "in the beginning") comprises several words: בשת (*boshet*, shame); ירא (*yirah*, awe or fear); תשב (*tashuv*, returns); תאב (*taav*, desires), as well as ישר (*yashar*, integrity). From this we understand that shame and fear of God help us to repent; that is, the desire to reveal integrity and truth in life motivates us to seek a new beginning.

The simple numerical value of the word בראשית is 913 (2 + 200 + 1 + 300 + 10 + 400), three hundred more than the number of mitzvot (613). The number 300 implies the perfection of the number 3, for multiplication represents an ordering of a higher world. This perfection refers to the perfection of the three levels of the soul: the נפש (*nefesh*), the רוח (*ruach*), and the נשמה (*neshama*). The perfection of these three levels raises a Jew to the point of בראשית, that is, a new beginning. The purpose of a person's existence is to constantly strive for repentance. This can be seen by the fact that the word בראשית is made up of the words ראש בית (*rosh bayit*, head of the home). The "head" (that is, the main aspect) of a person's "home" (that is, his existence in this world) is the striving for בראשית, a new beginning.

The full *gematria* of the word תשובה: תיו שין וו בית הי (400 + 10 + 6 + 300 + 10 + 50 + 6 + 6 + 2 + 10 + 400 + 5 + 10) equals 1215. The number 1215 is a possible numerical value of the word יראה; according to Kabbalah, the letter א can, at times, be considered equal to 1000. א is spelled אלף (*elef*, the Hebrew word for thousand); therefore, the word יראה may total 1215 (10 = י, 200 = ר, 1000 = א, 5 = ה).

Through יראה (*yirah*, fear or awe), a person can attain complete repentance. The fear of God (יראת ה', *yirat Hashem*) is dependent upon seeing God (ראית ה', *reiyat Hashem*) as the Source of everything. When a person recognizes the divine providence in all aspects of his life and the world, he is then able to be in awe and fear of God. This leads him to be בוש (*bush*, ashamed) of his evil deeds, which ultimately results in complete repentance (שוב, "return," has the same letters as בוש).

A special divine light is revealed to the true *baal teshuva*: The letters of the word ארה (*ora*, light) alphabetically precede those of the word שוב (*shuv*, return).

א precedes ב

ר precedes ש

ה precedes ו

The *Zohar* states that the verse: לחזות בנועם ה', "To behold the pleasantness of God" (Psalms 27:4) refers to the "pleasant" reward for repentance. When a person reflects on the ways of the world and sees divine providence within them, then he merits to see clearly the revelation of God in all His ways.

Faith: The "Mother" of Understanding

In order to merit יראת שמים (*yirat shamayim*, fear or awe of Heaven), a person must strengthen his אמונה (or אמנה; *emunah*, belief). The Ramah writes (*Shulchan Aruch*, Orach Chayim, 6):

When a person is aware that the great King, the Holy One, blessed be
he, who fills the whole earth with his glory, stands above him, and sees
his deeds . . . immediately he will become full of awe and will surrender himself (that is, his ego) to the fear of God, blessed be he.

Belief in the existence of God and his constant divine providence
is the beginning of the fear of God. The full inner *gematria* of the
word אמנה (לף ם ון י ;אלף מם נון הי = 30 + 80 + 40 + 50 + 6 + 10 = 216) is
the same as that of יראה (*yirah*, fear; 10 + 200 + 1 + 5 = 216), for fear of
God is a result of one's belief. The number 216 is also the numerical
value of the word גבורה (*gevura*, strength or control; 3 + 2 + 6 + 200 +
5), teaching us that by fear of and faith in God, a person is able to govern and control his evil inclination.

יראת שמים, the fear of Heaven, is most important at the beginning
of a person's life, as seen in its *gematria*:

1001 (10 + 200 + 1 + 400 + 300 + 40 + 10 + 40

This number represents "beginning": 1000 is spelled אלף (*elef*) in Hebrew; אלף spells the name of the first letter (א) of the *alef-bet* (the Hebrew alphabet). The numerical value of this first letter is, of course, 1.
Thus, we have twice א, emphasizing the importance of starting life
with יראת שמים, as it says: ראשית חכמה יראת ה', "The beginning of wisdom is the fear of God" (Proverbs 111:10).

Inasmuch as fear of God is indispensable for acquiring חכמה
(*chochma*, wisdom) and for improving and developing it, חכמה, in its
turn, amplifies and transforms יראה simple fear into the loftier concept
of awe of God.

Although fear of God is strengthened by means of חכמה (*chochma*,
wisdom), it also time improves and develops both חכמה and בינה, as is
written: אם אין חכמה אין יראה אם אין יראה אין חכמה, "If there is no wisdom,
there is no fear; if there is no fear, there is no wisdom" (Ethics of Our
Fathers 3:17). A primal fear of God is necessary to achieve wisdom,
but perfect fear or awe of God is only acquired through wisdom.

The full inner *gematria* of יראה (וד יש לף י ;יוד ריש אלף הי = 6 + 4 +
10 + 300 + 30 + 80 + 10 = 440) is the same as the gematria of the word
תם (*tam*, perfection): 400 + 40 = 440. The word אמת (*emet*, truth) is
made up of תם and א, which refers to the Holy One, blessed by he, the
Master (אלוף, the א) of the world. The perfect man is a man of truth.
The reduced *gematriot* of the words אמת (1 + 4 + 4) and אדם (*adam*,
man; 1 + 4 + 4) are the same. This teaches us that the essence of the
perfect man is the truth he acquires by יראת שמים, fear of Heaven.

A person's spiritual level is connected to his אמונה (*emunah*, faith). The talmudic Sage Resh Lakish says: כל העונה אמן בכל כחו פותחין לו שערי גן עדן, "Anyone who answers אמן (amen) with all his might causes the gates of the Garden of Eden to open for him" (Shabbat 119b), as is said: פתחו שערים ויבא גוי צדיק שמר אמנים, "Open the gates and a righteous nation who has kept the faith will come in" (Isaiah 26:2). Do not read אמונים (*emunim*, faithful), but אמנים (*amenim*, the amens we say in response to blessings). The gates of heaven open up for a person in the merit of his יראת שמים, as is written: זה השער לה' . . . פתחו לי שערי צדק צדיקים יבאו בו, "Open for me the gates of righteousness; this is the gate to God, the righteous will enter it" (Psalms 118:19, 20).

The word אמן is made up of אם–ן: "mother (אם, *em*) of the ן (*nun*). The letter ן, whose numerical value is 50, refers to נ' שערי בינה, the fifty gates of understanding (בינה).

אמונה (*emunah*, faith) also refers to the attribute of בינה (*binah*, understanding), as indicated by its letters אם (mother) and ן, both of which suggest בינה. Through contemplation a person comes to understand, thus increasing his awe and leading him to perfection. As it is said: סוף דבר הכל נשמע את האלקים ירא ואת מצותיו שמור כי זה כל האדם, "The end of the matter, when all is said and done: fear God and keep his commandments, for that is the whole of man" (Ecclesiastes 12:13).

The total spiritual structure (בנין, *binyan*) of a person is based on אמונה (*emunah*, belief). This is revealed by the proximity of the letters of the words אם to אמן, and בן to בנין. Just as a mother is essential to the development of her son, so is אמונה essential to בינה, for בינה is an outgrowth of the אימה (*aima*, fear) that a person has for his Creator. (ב follows א, and נ follows מ; both words include הי, a name of God.)

The Sabbath's Ability to Bring About Repentance

אמונה (faith) and תורה (Torah) are the basis of תשובה. This idea stems from the numerical value of תשובה (713), which equals the combined numerical values of תורה (611) and אמונה (102). During the holy שבת (Sabbath), one can sense and have a deep realization of Divine Providence. When a person experiences the holiness of *Shabbat*, his mind expands. This provides the impetus for becoming pure. He becomes free of the influence of the mixture of the knowledge of good and bad, thus returning to the initial point at which אדם הראשון (*adam harishon,* the first man, Adam) began before the Sin. The *Zohar Chadash* explains that even Adam realized that the Sabbath has an intrinsic ability to induce repentance. This is also stated in Midrash Rabba, Genesis, on the verse from Psalms 92: מזמור שיר ליום השבת טוב להודות לה׳, "A song for the Sabbath day: It is good to thank and praise God." The letters of the word שבת are the initial letters of שבת בו תשוב, "*Shabbat*, in it you should repent."

Shabbat is the time in which a person's נשמה (*neshama*, soul) is unified with its divine source. This can be clearly seen in the word שבת: שב–ת (*shav tav*, "return to the ת"). The letter ת, whose numerical value is 400, refers to the fourth dimension that transcends the natural world's three dimensions of length, width, and breadth. Thus, ת is a letter denoting עולם הבא (*olam haba*, the world-to-come). Consequently, when a person returns to the world-to-come (שב–ת), to the source of his נשמה, he is aroused to repent.

The letters of the word שבת (ש–בת, *shin bat*) also show how the Sabbath enlightens בת (*bat*, daughter), the souls of the daughters of Israel, with a double quantity of light. The triple-branched letter ש (*shin*), as written in the Torah, comprises the letters of the word זיו (*zeev*, shining). According to the *Sefer Yetzira*, the ש is the letter with which God created the element of fire. The shining light (the ש) of *Shabbat* and the supernal fire (that is, the spiritual source above of physical fire in this world, as represented by the letter ש) are kindled in the hearts of the daughters of Israel (ש–בת, "light for the daughter"), helping them to attain perfect repentance.

The numerals of the *gematria* of שבת (300 + 2 + 400 = 702) are the same as that of אור (*ohr*, light; 1 + 6 + 200 = 207). *Shabbat* is like a ray of light, full of lovingkindness. The *gematria* of the word חסד (*chesed*, lovingkindness; 8 + 60 + 4 = 72) contains the same numerals. It is God's attribute of lovingkindness that enables a person to repent.

In his book *Ateret Tiferet*, the Ben Ish Chai says that the aspect of knowledge and the connection of knowledge to *Shabbat* are hidden in the word שבת. The full inner *gematria* of שבת (שין בית תו; ו יׁת יׁן = 10 + 50 + 10 + 400 + 6 = 476) is the same as בדעת (*bidaat*, with knowledge: 2 + 4 + 70 + 400 = 476). This is also the full *gematria* of the letter י (יוד ויו דלת = יׁוד: (10 + 6 + 4 + 6 + 10 + 6 + 4 + 30 + 400 = 476). The letter י is symbolic of the upper world of אצילות (*atzilut*, the world of emanation, far more sublime than our world of action), which hints at the teaching that the spiritual light of that high world is revealed on the Sabbath.

inner full *gematria* of שבת = 476
gematria of בדעת   = 476
Full *gematria* of י   = 476

The sum of the ordinals of letters of שבת in the *alef-bet* are 45: ש is the twenty-first letter; ב, the second letter; ת, the twenty-second (21 + 2 + 22 = 45). Forty-five is the numerical value of the word מה (*mah*, what), denoting humility. שבת is a time when a person should be humble and surrender to God by realizing his dependence on God. The same applies to the principle of תשובה, repentance.

Clarity of the Mind Leads to Repentance

The letters of the word ראש (*rosh*, head) alphabetically precede those of the word תשב (*tashuv*, return), indicating that perfect repentance is dependent upon clarity of the mind (the head). According to our Sages, the letters composing ראש symbolize the primary rational attributes: כתר (*keter*, crown), חכמה (*chochma*, wisdom), and בינה (*binah*, understanding). These rational attributes are the source of a person's emotional attributes, by which all of life's actions are influenced.

ר precedes ש

א precedes ב

ש precedes ת

The letter ריש (ר, *raish*, symbolizing the head: ראש, *rosh*) symbolizes the concept of beginning (ראשית, *reishith*). It is stated: ראשית חכמה יראת ה' "The beginning of wisdom is the fear of God" (Psalms 111:10). The word ראשית denotes חכמה (*chochma*, wisdom), from which fear emerges. The א (*alef*), which is the central letter of the word ראש, refers to the אלוף (*aluf*, master)—that is, to God, the Master of the world, and, hence, to the attribute of כתר (*keter*, crown). The letter ש (*shin*) symbolizes the root of the word שנן (*shanan*, teach or instruct), as it appears in the expression from the Shema: ושננתם לבניך, "And you shall teach it to your sons" (Deuteronomy 6:7). This refers to בינה. This expression is used to show that one must teach clearly, so that the child will understand; שנן, then, refers to teaching that will result in clear understanding.

A perfect repentance emerges from the three rational attributes: כתר, חכמה, בינה. These three attributes are represented by the three

branches of the ש, the central letter of the word תשב (*tashuv*, return).
From this we conclude that the three attributes are central to *teshuva*,
the return to God.

Repentance has the power to elevate a person to the highest
worlds, as seen in Hosea 14:2: שובה ישראל עד ה' אלקיך, "Return, Israel,
to the Lord, your God." Our Sages remark: גדולה תשובה שמגעת עד כסא
הכבוד, "How great is repentance, for it reaches to the Throne of Glory
(כסא הכבוד, *kisai hakavod*)" (*Yoma* 86a). The *gematria* of the word תשובה
(*teshuva*, repentance; $400 + 300 + 6 + 2 + 5 = 713$) is the same as the
progressive *gematria* of the words כסא הכבוד:

כ כס כסא כסאה כסאהכ כסאהכב כסאהכבו כסאהכבוד; $20 + 80 + 81 + 86 +$
$106 + 108 + 114 + 118 = 713$.

Repentance has the power to bring about the redemption of the
world, as is said: ולציון גואל תביא ולשבי פשע ביעקב, "But to Zion a re-
deemer shall come, and to them that repent of their transgression in
Jacob" (Isaiah 59:20). According to our Sages, the source of גאולה
(*geula*, redemption) is connected to the world of *atzilut* and כתר (*keter*,
crown). The letters of כתר, according to the *Atbash* transformation, are
the same as those of גאל (*gaal*, redeemed: ל–א ר–ג ת–כ). Through perfect repentance, the repentant attaches himself to the world of כתר,
thus bringing redemption to himself and to the world. The word גאולה
is made up of the words גלה–א (*galeh alef*, the revelation of the א). The
letter א refers to God's being both the אלוף (*aluf*, master) and the פלא
(*pele*, wonder) of the world—the same letters rearranged. גאולה (redemption) emanates from repentance and attachment to the world of
אצילות (emanation).

Our Sages say (*Pirkei d'Rabbi Eliezer*): שובה ישראל עד ה' אלקיך,
"Return, Israel, to the Lord your God" refers to the One who told
you at Sinai: "I (אנכי) am God your God." אנכי (*anochi*, I), the first
word of the first of the Ten Commandments, is made up of אני (*ani*,
I) and the letter כ (*kof*), which refers to the world of כתר (*keter*). אני
refers to the innermost point in the souls of the nation of Israel,
which, when aroused through repentance, leads to their cleaving and
devotion to God.

This devotion to God is likened to purifying waters. Water is pu-
rified when it comes in contact with the source of pure water. Similarly, when the soul cleaves to the divine Source, the sins are rinsed
away, leaving a pure soul. On the verse in Isaiah: אנכי אנכי הוא מחה פשעיך
למעני, "I, even I, am he Who blots out your transgressions for my own
sake" (Isaiah 43:25), the *Zohar* states that this is the same אנכי as the

One who says: אנכי ה׳ אלקיך, "I am the Lord your God." That is, if the nation of Israel cleaves to God and fulfills the commandments that were given at Mount Sinai, then God will wipe away its sins.

The letters of the words אני (*ani*, I) and אין (*ayn*, nothing) parallel the three attributes of כתר, חכמה, בינה (crown, wisdom, understanding). The letter כ refers to כתר (*keter*, crown); the י to חכמה (*chochma*, wisdom), the ן to בינה (*binah*, understanding). When a person repents, he rebuilds his אני, his "I" or "self." Repentance is therefore considered to be like creation of יש מאין (*yaish m'iyin*, creation of something from nothing), which depends upon these three attributes.

The fact that the letters of the word אין (nothing) are the same as those of the word אני (self) teaches us that humility is the foundation needed to build the self, the אני of man. When a person nullifies himself before the Creator, putting himself in the category of אין, then he is able to find his אני. When a person is humble, he is able to achieve great things as a result of the light that emanates from the three attributes of בינה, חכמה, and כתר, which are parallel to the letters of אין.

This is similar to the process of seed growth. First, the seed rots, becoming part of the ground. Then, after it loses its identity as a seed, it is able to absorb water, its source of life, and grow. So, too, when a person nullifies himself and learns Torah (often referred to as water), he is able to draw down to absorb all available energies, and grow.

Our Sages say: קדושה מביאה לידי ענוה, "Holiness leads to humility" (*Avodah Zarah* 20b). The full inner *gematria* of האין (*ha'ayn*, "the nothing" a reference to humility) is 186 (הי אלף יוד נון : י לף וד ון = 10 + 110 + 10 + 56), which is the same as the full *gematria* of the letter קוף (ק: 100 + 6 + 80 = 186). According to our Sages, the letter ק represents holiness (קדושה, *kedusha*) (*Shabbat* 104a). Holiness, then, is achieved through humility.

The Sefat Emet explains how nullification, the basis of repentance, is revealed in the word תשובה. From the letters of the word תשובה, we can form the words תוהו (*tohu*, void) and בהו (*vohu*, emptiness). Says the Sefat Emet, the three branches of the letter ש (also found in תשובה) suggest the three attributes of כתר, חכמה, בינה (*keter*, *chochma*, and *binah*; crown, wisdom, and understanding). One can conclude that the words תהו and בהו refer to the humility and nullification in a person, and that the ש (which symbolizes these rational attributes) refers to the spiritual development of a humble person.

When a person makes himself unimportant, he may be likened to a שאר (*sh'ar*), a remnant. And when he then nullifies himself before his Creator, he merits the level of ראש (*rosh*, head). Once he attains this level, he is able to return (תשב, *tashuv*, whose letters follow those of ראש) further. So, too, can stage-by-stage repentance elevate a person to the exalted spiritual world of כתר (*keter*, crown), for the letters of the Hebrew word for crown (תגא, *taga*) follow the word תשב:

ש precedes ת, which precedes א

ר precedes ש, which precedes ת

א precedes ב, which precedes ג

Through the attachment of man to the other-worldly root of his soul, the spiritual patient is able to attain the cure (רפואה, *refuah*) and the healing (ארוכה, *arucha*) for his sickness. The root of the word רפא, רפואה, has the same letters as פאר (*p'er*, glory). The root of the word ארוכה is the same as the word ארך (*erech*), which, according to Kabbalah, symbolizes the attribute of כתר (*keter*, crown), which is also called אריך אנפין (*arich anpin*, long face).

The letters of the word פאר, which are the same as רפא (*refa*, healing), follow the letters of the word עתק (*atak*), which allude to עתיק (*atik*, ancient). According to Kabbalah, this also refers to כתר (also known as עתיקא קדישא, *atika kedisha*, the ancient Holy One). From this we can understand the words of our Sages: גדולה תשובה שמביאה רפואה לעולם, "How great repentance is, as it brings healing to the world" (*Yoma* 86a), that is, emanations from פאר and כתר.

The מחלה (*machla*, sickness) of man resulting from חול (*chol*, secular, profane, unholy) in his soul is taken away and healed by God in his great חמלה (*chemla*, mercy).

According to the Ben Ish Chai (Ben Yehoyada), the word רפואה may be divided to form the words אור (*ohr*, light) and פה (*peh*, mouth). This teaches us that truthful confession depends on the perfection of the light (אור) of the brain and the mouth (פה).

The Desire to Expose the Truth

In order to expose and perceive the truth, a desire to do so is necessary. This is revealed by the letters of the words חפש (*chipas*, searching) and חשף (*chasaf*, exposed). When a person tires of his constant searching, the light of truth is exposed to him. What's more, he then reaches his destination, which is חפש (*chofesh*, freedom) from the chains of the evil inclination, as our Sages say: הבא לטהר מסייעין אותו, "He who comes to purify himself receives divine assistance" (*Yoma* 38b). The similarity between the words אמץ (*ametz*, striving) and מצא (*matzah*, finding), as well as that between יגיע (*yagiah*, laboring) and הגיע (*higiah*, reaching), shows that if a person makes an effort, he will eventually reach his goal of truth.

The soul that seeks and desires truth will search and ask: איה מקום כבודו, "Where is the place of His glory?" This is the beginning of the road to repentance (*Likutai Halachot*, hilchot Rosh Hashana). The word איה (*ayeh*, where), an expression of wonder, conceals the answer in its very letters. These letters are the same as אהיה and יה, two of the names of God. Our forefather Abraham, who searched for the Creator of the world (referred to as "the Palace"), merited the revelation of the "Master of the palace" himself. Our Sages (Midrash Bereishith Rabba) relate that this is analogous to a person, walking along the road, who comes to a burning palace. "Doesn't this palace have a keeper?" he asks himself, and at that moment he is greeted by the master of the palace himself. Similarly, our Patriarch Abraham also questioned the existence of a world seemingly without a master. For this, he merited to have God reveal Himself to him and tell him: "I am the Master of the world!"

When someone has a חשק (*chaishek*, desire) for an object, this means that he has a connection, חישוק (*chishuk*, link), to that object, as is said: "According to the strength of his effort, so he achieves" (*Tzidkat Hatzadik*). The רצון (*ratzon*, will or desire) is the אנור (*tzinor*, conduit) and vessel for receiving spiritual abundance. Linked to the strength of this רצון is the ability of this צנור to receive. The word כלי (*kli*, vessel) is closely linked to the word כלה (*kala*, yearning). This alludes to the notion that it is according to the depth of the soul's yearning that the vessel can receive the light of abundance.

Just as חפץ (*chaifetz*, desire) is the same as and is connected to its חפץ (*chaifetz*, object), so, too, does a צמא (*tzameh*, thirsty person) or נפש צמא (*tzameh nefesh*, thirsty soul) find מצא (*motzeh*), the yearning of his soul. It can be said, then, that the חפץ (*chaifetz*, desire) of the heart, which leads to חפש (*chipas*, searching; צ and ש are interchangeable), results from חשב (*chashuv*, thinking; ב and פ are interchangeable).

The importance of searching for the truth in the process of repentance is revealed in the word תשובה (*teshuva*, repentance). This word contains within it the words תהו ובהו *tohu u'vohu*, void and emptiness) and the ש (*shin*), the letter of building. These words (תהו ובהו)

allude to the person who, amazed and wondering (תהה בהה, *taha baha*), searches for the ש, the letter symbolizing שרש (*shoresh*, root). Repentance is the search for the source, the root of all: God.

A similar idea is found in the book *Shaarai Teshuva* by Rabbi Yaakov Abuchazira, who points out that the letter ש represents שנן (understanding); that is, by doing תשובה (repentance), the negative situation of תהו ובהו is corrected.

King David's request and search for the Temple led to the revelation of God, as is suggested in the verse: לשכנו תדרשו ובאת שמה, "You shall seek Him at His dwelling, and there shall you come" (Deuteronomy 12:5). Whatever one searches for is revealed. Zion, too, is attained through search, as the verse of rebuke suggests: ציון דורש אין לה, "Zion, no one searched [that is, cared] for it" (Jeremiah 30:17). Our Sages say: "You have to demand it" (*Sukka* 41a), meaning that if a person desires something, it will be attained.

תקוה (*tikvah*, hope) creates a קו (*kav*, a line or connection) to the desired object, as the verse suggests: ויש תקוה לאחריתך נאם ה' ושבו בנים לגבולם, "There is hope for your future, that the children come back again to their own border" (Jeremiah 31:16). Our Sages learn from this verse (Yalkut Aicha) that the generation that sincerely awaits the kingdom of God will immediately be redeemed. The redemption resulting from repentance (תקוה implies תשובה) is dependent upon the Jewish people's will and yearning to be pure.

According to Rabbi Abuchazira, the letter ש, equal to 300, symbolizes רוח אלקים (*ruach Elokim*, the spirit of God; 200 + 6 + 8 + 1 + 30 + 5 + 10 + 40 = 300), all of which is concealed in the ש of תשובה.

3

The Three Stages
of Repentance

Regret Causes a "Hole in the Clay"

ACCORDING TO *Letters of Rabbi Akiva*, the letter ט (טית, *tet*) is related to
טיט (*teet*, clay), which refers to materialism, as is said: תקרי טית אלא טיט
אל, "Don't say *tet*, but rather say *teet* (clay)." It also represents טומאה
(*tuma*, impurity), whose root is טמא, which causes a person to tend toward materialism. The root טמא is made up of אמ-ט (*em tet*, mother of
the clay), the source of materialism (clay). חטא (*chet*, sin) is א–טח—the
plastering over of a person (א), which prevents the light of repentance
from penetrating him.

For a person to break through the barrier of materialism surrounding his heart, he must first acknowledge truth and then feel
heartfelt חרטה (*charata*, regret; from the root חר-ט, *chor tet*, "hole in
the clay"). Rabbi Eliyahu Dessler states (*Michtav MiEliyahu*): "To the
same extent that a person manages to open his heart, thereby allowing
the pure truth to penetrate, so too are the gates of heaven opened."
The letter ר (ריש, *raish*) in the root חרט (*charat*) separates the letters חט,
the negative letters of the word חטא (*chet*, sin). A person's intellect,
symbolized by the ר (ראש–ריש, *rosh*, head), allows him to observe and
realize the negative implications of the sin (symbolized by the letters
חט). Regret, therefore, brings about the nullification of the evil power
of the sin.

Rabbi Dessler adds that if the Jewish people were to shed sincere
tears on Tisha B'Av (the ninth day of the month of Av, when both

Temples were destroyed), the materialistic shells of evil would break, thereby bringing redemption. Similarly, tears of true regret cleanse and purify the soul. The letters of the word גלה (*gala*, revealed) follow those of the word בכה (*bacha*, cried), teaching us that regret of or pain from our sins will uncover and reveal the coarse materialism covering our hearts. Crying, as a rectification of sin, is seen in the similarity of the words נתוק (*nituk*, cut off as a result of the sin), קינות (*kinot*, crying, lamenting) and תקון (*tikun*, rectification). Through sin, we are נתוק (cut off); through קינות (lamenting), we return and are brought to תקון (rectification).

The holy Ari said that one of the most important means of תקון of one's character is טרחה (*tircha*, effort) in fulfilling the *mitzvot* (commandments) in general, and by learning Torah in particular. The letters of the תרחה are the same as those of חרטה (*charata*, regret). The letters of חרט (*charat*, the root of חרטה) are similar to those of טהר (*tahor*, spiritually pure; the ה and ח are interchangeable). Purity (טהרה) of the soul, then, is the result of heartfelt regret (חרטה) combined with increased effort (טרחה) at fulfilling the *mitzvot* of the תורה (Torah; the ת and ט are interchangeable).

The Importance of the Alphabetical Order of the Vidui

There is a strong connection between verbal confession (וידוי, *vidui*) and complete repentance, as is said in Hosea: ישראל עד ה' אלקיך כי כשלת בעונך שובה, "Return, Israel, to the Lord your God, for you have stumbled in your iniquity" (Hosea 14:2). We also have the verse אל ה' קחו עמכם דברים ושובו, "Take with you words and turn to the Lord" (Hosea 14:3). The injunction "Take with you words" refers to verbal confession, an essential aspect of repentance leading a person back to God.

After a person has repented, he is likened to a new creation. This is indicated in Midrash Rabba on Leviticus 30:3, which comments on the verse: ועם נברא יהלל יה, "A created nation praised God" (Psalms 102:19). That is, in the future, God will recreate those who repent (*baalei teshuva*) into new creatures. That the letters יה (a name of God; 10 + 5 = 15) are equal to those of ודה (*vadah*, confess; 6 + 4 + 5 = 15) indicates that וידוי causes God's light to be revealed in the soul of a person.

The book *Reishith Chochma* says:

> It is customary to confess in alphabetical order, since all the worlds were created with these twenty-two letters, as it is explained in *Sefer Yetzira*. It is written in the *Zohar* that sin blemishes all the worlds. It is, therefore, fitting to confess in alphabetical order.

The Ravad writes that "one should know that the נשמה (*neshama*, soul) is woven together by the holy letters [like the genetic code of a person's physical body]." If a person transgresses the Torah, the sequence of the letters of his soul are changed; his sin is encoded within him (like certain types of genetic mutations). It is written: ותהי עונתם על עצמותם, "and their iniquities will be upon their bones" (that is, their נשמה, soul) (Ezekiel 32:27). God, the Master of lovingkindness, removes himself from the sinner, causing the spiritual "limb" to die, to be cut off (כרת, *karet*) or to be debilitated. Sin disrupts and damages the original sequence of the holy letters both in the soul and in the world. When a person confesses by saying וידוי (*vidui*, the alphabetical confessional prayer) from the depths of his soul, with sincerity and remorse, he rectifies the sequence of the soul's letters, which was distorted as a consequence of his sin.

The *M'or Ainiyim* (on Vayetzai) says: "The main thing is to verbally confess before one's Creator in complete truth, with a perfect heart and with deep remorse; then that which he damaged is rectified." When a person sins, he blemishes the Torah. The Torah is an expression of the twenty-two letters of the אלף בית (*alef-bet*, the Hebrew alphabet) with which the heavens and earth were created. Sin diminishes the amount of letters in the upper Torah. This means, for example, that if a person steals, thereby transgressing the commandment לא תגנב ("You shall not steal"), he separates those particular letters from the Torah and from the corresponding portion of his soul, which is composed of letters. When he has remorse for something he has done wrong, he must confess orally, because the confession is also made up of these letters. By remembering the sin orally, the repentant rectifies that which he blemished, thereby returning the letters to their rightful place.

This fundamental idea, that sin blemishes the letters of the אלף בית, is also found in the Talmud. Rabbi Yochanan asks: "Why were we afflicted alphabetically [referring to the fact that the Book of Lamentations is written in alphabetical sequence]?" (*Sanhedrin* 104a).

He answers that it is due to the fact that we transgressed the Torah, which was given by means of the *alef-beit*.

Confession: Changing Spiritual Pain into Spiritual Glory

וידוי (*vidui*, verbal confession) has the power to change the darkness caused by sin into the light that illuminates the soul (*neshama*). If we change the sequence of the letters of the root of the word ודה (*vadah*, confess), we form the negative word דוה (*dava*, grief or pain) and the positive word הוד (*hod*, glory). This implies that sin distorts a state of glory (הוד) into a state of pain (דוה), which can be rectified through confession (ודה), as is seen in the words תקון and קינות. The sequence and arrangement of these energies is important. Sin distorts the arrangement of letters that constitute the essence of man and the world, thus changing a state of glory (הוד) to one of grief (דוה). The letters can be returned to the source of their original state and the root of their existence by means of וידוי (confession). That is, through וידוי (confession), spiritual pain (דוה) is changed to spiritual glory (הוד).

The *gematria* of the word וידוי (6 + 10 + 4 + 6 + 10 = 36) is the same as the number of righteous people for whose sake the world is said to exist. Thirty-six is the number 6 squared ($6 \times 6 = 36$). This number, according to Kabbalah, is the number representing purity and holiness.

The numerical value of the word אהל (*ohel*, tent; 1 + 5 + 30) is also 36. Mystically, this refers to the two parts of the soul: the halo (הלה) and the אורה (*ora*, light, aura) that surround a person like a tent. This teaches us that, through proper confession, a person can attain a very high spiritual level.

The small *gematria* of the word וידוי (6 + 1 + 4 + 6 + 1 = 18) is the same as the numerical value of the word חי (*chai*, life; 8 + 10 = 18). When a person confesses, he is able to achieve a true and full חיים (life), for life is the essence of a righteous person, as is said: חי צדיק איש (*tzadik ish chai*, a righteous person lives). The letter צדי (צ, *tzadi*) represents the righteous person and is the eighteenth (חי) letter in the *alef-bet*.

The progressive *gematria* of the word וידוי (ו וי ויד וידו וידוי; 6 + 16 + 20 + 26 + 36 = 104) is the same as the full numerical value of the letter צדי (90 + 4 + 10 = 104), which teaches that confession elevates a person to a level of righteousness.

The destructive energies produced by the sins of Israel caused the destruction of the Temple (Beit Hamikdash). The Temple was referred to as הוד (*hod*, glory), as the Sages say: לך ה' הגדולה הגבורה התפארת והנצח וההוד, "Yours, God, is the greatness, the power, the beauty, the victory, and the glory" (Berachot 58a). The destruction of the Temple caused Israel to lament and to grieve, as it says in Lamentations: על זה היה דוה לבנו על אלה חשכו עינינו, "For this our hearts grieved (דוה, *dava*), for this were our eyes darkened" (Lamentations 5:17). The pain (דוה) that was caused by the destruction of הוד—the Temple—was due to sin. The reparation and return of הוד (glory) to its former state comes through וידוי (verbal confession). ודה (*vada*, confess) is also related to the word הודאה (*hodaa*, acknowledgement) because, during confession, a person acknowledges the truth of his deeds.

In the sequence of their letters, the words הוד and דוה express positive and negative attributes, respectively. In the word דוה (suffering), the primary letter, ד (*dalet*) controls the letters ו (*vav*) and ה (*hei*). The ד symbolizes the four elements (ד = 4): fire, air, water, and earth. From their spiritual source Above, these elements become progressively more physical as they descend through the worlds of emanation, Creation, and formation (אצילות בריאה יצירה). Finally, in our world of action (עשיה, *asiyah*), the lowest of all the worlds, these four elements adopt their common physical forms, thereby establishing the physicality of the universe. It is in this low, physical world of action that these four elements give expression to their four evil qualities in man: pride (from fire); frivolity (from air); lust (water); and laziness (earth).

The ו and ה, two letters of God's name (יהוה), hint at the six emotional attributes (ו = 6): חסד (*chesed*, lovingkindness); גבורה (*gevura*, strength or power); תפארת (*tiferet*, beauty or harmony); נצח (*netzach*, eternity or victory); הוד (*hod*, glory); and יסוד (*yesod*, foundation). In addition and subsequent to these is the attribute of מלחות (*malchut*, kingdom), symbolized by the letter ה. When the four elements (represented by the letter ד) influence these seven emotional attributes of man, the state of דוה (*dava*, suffering) may result.

According to the *Zohar*, דוה is another name of Amalek, the one who causes pain to the nation of Israel. Lamentations states: השיבני אחור נתנני שממה כל היום דוה, "He has turned me back, made me desolate all day in grief" (Lamentations 1:13). The evil power of גאוה (*gaava*, pride) causes דוה, as can be inferred from the equivalent *gematriot*:

דוה: 4 + 6 + 5 = 15
גאוה: 3 + 1 + 6 + 5 = 15

The reduced *gematria* of the word Amalek (עמלק) is also 15 (70 + 40 + 30 + 100 = 7 + 4 + 3 + 1), thus showing the connection between pride and suffering and the evil Amalek.

It is interesting to note that the *gematria* of Amalek (עמלק, 70 + 40 + 30 + 100 = 240) is the same as that of רם (*ram*, proud; 200 + 40 = 240). Furthermore, the letters of רם, reversed, read מר (*mar*, bitterness), once again showing that pride brings the bitterness of suffering.

The word גאוה (*gaava*, pride) shows how pride increases a person's lust and ambitions. It is built from ג-אוה, the ג (*gimel*, representing growth and greatness) of אוה (*avah*, desire). Pride increases desire in a person to such an extent that he is never able to fulfill all his ambitions. This leads to constant frustration and depression. Pride brings pain to a person, as can be seen in the alphabetical order of the letters גאוה (*gaava*, pride), which precede דאוה (*dava*, pain).

The danger of pride causing sin can be seen clearly from King Solomon's wisdom: רום עינים ורחב לב נר רשעים חטאת, "A haughty look and a proud heart are the sinful growth of the wicked" (Proverbs 21:4).

The *gematria* of Amalek (15) is also that of God's Name (הי; 10 + 5). Amalek's desire is to obscure God's presence in the world, as is said: כי יד על כס י-ה מלחמה לה' בעמלק מדר דר, "The hand is on God's [יה] throne. God shall be at war with Amalek for all generations" (Exodus 17:16). This verse reveals much: The word כס (*kais*, throne) is related to the root כסה (*kasa*, covers), and, therefore, hints at Amalek's desire to obscure godliness in the world. Also, the name for God here is הי, a covering up of the full, four-lettered name of God.

Amalek is the root of evil in the world, and the source of sin. חכמה (*chochma*, wisdom), symbolized by the letter י (*yud*), together with בינה (*binah*, understanding), as represented by the letter ה (*hei*, both הי being component letters of the name of God), are able to overcome the evil force of Amalek and, hence, that of דוה (*dava*, suffering).

In sharp contrast to the negativity of דוה is הוד, in which the positive letters ה and ו dominate the letter ד, the foundation of the material world. Realizing this situation leads to brightness and glory (הוד).

The strength of חכמה (*chochma*, wisdom) and בינה (*binah*, understanding) is revealed in the verbal confession of the sinner. The greatness of his wisdom and understanding cause him to reflect upon and appreciate his wrongdoing to the extent that he is filled with true remorse, which leads him to a confession of his sin. This ודה (*vadah*, confession) increases his ודע (*vadah*, awareness), and vice versa (the letters ה and ע are interchangeable); his ודע makes him fully realize the depths and significance of the sin, leading him to confess (ודה) to the wrong he has done.

The full inner *gematria* of ודה; הה דלת וו: ה לת ו (6 + 430 + 5 = 441) is the same as the primary *gematria* of אמת (*emet*, truth; 1 + 40 + 400 = 441). Confession (ודה) is an admission of אמת (truth). Alphabetically, the letters of the word ודה follow those of הגד (*haged*, to make known or to expound that which lies within).

ו follows ה

ד follows ג

ה follows ד

Verbal confession, then, is a deep inner revelation of thoughts, in the category of הגדה (*hagada*, profound expounding). The root הגד is connected to the word גיד (*gid*), a sinew that meanders at length in a deep and hidden manner in the body, just as הגדה elaborates on a deep, inner meaning of Torah, thereby making the hidden revealed.

According to the early commentators, ענוה (*anava*, humility) has the power to nullify evil forces. Its numerical value (70 + 50 + 6 + 5) is 131. King David speaks humbly: ולא רמו עיני ולא גבה לבי הלכתי בגדלות ובנפלאות ממני, "My heart is not haughty, nor mine eyes lofty; neither do I exercise myself in things too great, or in things too wonderful for me" (Psalms 131:1). But ענוה also has the same *gematria* as the name of the evil angel סמאל (Samael; 60 + 40 + 1 + 30 = 131). Samael, who is generally known to be the source of all sins, is connected to Amalek, the source of impurity and pride.

The full *gematria* of the word ענו (*anav*, humble person; עין נון וו = 130 + 106 + 12) is 248, the number of positive *mitzvot*. Through humility, a person can achieve a great level of holiness by simply fulfilling the Torah's positive *mitzvot*. The power of a humble man is also evident in the name אברהם (Abraham), which is composed of the words אבר מה (*ever mah*, organ of "what"), which indicate humility. Our forefather Abraham was a complete ענו; he was so nullified of self that he became a selfless organ of God. The numerical value of אברהם is also 248 (1 + 2 + 200 + 5 + 40 = 248).

Three Types of Sin, Three Types of Repentance

חטא (*chet*), און (*avon*), and פשע (*pesha*) are three different levels of evil, each of which has relevant levels of atonement. The type of atonement determines the negative effect that the sin has on a person and on the world. חטא (unintentional sin) causes damage to the soul itself; עון (iniquity) creates a distance between a person and his Maker; and פשע (crime) produces prosecutors and harmful forces that oppose a person and the nation of Israel.

חטא is a sin in which a person's intention and heart were not involved, but which nevertheless causes damage to the soul. This is similar to the damage caused by ingesting poison unintentionally. עון, related to the letter ע (*ayin*, also the word for "eye"), not only damages the soul but also spoils the heart, from which stems the desire to carry out the sin. A person's malicious intention, which is in opposition to God's will, creates a distance between him and God. פשע is the outcome of יודע את בוראו ומתכוון למרד בו, "He is aware of his Creator but intends to rebel against him," as it is written about Nimrod the wicked. When a person falls to the spiritual depth whereby his intellect participates in the evil act, causing him to do a פשע, then the harsh divine attribute of judgment is aroused against him. (In each of these three types of sin, a different divine attribute is dominant.)

עון involves intention, and suggests misjudgment of the עין (*ayin*, eye). The positive and negative meanings of the letter ע (also pronounced *ayin*) can be seen in the words עשר (*osher*, wealth) and רשע (*rasha*, wicked). עשר results when the eye (the ע) rules and controls the שר (*sar*, ruler). The רשע, on the other hand, is dominated by the ר, the nonintellectual, as found in (*regesh*, emotion). Furthermore, the רשע is the outcome of a "permissive eye" (עין מרשה, *ayin marsha*). Interestingly, the root of רשע is רשה (*resha*, permits). That the ע in the word רשע is more emphatic than the ה in the word רשה teaches us that permissiveness brings a person to wickedness.

Just as עון is the negative aspect of the letter ע and the concept of "eye," so, too, is פשע related to the concept of sight. The word can be seen as פש-ע (*pash ayin*, a "spread" or expansive eye), one of the evil qualities of Bilaam the wicked.

פשע is much more serious than עון, for it is an evil deed carried out with intention, thought, and rebelliousness. פשע is closely related to the word בצע (*betza,* ill-gotten gain; the ב and פ are interchangeable labial letters, and the צ and ש are interchangeable sibilant dental letters). Both are related to פצע (*petza,* wound), teaching us that sin, iniquity (פשע), wounds (פצע) the soul of man.

שפע (*shefa,* abundance), related to the שפל (*shafal,* humility) can be seen as שף–ע (*shaf ayin,* lowering of the eye). A person's humility allows him to receive divine abundance (שפע). It is clear that both שפע and פשע are dependent on a person's eye—that is, on the way that one perceives the world. The full inner *gematria* of the word שפע (שין יי ין; פי עין = 60 + 10 + 60 = 130) is identical to the *gematria* of the word עין (eye; 70 + 10 + 50 = 130). From this we see that עין טובה (a "good eye," humility) is the source of שפע (abundance), whereas עין–רעה—a "bad eye"—results in פשע (crime).

A similar idea can be found by rearranging the letters שפר (*shaper,* improve). When the ש (*shin*) precedes the פ (*peh*), then שיפור (*shipur,* improvement) comes about. When the פ precedes the ש, however, the contaminated פרש (*peresh,* waste product) results.

Permissiveness, as a root of crime, can be seen by the ר of פרע (*pera,* wild, uncontrolled) preceding and leading into the ש of פשע. What's more, when the eye (ע) is ruled by the storm (רעש, *raash*) of inclinations, the person becomes like a poor man (רש, *rash*) who is never satisfied with what he sees.

סלח (*selach,* pardon) can be transformed by exchanging the letter ס with צ and ש (all are interchangeable sibilant letters), thereby forming the words צלח (*tzalach,* crosses a river) and שלח (*shalach,* sent). Both of these words express liberation and unloading, or throwing off of לחץ (*lachatz,* pressure). סליחה (*selicha,* forgiveness) liberates the spirit from the pressure of the impurity of the sin.

מחל (*machal*) is forgiveness of a debt owed. This is similar to what results when a person owes a debt to another: It creates a distance between them. When a person sins intentionally (עון), he creates a debt between him and his Creator. Forgiveness of the sin (מחילת עונות, *mechilat avonot*) restores the union. The letters of the word מחל, rearranged, form the root of the word הלחמה (*halchama,* soldering). Asking for forgiveness leads to חמלת (*chemlat Hashem,* God's mercy) and a "resoldering" of the bond between the sinner and God.

כפר (*kfar*) means "cover," as is said regarding Noah's ark (Genesis 6:14): וכפרת אתה מבית ומחוץ בכפר, "And you shall cover it inside and outside with tar" (Genesis 6:14). כפרה (*kaparah*, forgiveness) conceals the evil forces and prevents them from harming a person or the world.

When a person says וידוי (*vidui*, verbal confession) and enunciates the words חטאנו, העוינו, פשענו (*chatanu*, we have sinned; *he'evinu*, we were iniquitous; and *peshanu*, we did evil), he is admitting to the three kinds of sin. He is then forgiven with the corresponding types of forgiveness: סליחת חטאים (*selichat chataim*); מחילת עונות (*mechilat avonot*); and כפרת פשע (*kaparat pesha*). These are actually three levels of forgiveness, and each is an atonement for the person's body (חטא), heart (עון), or brain (פשע), respectively—whichever was principally involved in bringing the person to sin.

Three Parts of the Body, Three Stages of Repentance

The three major stages of repentance—חרטה (*charata*, regret); וידוי (*vidui*, confession); and שינוי מעשה (*shinui maaseh*, change of action)—correspond to the מח (*moach*, brain), the לב (*lev*, heart), and the גוף (*guf*, body). חרטה is aroused in a person by the intellectual awareness of the seriousness of his sin and its negative effect on man and the world. The וידוי, resulting from דוה (*dava*, pain), purifies and cleanses the stain caused by the negativity of sin. A person's actions (מעשה) are changed as a result of his regret and confession, which leads to the perfection of his body.

When a person regrets his sin, confesses, and changes his actions through repentance, prayer, and charity, the evil decree against him is nullified. תשובה (*teshuva*, repentance) is the direct result of a person's intellectual (מח) regret of his evil deeds. Verbal prayer (תפלה, *tefillah*) by means of the mouth (פה, *peh*) is an expression of the heart (לב). In the Talmud, our Sages question the verse: לעבדו בכל לבבכם, "And you shall serve Him with all your heart" (Deuteronomy 11:13). The Talmud asks: "What is the 'service of the heart'?" It answers: "Prayer (תפלה)!" (*Taanit* 2a).

The main purpose of giving charity (צדקה, *tzedakah**) is to perfect a person's deeds. The power of charity is as potent as fasting in bring-

---

*צדקה: For lack of an equivalent English word, we define the holy concept of צדקה as "charity." צדקה means "justice" or "righteousness," and as such is far more sublime than the mere giving of alms. The commandment to give צדקה stems not from our compassion for the poor but from God's demand for justice; God grants us more than we require and trusts us to distribute judiciously to those in need.

ing a repentant back to God. This is seen in the phrase עני תת (*tet oni*, giving to the poor), which has the same letters as תענית (*taanit*, fasting).

As noted in the מחזור (*machzor*, the prayerbook used for the High Holidays), above the words צדקה, תשובה, תפלה are printed the words ממון (*mamon*, money), קול (*kol*, voice), and צום (*tzom*, fasting), respectively. The numerical value of each of these words (ממון, 40 + 40 + 6 + 50; קול, 100 + 6 + 30; and צום, 90 + 6 + 40) is 136, the same as that of the word סולם (*sulam*, ladder; 60 + 6 + 30 + 40 = 136). This teaches us that תפלה, צדקה, תשובה are similar to a ladder that elevates a person to higher spiritual worlds. These spiritual worlds parallel man's brain (מח), heart (לב), and liver (כבד, *kaved*), which represent the body. The importance of the brain, heart, and liver in the elevation of man is seen in the numerical value (112) of the words מח, וכבד, לב (40 + 8 + 30 + 2 + 6 + 20 + 2 + 4). The number 112 is the numerical value of three names of God—אדני, יהוה, and אהיה (21 + 26 + 65 = 112)—and are connected with the three main spheres, respectively: כתר (*keter*, crown), תפארת (*tiferet*, beauty) and מלכות (*malchut*, kingdom). Those spheres are the main rungs on the ladder (סולם) that elevate a person as he returns to God.

The number 136 multiplied by three (136 × 3) is 408, which is the numerical value of the word זאת (*zot*, this). This alludes to the Torah: וזאת התורה, "And *this* is the Torah" (Deuteronomy 4:44). The Chida teaches us that through the power of Torah study, a person can achieve the three perfections normally attained through repentance, prayer, and charity. Learning Torah involves concentration of mind, deliberateness of speech, and bodily effort, each of which perfects the three representative parts of the body that have been negatively affected by sin.

At the beginning of the month of אלול (Elul), people begin to work on these three areas. The letters of Elul are the initial letters of the verse: אני לדודי ודודי לי, "I am my beloved's and my beloved is mine" (Song of Songs 6:3). This hints at תפלה (prayer), which arouses a person to come close to his beloved—that is, to God.

From Deuteronomy: ומל ה' את לבבך ואת לבב זרעך, "And God will circumcise your heart and the hearts of your descendants" (Deuteronomy 30:6). This verse suggests תשובה (*teshuva*, repentance). Circumcision is a process, like ברית מילה, that perfects and completes the human being.

איש לרעהו ומתנות לאבינים, "Every man to his friend and gifts to the poor" (Esther 9:22). Can you see why this verse hints at the connection of אלול, the month of repentance, and the giving of צדקה?

When the brain (מח), heart (לב), and body (גוף) are perfected, then a person becomes complete, as seen by the letters of the word for man: אדם (*adam*). Our Sages teach that אדם is a term denoting perfection: the א (*alef*) refers to the brain (מח), which is the storehouse (אולפן, *ulpan*) of wisdom and the foundation of thought. The ד (*dalet*) refers to דבור (*dibor*, speech), the expression of the heart. The מ (*mem*) refers to מעשה (*maaseh*, action), the expression of the body. The numerical value of the word אדם (1 + 4 + 40 = 45) equals that of the word מה (*mah*, what; 40 + 5 = 45), alluding to the humility one achieves through perfect repentance.

By the order of its letters in the *alef-bet*, the word אדם equals 18 (that is, א is the first [1] letter; ד, the fourth [4] letter; מ, the thirteenth [13]; 1 + 4 + 13 = 18), the same *gematria* as the word חי (*chai*, life).

The Three Dimensions of Creation

The words עולם, שנה, נפש (*olam, shana, nefesh*; world, year, spirit) hint at the hidden forces of nature at work in the world. These forces were created at the time of the Creation of the world, and are continually strengthened by people's sins (חטאים, *chataim*). The word חטא is made up of טח-א (*tach alef*, coating of the *alef*), a reference to the fact that sins "coat" and conceal (an expression of materialism) the א, the אלוף (*aluf*, master) of the world: God. This materialistic covering is like smoke (עשן, *ashan*, from the initial letters of עולם, שנה, נפש) that conceals God's presence, thus bringing punishment (עונש, *onesh*) on man and the world.

The force of the עולם (*olam*, world) conceals (העלם, *helaim*, from the same root as עולם) the godly creative force. The word הטבע (*hateva*, the nature; 5 + 9 + 2 + 70) is equal to the word אלקים (*elokim*, the Creator—that is, the name of God that refers to his creative, worldly, physical presence); both total 86. שנה (*shana*, year) is the concealment of time, which is what influences the brain and the thought processes. נפש (*nefesh*, spirit), a person's physical desires, are what ultimately influence his outer behavior. During the Days of Awe, we request in our prayers וכל הרשעה כעשן תכלה, "And all evil, like smoke, will cease." When the משיח (Messiah) comes, this promise will be realized, and עשן, the smoke of wickedness, will be removed. The letters of the word עשן are the same as the letters of the word ענש (*anash*, punish), alluding to the concealment of God's light by חטא (sin).

The similarity of עשן (smoke) and ענש (punish) teaches us that a person's sin creates the punishment. חטא (sin) creates עשן (smoke) and then עונש (punishment). The same idea is found in the word עברה (*evrah*, wrath): It refers to the anger of God at the sinner, and is related to the עברה (*aveira*, iniquity) of the sinner.

The full numerical value of the word עשן (עין שין נון: 130 + 360 + 106 = 596) is the same as that of the word ירושלים (Jerusalem; 10 + 200 + 6 + 300 + 30 + 10 + 40 = 596). Jerusalem is the symbol of מלכות (*malchut*, kingdom) and קדושה (*kedusha*, holiness). The numerical value of the word מלכות (40 + 30 + 20 + 6 + 400 = 496), plus the value of the letter symbolizing holiness (ק, 100, from קדושה), equals the numerical value of ירושלים (496 + 100 = 596).

The עולם (*olam*, world), שנה (*shana*, year), and נפש (*nefesh*, soul) are the foundation of Creation, as is explained in Sefer Yetzira. It is stated there that the twenty-two letters of the *alef-bet* are the basis of the creation of the twelve מזלות (*mazalot*, signs of the zodiac) in the world. "Twelve months in the year, twelve rulers in the soul, seven stars in the world, seven days in the year, and seven gates to the soul."

The Creation is based on the foundation of the three physical elements symbolized by the letters אמש, a mnemonic for the words מים, אש, אויר (*avir*, air; *esh*, fire; and *mayim*, water). One of these letters is included in the Hebrew words for earth (אדמה, *adama*), world, year (that is, time), and soul (נפש, *nefesh*). The fourth element, עפר (*afar*, earth), is not considered here, as it is nothing on its own and takes its form and shape only from the other elements (*Beer Moshe*, Genesis).

Complete repentance (as revealed by the articulation of the twenty-two alphabetical expressions of the וידוי confessional prayer) reveals the godly source in man, in the world, and in time. It removes the covering of materialism (חמר, *chomer*) from the world. That the word חמר indicates sin can be seen from in letters שטן (Satan), which follow its letters in the *alef-bet*:

ט follows ח

ן follows מ

ש follows ר

4

The Days of Awe

The Symbolism of the Four Holy Days

ACCORDING TO OUR HOLY BOOKS, the four festivals ראש השנה יום, (כפור, סוכות, שמיני עצרת)—Rosh Hashana, Yom Kippur, Sukkot, and Shemini Atzeret) correspond to the four letters of the tetragrammaton, God's holy name: יהוה. The י (*yud*), the letter at the head or beginning of the name, corresponds to Rosh Hashana, the head of the year. Yom Kippur (whose full name is יום הכפורים, *Yom* Hakipurim) corresponds to the heart and understanding, and is symbolized by the letter ה (*hei*). Sukkot corresponds to the ו (*vav*), a letter symbolizing the attribute of glory. And Shemini Atzeret relates to the ה, the last letter of God's name, the letter of kingdom.

Yom Kippur, the day set aside for complete repentance, returns the ה—the holiness of the heart—to its place. The עשרת ימי תשובה, the Ten Days of Repentance between Yom Kippur and Rosh Hashana (the numerical value of the letter י), leads to the perfection that only Yom Kippur has the potential to bring about. The letter ה, having the numerical value of 5, refers to the perfection that can be achieved during the five days between Yom Kippur and Sukkot.

The numerical value of the initial letters of these four festivals (ר, כ, ס, ש; 300 + 60 + 20 + 200 = 580) is the same as that of the word תפילין (*tefillin*, phylacteries; 400 + 80 + 10 + 30 + 10 + 50 = 580). The *tefillin* consist of four sections that correspond to the four letters of God's name. The number 580 is also the numerical value of the words: סם לילית (Sam and Lillit; 60 + 40 + 30 + 10 + 30 + 10 + 400 = 580), which are the evil forces of שעיר (Seer, the dwelling place of Esau the wicked; 300 + 70 + 10 + 200 = 580). The letters in the word שעיר, when rearranged, spell יש רע (*yaish ra*, there is evil), hinting at the intrinsic evil power of that place. These forces have the ability to nullify the holiness contained in these four festivals.

According to Kabbalah, the number four relates to the four letters of the name of God that reveals his attribute of pity and kindness. This number refers to the four white garments that were central to the High Priest's service on Yom Kippur. The color white is also symbolic of pity and kindness. The High Priest's four golden garments represent the four letters of God's name that reveals his attribute of judgment: אדני. This name relates to Rosh Hashana, the Day of Judgment. The numerical value of these two names of God (יהוה and אדני; 26 + 65 = 91), combined, is the same as that of the word אמן (*amen*; 1 + 40 + 50 = 91). Amen, the traditional response to any blessing that mentions God's name, is also the root of the word אמונה (*emunah*, faith). What's more, the *gematria* of these names is equal to the word סוכה (*sukkah*, tabernacle or booth; 60 + 6 + 20 + 5 = 91), known as the צילא דהימנותא, the shade of faith.

Yom Kippur: Revelation of the Light of Truth

According to our Sages, the attribute of truth is the basis of the atonement of Yom Kippur. The Divine soul of the Jewish nation has its source in truth. All the sins and iniquities that cling to the soul are a result of the influence of the יצר הרע (evil inclination) and שטן (Satan, adversary). In the Midrash (Bereishith Rabba on Vayishlach), our Sages say that the relationship between the brothers עשו and יעקב (Esau and Jacob) can be compared to two men standing near a threshing-floor. One man is hairy; and other is bald. When the wind blows, it blows the chaff onto their heads. In the hairy man's hair, the chaff becomes so entangled that it cannot be removed; the bald man, however, has only to pass his hand lightly over his head to remove the chaff. The "bald" man, Jacob (whose other name Israel makes him the namesake of the Jewish nation), has only to pass through Yom Kippur in order to remove the chaff of his sins. On Yom Kippur, the spirit of purity removes all stains from the nation of Israel, for the souls of His people are pure, and impurity of sin is but external and superficial.

On Yom Kippur these sins are removed from the soul of the Jewish nation, and are then cast onto עזאזל (Azazel), a goat chosen for abandonment in the desert. Such is his fitting end, for he is symbolic of Satan and the evil inclination, who bear responsibility for Israel's sins; only through their cajolery and collaboration is Israel enticed to do evil.

According to the *Shem MiShmuel*, the three festivals (Rosh Hashana, Yom Kippur, and Sukkot) are parallel to the three pillars on which the world stands: דין (*din*, judgment), אמת (*emet*, truth), and שלום (*shalom*, peace). From this we can see that the attribute of truth is embodied in Yom Kippur itself. The essential nature of the Jewish people, whose shining attribute is truth, is revealed on Yom Kippur. The Jews are essentially pure, and their sins are due only to the fact that the non-Jewish nations spiritually pollute the air with their evil deeds.

The central service of Yom Kippur was the offering of the incense by the High Priest in the Holy of Holies. The ability of the Jewish people to unite with the source of their soul on Yom Kippur is hinted at in this holy service. The root of the word קטרת (*ketoret*, incense) is קטר (*keter*), meaning קשר (*kesher*, connection). The rising incense symbolized the connection that the souls of the Jewish people below have with their Source above—that is, with God.

The Chatam Sofer explains that the spoonful (כף, *kof*) of קטרת that was offered is symbolic of the nation of Israel. The letters following the letters קטרת-כ in the *alef-bet* (the כ refers both to the letter and to a spoon) spell the word ישראל (Israel).

ל follows כ

ר follows ק

י follows ט

ש follows ר

א follows ת

The spoonful (כף) of קטרת raises the root of the soul of the Jewish nation heavenward. This idea is also suggested by the fact that the initials of the word ישראל are a mnemonic for יש ששים רבוא אותיות לתורה, "There are six hundred thousand letters in the Torah." The number of souls of Israel who received the Torah at Mount Sinai was also 600,000.

The numerical value of the word כפר (*kiper*, atoned; 20 + 80 + 200 = 300) is the same as that of the letter ש (*shin*), which represents truth. This equality of numerical values teaches that the foundation of כפרה (*kaparah*, forgiveness) on Yom Kippur is connected to the attribute of truth.

ש (*shin*) is the twenty-first letter in the *alef-bet*; 21 is the numerical value of God's name אהיה (1 + 5 + 10 + 5 = 21). This name is connected to the attribute of כתר (*keter*, crown), the source of all the attributes from which emanate the souls of the nation of Israel. The numerical values of the names יוסף, יעקב, יצחק (Joseph, Jacob, Isaac) are equal to twenty-one times the name of God (יהוה) that equals 26:

$$יצחק = 10 + 90 + 8 + 100 \quad = 208 = 8 \times 26$$
$$יעקב = 10 + 70 + 100 + 2 \quad = 182 = 7 \times 26$$
$$יוסף = \quad\quad 10 + 6 + 60 + 80 = 156 = 6 \times 26$$

The nation of Israel is essentially connected to God. If the numerical values of the two names of God—אהיה (1 + 5 + 10 + 5 = 21) and יהוה (10 + 5 + 6 + 5 = 26)—are multiplied together (21 × 26 = 546), the total equals the numerical value of ישראל (Israel; 10 + 300 + 200 + 1 + 30 = 541) plus the number (5) of that word's letters (541 + 5 = 546).

Rosh Hashana represents strict דין (judgment); Yom Kippur, the day of forgiveness of sin, represents the great חסד (*chesed*, lovingkindness) of God, for he himself forgives and purifies the nation of Israel. Our holy books relate that the four special white garments that the High Priest wore on Yom Kippur are parallel to the four letters of the holy name of God. The four golden garments suggest the strict judgment parallel to God's name אדני. The *sukkah*, which is the central theme of the festival of Sukkot, shows the unification of God's name of lovingkindness (יהוה) with his name of judgment: אדני. The numerical value of the word סוכה (*sukkah*, booth; 60 + 6 + 20 + 5 = 91) is the same as the value of these two names together (אדני: 1 + 4 + 50 + 10 = 65; יהוה: 10 + 5 + 6 + 5 = 26; 65 + 26 = 91). The expression "peace between judgment and lovingkindness" refers to the *sukkah*, as we read in the Sabbath blessing called השכיבנו (Hashkivainu, "Let us lie down"): הפורש סכת שלום עלינו, "Who spreads over us the shelter of peace."

The numerical value of the word תשרי (Tishrei, the name of the month that contains these festivals), is 910 (400 + 300 + 200 + 10). In this month, these attributes of God attain perfection. Multiplication of a number by ten reveals the perfection of that idea; The value of 910, being ten times the combined numerical value of these holy names of God, represents the perfection of the godly attributes contained in these names.

It is also interesting to note that the zodiac sign for this month is מאזים, the Scales. Lovingkindness is weighed on the right side of the scale, and judgment is weighed on the left. Counting from the month of Nissan, Tishrei is the seventh month. According to our Sages, seven is a special number representing the kingdom, the attribute of unification and balance between lovingkindness on the right and judgment on the left.

The verse תקעו בחודש שופר בכסה ליום חגינו, "Blow the *shofar* on the new moon, on the designated day of our feast" (Psalms 81:4) refers to the judgment of Rosh Hashana. The Talmud says that the festival falls at the time of the new moon, when the moon is "covered" (כסה, *kasa*). This is the time when the God of Isaac judges His people. The word כסה resembles the word כסא (*kisai*, chair), a reference to the throne that God sits upon when he judges his people. The righteous ones recite the verse: ליום הכסא יבא ביתו, "He will come home at the full moon" (Proverbs 7:20)—an allusion to the seat of judgment used on this day. The word כסא has the same root as כסוי (*kisuy*, covering); on Rosh Hashana, God "covers" the sins of the children of Israel, bringing them to repentance and complete forgiveness.

Yom Kippur: Wiping and Cleaning

The root of the word כפור (*kippur*) is כפר (*kapar*), to wipe or rub out, as in the verse: אכפרה פניו, "I will remove the fury from His face" (Genesis 32:21). Yom Kippur is the day when the stains caused by sin and iniquity are removed from the Jews. Jacob sent the gifts in order to appease Esau ("clean his face"). The *Zohar* compares the gifts that Jacob sent to the casting of the goat to Azazel on Yom Kippur; both were merely a bribe to Satan, the ministering angel of Esau. On Yom Kippur, the spirit of purity rubs away the stain of sin only after a person repents and breaks his heart in self-nullification before the Holy One, blessed by he. If he does not repent before Yom Kippur, then even the pure spirit of the day will not remove his stain. Commenting on the verse תשובה תולה ויום הכפורים מכפר, "Repentance is tentative and Yom Kippur atones," our Sages say: "The action of repentance is merely to remove the poison of the evil deed from the internal part of man" (*Yoma* 86a). It is Yom Kippur, the Day of Atonement, that brings about כפרה (*kaparah*, atonement) through the erasure of the stain of sin.

A person whose transgressions are of a more serious nature needs more than just repentance to remove the stain of his sins. In such a case, one needs יסורים (*yesurim*, sufferings) sent from Above to scrub and polish the soul. Only after these financial or physical sufferings can a person be completely forgiven on Yom Kippur. The gravity of sin resulting from transgressing a prohibition (אסור, *issur*) instills ארס (*aires*, poison) and אסר (*asar*, imprisonment) in the inner-most part of the soul of man and necessitates an extra cleansing to remove it.

The root כפר (from יום כפור) hints at a time when the brute ani-mal force that causes sin (פר, *par*, bullock) kneels down to the forces of holiness. כפר can be read as כף פר (*kaf par*, "(the) bullock bows"). The numerical value of the word פר (*par*, bullock, the representative of brute force) is 280 (80 + 200 = 280), which is ten times that of the word כח (*koach*, strength; 20 + 8 = 28 × 10 = 280). The word פר, then, symbolizes the perfection of the power of strength and judgment. The central portion of the Yom Kippur service was the slaughtering and offering of the פר, a clear illustration of this same idea.

According to our Sages, Satan and his accompanying powers want to prosecute the nation of Israel on Yom Kippur, but are unable to accuse or denunciate Israel or speak evil against it. Their evil power is nullified against the nation of Israel on this day. This can be seen by reading the word כפר as כף-ר: "the ר (*raish*) is bent over." The Talmud (*Shabbat* 104b) says that the letter ר symbolizes the רשע (*rasha*, evil one). On Yom Kippur, the evil one is "bent over," humbled. On Yom Kippur the שעיר (*s'eer*, goat) is sent to Azazel, which is symbolic of the Satan. The word שעיר is composed of the same letters as the word רשע (evil one), indicating its root in evil.

The numerical value of the word השטן (5 + 300 + 9 + 50 = 364) is one less than 365, the number of days in the solar year. Our Sages say that this alludes to the fact that Satan does not have an effect on this unique day of the year.

The full numerical value of the word כף פי ריש :כפר (20 + 80 + 80 + 10 + 200 + 10 + 300 = 700) is the same as that of the word שת (*shat*, foundation; 300 + 400 = 700). The word שבת (*Shabbat*) comprises the words שת-ב (*shat bet*, foundation of the ב). The letter ב refers to בית (*bayit*, house). The שבת, then, may be seen as שת-ב, "the foundation of the structure of the world." Yom Kippur, known as the source of all the Sabbaths, is שבת שבתון, the Sabbath of Sabbaths. This is the day on which a person achieves the holiness of the Sabbath by complete atonement. The full numerical value of the word כפרה is 706 (*kaparah*, atonement; כף פי ריש הא; 20 + 80 + 80 + 10 + 200 + 10 + 300 + 5 + 1); with the addition of the *kollel* it totals 707, the same as the word השבת (5 + 300 + 2 + 400 + 1 [*kollel*] = 707). Complete atonement expresses the holiness of *Shabbat* that can be revealed to man and to the world.

The unique quality of Yom Kippur above all the other days of the year is suggested in the verse: ימים יצרו ולא אחד בהם, "Days were created and not one of them" (Psalms 139:16). The *Tanna d'Vai Eliyahu* says that the phrases "days were created" and "not one of them" refer to Yom Kippur, a unique day with unique nature. It is the day when the nation of Israel cleaves to God without any intervening substance or powers of nature. On this day, שטן, the יצר הרע—all opposing forces—are at rest (שבת). For this reason, Yom Kippur is likened to the Sabbath. On Yom Kippur, the evil forces cease doing harm; every Jew merits the holiness of the Sabbath. Indeed, the Torah calls Yom Kippur a *Shabbat*. The special holiness of the day raises it above the other six festivals of the year, just as *Shabbat* is raised above the other six days of the week. The holiness of Yom Kippur is above all the forces of strength and nature of this world. It is this day that attains the world-to-come.

Our Sages say that, in the future, all the festivals of the year will be annulled, except for Yom Kippur and Purim (פורים) In both of these festivals, the power of the פר (the animal strength of the physical world) cannot oppose the holiness of the day. (An allusion to this is found in the full name of Yom Kippur—יום הכפורים, *Yom Hakippurim*, which can be read as "the day that is like [כ, the abbreviation meaning "like" or "similar to"] פורים.") The unbounded holiness found in the joy and gaiety of the Purim festival, not the somber atonement of Yom Kippur, is most like the spiritual gifts awaiting us in the world-to-come.

The Sages of Kabbalah say that the day of Yom Kippur will change from a harsh judgment to a רפה (*rafeh*, weak) judgment; through the attribute of lovingkindness, the power of the פר that rules on Yom Kippur is changed to רף. This is seen in the unique ritual of the Yom Kippur service performed by the High Priest. Dressed in his special white garments (the color white is symbolic of lovingkindness), the High Priest's service on this day diminishes the harsh attribute of judgment leading into Yom Kippur.

Index

About the Author

Rabbi Matityahu Glazerson was born and educated in Israel. He studied at Medrashiat Noam in Pardes Chana, and at various yeshivot, including Kfar Chassidim, Ponievez, and Chevron. Today he is involved in teaching in a Kollel, and lecturing at various institutions, like Neve Yerushalayim, Ma'ayonot Yerushalayim, and Kol B'Rama. He is instrumental in paving a new way toward the instillment of Jewish values. Rabbi Glazerson is the author of many books including *The Secrets of the Haggadah; Torah, Light, and Healing: Mystical Insights into Healing based on the Hebrew Language; Above the Zodiac: Astrology in Jewish Thought;* and *Music and Kabbalah.*